DON'T BUNCH UP*

DON'T BUNCH UP*

One Marine's Story

*and some notable exceptions

William Van Zanten

Foreword by
General P. X. Kelley

Archon

1993

First published 1993 as an Archon Book, an imprint of
The Shoe String Press, Inc., Hamden, Connecticut 06514

Printed in the United States of America

The paper used in this publication meets the minimum requirements of
American National Standard for Information Sciences—Permanence
of Paper for Printed Library Materials. ANSI Z39.48-1984 ∞

Library of Congress Cataloging-in-Publication Data

Van Zanten, William
Don't bunch up : one Marine's story and some
notable exceptions / by William Van Zanten.
p.   cm.
1. Vietnamese Conflict, 1961–1975—Personal narratives, American.
2. Van Zanten, William.   I. Title
DS559.5.V37   92-25175   959.704′38—dc20
ISBN 0-208-02347-X (alk. paper)

This book is dedicated to my wife, Myrna, my friend and helper. Pray that when life puts a thorn in your paw, she is close by to pull it out. And to the guys on the Wall.

CONTENTS

Foreword

During the first half of 1966, I was honored to command the "Magnificent Bastards" of 2nd Battalion, 4th Marines, in the Republic of Vietnam. These were among the finest marines in our Corps at that time, seasoned combat veterans like Major Ernie Defazio, Lieutenant Gary Brown, Gunnery Sergeant Billy Howard, and Lance Corporal John Bianchini, to name but a few. They were men of courage, dedication, and determination. And, as strange as it may sound to some, they were men of concern and compassion. Bill Van Zanten was one of those marines, and his story is a poignant and accurate portrayal of noble men in combat. It is an important story, for it provides a necessary counterpoint to the Hollywood hype which has been force-fed to the American public in our theaters and on our televisions.

No group is closer to the horrors of war than infantrymen. They alone are the ones who close with and destroy the enemy. In doing so, they are constantly exposed to death and human suffering. Bill Van Zanten tells you about the good times and the bad times, providing the uninhibited insights of a fine young infantry officer in combat.

Marines have always taken pride in their extraordinary preparations for conflict. From the first day in uniform, they are convinced that they can accomplish tasks previously thought impossible. Other services use the vigorous training of our boot camp as the exacting standard which must be met to instill esprit and confidence. *Don't Bunch Up* is replete with stories, many of them humorous, about how this training paid off for marines in war.

This is also a story of how marines won tactical victory after tactical victory on the battlefields of Vietnam. What is not said, however, is that the United States did not achieve its strategic objectives in the Republic of Vietnam, and ultimately abandoned that tiny nation and its people. The real heroes of this struggle were the American men and women who served their country in what can honestly be described as the toughest war we have ever fought. They endured prolonged and difficult combat—over 58,000 made the supreme sacrifice; the rest returned home to find themselves largely forgotten and unwanted. In reality, they were proud soldiers, sailors, airmen and marines who were given a lousy job to do, and they did it superbly.

The author does not pretend to be a spokesman for his generation and he makes no apologies. His is a story about young officers and enlisted men who shared an extraordinary experience in a far-off land over two and a half decades ago.

With the exception of serving together for several months in combat, Bill Van Zanten and I have met on only one other occasion. We have, however, kept in telephone contact and followed each other's careers. Like the majority of Vietnam veterans, he went on to live a useful and productive life. Not everyone did. Unfortunately, some came back with physical and mental scars.

The American fighting man from the Vietnam era deserves to be honored. *Don't Bunch Up* does just that, and does it with style and candor. I have no doubt that it will take its rightful place in the long and proud history of one of America's most cherished institutions—the United States Marine Corps.

P. X. KELLEY
General, U.S. Marine Corps (Ret.)
28th Commandant of the Marine Corps

Acknowledgments

This book could never have been completed without the assistance and unwavering support of my wife, Myrna. She read every word three or four times as we pored over the changes that were part of the effort. She tolerated my many hours in the den, away from the family and her, as I struggled through each word and page. She pushed me forward when quitting would have been more tolerable. She laughed and humored me when she reviewed every new chapter. She transcribed some of my horribly scribbled notes, at great pain. She understood my compulsion to finish this work. I will be forever grateful.

I also wish to thank some wonderful friends, who have shown great tolerance for pain in reviewing and editing and making suggestions and putting up with my horrible spelling. Dr. Bill Ferrell had many good, practical suggestions and encouraged even my earliest efforts. And Dr. Bob Brouwer, an enduring friend, always sounded enthusiastic even when he shouldn't have been. And Dr. Glen Toney, for his thoughtful and encouraging comments. And Lou Liedman, who not only encouraged me but helped me in my struggle to master the computer and the printer. And Amar Singh, who offered so many good suggestions.

And to those who helped me live this wonderful experience.

And to my children, who inspired me to start on this project. I'm glad you became part of my life. May this book help you understand the wonderfulness of life as I saw and lived it, and may it bring us closer together.

Preface

This book is unabashedly autobiographical. It is not an auto-biography. It is historical, yet not a history book. It is my history. My truth. My side of the story. The idea started innocently enough. I wanted very much to describe these parts of life to my children, who know me, yet don't. Writing down descriptions of some of the events seemed like a great idea. It blossomed into a project that was far more involved than I had ever imagined. It was taking longer to write it than to live it. But I plodded on, hoping to finish it before my judgment day.

The first 26 years of my life were so fundamentally different from the same years in my children's lives that it seems to me to be completely impossible for them to comprehend. Like most Americans, they have not been part of the U.S. Marine Corps, with all of its history and tradition in service to our great country. Respected and feared by friends and enemies of this nation, this organization has always represented the best we have to offer. Marine Corps Boot Camp is still talked of as the toughest test of manhood. Service to country is the principal mission, a mission and a commitment which has lasted more than 200 years. The Corps took me and molded me and made me tough where no toughness had existed. I loved or at least respected every minute of every day that I served and could never be more proud of any accomplishment in life than the knowledge that I served the Corps and my country well.

As a marine, I served a year and some in the Republic of Vietnam. No other endeavor I know could possibly have the same lifelong effect these months have had on my life and my being. The events of that year will forever live in my memory. I learned to kill. I learned to kill extremely well. I also learned to face death. I learned to face death and not be paralyzed. I was prepared to die, if necessary, not because of some suicidal impulse or insane death wish but because it looked on several occasions as though that was the way my life was going to be played out. And I was ready. I knew God and was ready to meet Him. I felt He was ready for me and that he would be somehow proud of my being there. We were the good guys, weren't we?

The Vietnam War has been terribly misunderstood in many ways. Books and movies galore have degraded and I believe misrepresented many of the events of that sad period of our history. None has ever come close to capturing the heart and soul of what I saw and felt. None has begun to capture the spirit of the dedication to decency and fairness that I saw in the people that I saw fight there with their courage and unselfishness. Of course there were some I didn't like or respect. To protect those few I have changed a few names and unit designations to prevent hard feelings. None of them were that bad or deserve any embarrassment from the contents of this book.

My year there was spent as part of a hard-fighting Marine infantry battalion, each and every day in harm's way, every minute, every hour. We did our jobs as well as we knew how. We got our butts shot off and blown to bits. We got scared beyond description. We took home scars that will never disappear and got a few more for good measure once we got back home. Yet in some very strange way those days represented the best of what we were and ever will be. The movies I've seen do not leave that kind of impression. I want my kids and anyone else who cares to have my views of that experience. It is markedly different from the easy debunking and simple-minded whining of ideologues and adolescents.

After all these years I'd like to start sharing some of the experiences. It hasn't been easy up to now. After the war, and for many years later, nobody was especially interested. Like most veterans, I have always found it difficult to talk about these things with someone who wasn't there. It is time for me to let go and at the same time to set the record straight from my perspective. I do not pretend at all to offer LBJ's truth, the whole truth, or anyone's version but my own. And perhaps, in some strange way, to help the wonderful people I served with during that unimaginable year.

1

First to Fight

The hangar deck of the USS *Iwo Jima* was a jumble of humanity. One thousand marines, all dressed up for combat. Packs were packed, helmets pulled on tight and cartridge belts filled with a large assortment of rifle magazines, hand grenades, flares, mortar shells and machine-gun bandoliers. Everything in its place, neatly stored for easy use. We looked sharp.

This wasn't a parade and no well-defined lines existed, but we knew exactly what we were doing and where we were going. Random, yet well-defined motion in all directions. It may have looked like mass hysteria to an outsider. Nothing could have been further from the truth. This movement was part of the overall plan, a very precise drill. Each movement had a purpose. A deadly purpose.

We had practiced this exercise hundreds of times, but could all that practice prepare us for the real thing? This time our M-14 rifles were loaded with live ammo. This would be the first shooting war with this new-model rifle and its 20-round, bottom-loaded magazine. It was very accurate at 500 yards and more but this wasn't target practice. This time somebody might be shooting back. This time people were probably going to get hurt.

It was June 5, 1965, and we were about to introduce South Vietnam to the 3rd Battalion, 7th Marine Regiment. OPERATION STARLITE was officially under way. We would participate in the first large military operation of the war. Other American troops were on Vietnamese soil and had been for a couple of months, but up until now military activity had been confined to a rather large-

1

scale show of force. Forces from the Pacific had been deployed throughout the area for just exactly this contingency. We were the first forces sent from the mainland U.S.A. We weren't here to show force. We were here to *do* force, in a big way. We all wanted to perform well. We all wanted to stay alive. Maybe we'd get this over and be home in a couple of months. Maybe the bad guys would turn and run for cover. The Marines had arrived. Wouldn't LBJ be pleased if we got this over in a hurry? Wouldn't we all.

After a hurried departure from Camp Pendleton, California and 17 days at sea, we stood approximately three miles off the coast of what would turn out to be a hard-to-forget, easy-to-hate part of the world. We were tired of being honored guests of the U.S. Navy, even though a converted aircraft carrier was more hospitable than some of the other crap the Navy used to move marines around the world. We were ready. We were confident. And we were scared.

Intelligence reports indicated that the 7th Marine Regiment, with two of its three battalions already ashore, was head-to-head with two hard-core North Vietnamese regiments. Butt-kicking time. The previous evening, the Battalion Commander had conducted a short briefing for the battalion's officers in the ship's main wardroom.

"We'll be landing by helicopter at first light, just west of the Viet Cong's main force," the Battalion Commander, Lt. Col. Richard Owens, had said, opening his operational briefing session and mentioning for the first time the name of our adversary on this landing. "Viet Cong" was the South Vietnamese guerrilla forces. We would come to know them as the VC or Victor Charlie or just Charlie. His counterpart from the North was known as the NVA (North Vietnamese Army). We called either of them anything that came to mind, not often making any big distinction between the two. "Our mission will be to form a blocking force and to seal off any escape route they might attempt to use," Owens continued. "Fighting has been going on since yesterday and the 7th Marines and elements of the 4th Marines have received their first wartime casualties since Korea," he added, in a deep, full, stern voice that he must have been practicing since the night before. This was the real thing. Most of the young lieutenants, like myself, normally had a tough time taking the Colonel very seriously, but tonight was different. We could still clown and make jokes but we knew we had to buckle down now. Humor had a way of containing the pressure, making the tension more tolerable.

During the briefing, Tommy "Max" Sanders and I were included in a small group in the back of the wardroom participating in one of our favorite pastimes: imitating the Old Man. His overstated mannerisms and tough-guy style were an easy target. We made little attempt to hide our dislike for him, even though disrespect of a superior officer was a crime punishable by death or something even worse. After all, this was the Corps, and it just wasn't permissible to criticize your superiors. If you were very clever and careful, as we certainly were, you could go right up to the line of disrespect without actually crossing over into the land of military justice.

"Do you suppose he's going to ask us to sing 'The Star Spangled Banner'?" Max asked nobody in particular.

"I'm betting on the Marine Corps Hymn," I countered.

"You're on for five," he answered. We were very careful with this kind of stuff, except in the privacy of our quarters. Besides, we were good officers ourselves and really did love the Corps, rules and all. But this jerk really deserved our nonsense and it helped relieve the tension. And the tension was suffocating.

Max was my best buddy, a bullheaded but easy-to-like product of San Angelo, Texas. His long sentences usually ran no more than four or five words. Beating around the bush was not his strong suit. He had an especially low tolerance for anything Mickey Mouse. The perfect material for the making of a good Marine officer.

Nothing in life had come particularly easy for Max. An undersized, former high school football linebacker, he had to fight his way onto every team he ever tried out for, including the Marines. He made up for his lack of size with Texas-sized grit, an innate toughness and a dogged determination. A below-average student and dirt poor during his days in San Angelo, he was given no chance to go to college but did anyway and in four long, tough years of near-starvation and constant study he received a degree from the University of Texas. He had learned to scratch and claw for whatever he wanted in life.

The Marines offered him yet another opportunity to butt his head against a wall and he took to it with the same determination and doggedness. The Corp's demand for total conformity occasionally came into conflict with his free spirit but its demand for dedication, hard work and taking on impossible missions fit him perfectly. He found a home in the Marines. We'd served together around the world for nearly three years and had learned much of our craft as Marine infantry officers together in the boondocks of Camp Pendleton, Okinawa, Taiwan and the Philippines. Max loved it when the time came to put on the helmet and our green fatigue work uniforms. He felt somewhat out of place and uncomfortable in spit-shined shoes and our world-famous dress blue uniform. He liked to get dirty and flop around on the ground, as we were frequently required to do. A certifiable nut case, but just the kind you'd like covering your butt in times of trouble. Tomorrow he'd be covering mine.

Tom Draude, the third member of what had become our special, private brotherhood, had also been with Max and me for the last three years. A graduate of the Navy Academy, he always looked and acted more serious than the rest of us did. He was. But through it all he maintained his considerable sense of humor and put it to good use whenever he could, which wasn't often since he had become the Battalion S-1 (Administration) Officer, and found himself spending most of his time running errands for Colonel Jerk. While the rest of us were off screwing around whenever we had a break, you could always find Tom with his nose in some military manual, studying some new way to serve the Corps more competently. Raised on the south side of Chicago, Tom was a staunch Catholic and the ultimate overachiever. He didn't know how to be number two at anything he did. He knew exactly what he wanted and went after it. He never gave himself much time to smell the roses. Not antisocial but with little time for social events, Tom was surprisingly well liked by everyone. Always pleasant and in control, he never seemed to struggle with any aspect of life. He loved every aspect of being an officer and a gentleman.

During the briefing, Tom was at the front of the wardroom next to the Old Man, looking very businesslike and trying very hard to avoid eye contact with Max and me. We normally had no particular problem getting him to crack up, but tonight he didn't feel like playing our silly games. Tom was very much a product of his middle class Catholic upbringing and the Academy had only served to strengthen his already strong work ethic. It was time to go to work and he was all business. Nevertheless, Max and I did our best to keep it loose. We had to do something. We were sitting on this immense war machine, somewhere in the South China Sea, 8,000 miles from home and about 10 hours away from losing what little virginity we had left. If we could have envisioned the events of the next 13 months we would have been even more concerned.

"Ask a question," I said to Max.

"OK," he replied, ready for some fun. "Sir, do you anticipate that we'll get any liberty this weekend, after we land?" Max knew this would probably set the Colonel off on a pretty good tirade, but he was enjoying the round of snickers the question raised in the room.

"Lieutenant Sanders, I'm not going to honor that question with an answer. This is war, gentlemen. No time for thinking about getting liberty or time off. We have a job to do. An important job and one which we will be proud of," the Old Man blurted out, never aware that his leg was being pulled.

Tom grimaced in our direction. We smiled and waved back, glad to have finally gotten him to look at us from his position near the map the Colonel was using for the briefing. Max flipped him the bird. A faint smile came to the corner of Tom's mouth.

Our last night aboard ship was spent sleeping on mattresses and sheets. It would be the last time for a while. My 15 trips to the "head" that night were made in the relative comfort and style afforded an officer and a gentleman on a U.S. naval vessel. For the next year, minor events such as taking a crap would be much less comfortable, unless you enjoyed sharing your most private human functions with 800 million flies and an occasional water buffalo.

The Navy always saved its best meals for moments like this. I believe it is the same tradition carried out in our prison system just prior to throwing the big switch. Unfortunately, the thought of food at this very moment provoked nothing but nausea. Coffee went down well but went right through you. The Navy always had lots of coffee available. Also, lots of places to take a leak. These places were all highly utilized the last night aboard that ship.

It was impossible to sleep after the Old Man had done his John Wayne impression in the wardroom. We passed the remaining hours talking with the troops, making final plans and going over the last-second changes. People were added and deleted from rosters every 10 minutes. Equipment appeared and disappeared. Sergeants shouted orders at no one in particular, and the troops bitched. They'd do anything to get off this boat.

Back in the privacy of our sleeping quarters, we wrote letters, checked equipment for the tenth time, listened to Max's garbage about the superior quality of high school football in Texas, made more trips to the head and tried to forget our fears.

"What's the Old Man think is going to really happen tomorrow?" I asked Tom, who was stretched out in the rack above me, knowing that because of his job, he might have some secret insight into what was really going on, beyond the normal party line.

"I think he feels like most of the fighting will already be over by the time we get in there," he answered, not bothering to look up from the letter he was writing.

"I hope it is," Max stated.

"Me too," I offered.

"I thought you guys were dying to be highly decorated war vets," Tom jabbed.

"Not me," Max answered.

"What do you want, Tom?" I asked seriously, as I got up to pace around the room one more time.

"I just want us to do well, whatever happens," he said, sounding a little perturbed by all the questions.

"Think we'll do OK?" I asked, hoping my own self-doubts didn't show too much.

"Damn straight," Max spit out, without thinking twice. "By the way if you get killed tomorrow, Van, can I have your watch? Mine seems to have gone on the blink," he added, as he threw his Marine Corps supplied timepiece in the wastebasket.

"I ain't gettin' killed and you ain't gettin' no damn watch," I responded, without losing a step in my pacing around the room.

"Will you guys knock it off? You're driving me crazy. We're going to all do just fine tomorrow. We're marines aren't we?" Tom said, sounding very confident, as usual.

"Why don't you do something useful, like get us a cup of coffee?" Max asked. "I can't stand watching you walk the room much longer."

"Get your own damned coffee. Pacing is what I do best," I answered.

"Could you guys knock off the shit? I'm trying to compose a

letter to Sandi and I can't think with all this racket going on," Tom pleaded.

"That girl doesn't want any letters from any marine. She ain't going to marry into the Corps," Max poked.

"She's in love with this marine and she can't help herself," Tom boasted, trying to hide the one area in his life where he didn't have complete confidence.

"You're dreaming," I said, trying to get in one more dig, before I stepped out into the passageway, on my way up to the flight deck for one last breath of fresh air. It was a long walk, but who could sleep.

A large number of people were walking around the ship alone and in small groups, an unusual occurrence for 0200. Not much sleeping going on. Mostly thinking. And praying. Mostly in private. The prayers were, I'm sure, largely identical. Please Lord, don't let me get hurt too bad and please, please Lord don't let me screw up. If it's time to die, Lord please let me do it with some dignity. Don't let me be a coward. Amen. Letters home were similar. Dear Mom and Dad, Tomorrow your son will be going into Vietnam. Doesn't look too serious. I'll be careful. Whatever happens, I love you.

It was extremely hot on the hangar deck. Our uniforms were drenched with sweat and stuck to our bodies. People took off packs to use as a seat on the deck and seconds later they put them back on, a reaction to the nervous tension. Staying in one spot or position for more than a few seconds proved impossible. It was impossible to get comfortable. Though the large holes in the side of the ship on the hangar deck were open to the outside, back in the corner near the aft section where I was standing the air was completely still and stale from the glut of humanity that was using it. It had been weeks since we left California. It would be months before most of us would see it again. We were in great shape despite being largely inactive for the last 17 days and the hot weather had little effect on our ability to operate. The loss of one night's sleep and gallons of sweat was just a nuisance. We were ready. We'd been trained for exactly this moment. No more warm-ups. No more practices. I hoped I didn't forget what I was supposed to do.

Marines claim to be the world's best fighting force and they believe it. Confidence had been built into all of us through months of drill and practice. Confidence, as the Marines very well knew, had always and will always be fundamental to winning when the bullets start to fly. Searching the young faces, as we mustered on the open hangar deck 50 feet below the flight deck, I could see the pride and the preparedness.

As the Executive Officer of India Company, I had a special, unhurried view. Four young second lieutenants each herded groups of 50 or so of these green-clad fighting men from station to station, as we moved smoothly through the South China Sea at a brisk 20 knots. They were doing all the important work. I had very little of importance to do except help the Company Gunnery Sergeant oversee the issuance of rations, special equipment, live ammo, and weapons. We had lots of every kind of special fighting tools in addition to our normal issue of rifles, food, helmets, flakjackets, cartridge belts and canteens. Every marine carried at least 75 pounds of equipment on his back, some even more. How in the hell are we going to move once we exit the chopper? I thought to myself, as I strapped on one more hand grenade. Adrenaline and well-conditioned muscles would work wonders once we hit the dirt of South Vietnam, now only a few miles away.

Getting 1,000 men into the correct helicopter and that helicopter into the right place on the ground five miles away is one complex problem. Fortunately we'd been through the exercise many times in many different places around the world, but never with quite this much intensity and seriousness. The prospect of combat concentrates the mind wonderfully.

We somehow stumbled into the right area on the hangar deck. Each assembly area is marked on the deck with bright red paint to identify the station number and unit. We have been memorizing these markings for three days. We've walked through the drill five times. This time people pay more attention and find their places on the deck without too much fumbling around. Nobody wants to get lost from his unit.

As units are called and start to make their way from the hangar deck up to the flight deck, some 50 feet above us, people cling to each other, afraid to let even a few feet separate you from the guy in front. The realization of what I'm about to go through starts to set in. I'm scared but I'm not supposed to show it and try not to. I have to lead. To set the example. To always look like I know exactly what I'm doing. I've had three years to get ready. I could use three more. The pair of single silver bars on my collar designated me as a first lieutenant, and reminded me and others of my responsibility and assumed readiness for this role.

Self-doubts fill my consciousness. I hope it isn't too obvious to others. Watching the troops and my friends go about their jobs helps. These are good people. I'm counting on that. They'll be counting on me. The ultimate team sport.

Before going topside, I made one last check with the Company Commander. He was ready. He was nervous too but had a great ability to channel the fear into action and intensity, which had a positive effect on all of us. He gave last-minute instructions in a forced, slightly unnatural, higher-pitched voice.

Captain Ronald Swenson was an eight-year veteran of the Corps and was well prepared for the task ahead. A native of Minneapolis and a graduate of the University of Minnesota, Captain Swenson was a tall Nordic blond who looked like he could chew nails. He had joined our unit just before we left Camp Pendleton and was still finding his way around the company, but his precise military manner and his quickness to smile had made him a popular commander from the first minute he had arrived. He was a confidence donor and he was totally in control.

"I'm not waiting for you on the ground," he told me once again. "Once I have two platoons ready to go, I'm moving out. I'm counting on you to get the rest of the company together and catch up," he added. I nodded my agreement on the plan, which had already been given several times, and waited to hear any last-minute changes. There weren't any.

Assignments are double-checked with the platoon commanders and objectives are marked on maps which we'll find out later barely resemble the terrain they're supposed to describe. This is critical stuff. Finding the proper position in a totally strange location is always tricky. Bullets flying around may make it a touch more difficult. There will be hundreds of nervous, well-armed marines on the ground, and trying to avoid getting shot by your own people because you're out of position is a full-time job.

Once on the ground it's important to quickly get back into our proper unit groupings and move out towards our first objective, while avoiding getting too bunched up. Just like we've practiced.

Don't make it any more difficult than it needs to be. Just get it done.

I'll be going in on a chopper which will arrive on the flight deck at Station Blue 10. The Company First Sergeant and I will be with eight or nine other marines from the 2nd Squad of the 3rd Platoon. We'll be landing in the third wave. The Skipper and the first two platoons will go in first.

We watch the first group ascend the passageway, wondering how experienced they'll be by the time we arrive some 15 minutes later. It'll take the choppers 10 trips and three hours to get the whole battalion ashore. The 15-minute wait for our turn is an eternity.

Finally, a call came over the ship's overhead microphone system and our group moved forward and up 50 feet, by ladder, to the flight deck, which was now devoid of aircraft and strangely quiet. The carrier was moving into the wind very smoothly and peacefully, seemingly oblivious to the death and destruction that may be going on a few miles away. It was blistering hot. The wind moving across the flight deck provided some temporary relief. The flight deck crews were taking a small break from the heat and the frantic activity that had been going on here since dawn and that would take place again in a couple of minutes when the choppers found their way back to the ship and its huge flight deck.

We ran from the top of the ladder along the side of the flight deck until we reached the Blue 10 Station on the starboard side of the ship and gathered in a small group, slightly forward of the ship's control tower and out of the way of the deck crews and the helicopter blades that would soon come flashing onto the enormous steel deck. Most of us knelt or sat to get some relief from the crushing weight on our backs. Breathing came with some difficulty. Nobody talked. A sergeant moved silently among his troops adjusting equipment and checking safety catches on rifles. It was very quiet except for the rushing of the wind across the flight deck.

The returning choppers finally appeared on the horizon, looking like a small swarm of insects against a mixture of a bright blue sky and intermittent, large, white, billowing clouds. Pulse rates and blood pressures increased, as did activity from the deck crews.

Twenty-five of these choppers would shortly come hurling sideways and forward onto the moving deck, at predesignated locations along the entire length and breath of this seagoing monster. The pilots made it look easy. It wasn't.

The noise of the arriving choppers increased to ear-shattering levels, as each of the machines grunted and groaned to hit their moving target and also miss the other 24 aircraft. Nobody moves until these babies are on the deck and stable. One wrong move and you get a rotor blade in the mouth, a disaster even for a tough, hardheaded marine.

All of the birds eventually got safely into position and the signal came to load up. We stood and began to run in an uncomfortable crouching position to our assigned aircraft. I followed the First Sergeant along the thin yellow lines painted on the deck. He moved pretty well for a 40-year-old, 22-year-veteran of the Corps. He'd seen this drill before. Might be a good idea to keep my eye on him for a while when we get on the ground. He knew his job just like the rest of us, only better.

Getting 12 combat-equipped marines settled in the belly of an HR34 Sikorsky was a tight fit. Finding the matching ends of seat belts was an impossible task without the aid of the two helicopter crew members who accompanied us on the journey. The two pilots sat up front and slightly above us. All we could see of them was their boots. The two crewmen repeated orders to us from the pilot, but the orders were largely unheard over the din caused by the increased noise of the engine as the pilot began to apply more power. The crew members finished getting us buckled up, then took their assigned positions, one near the door and one in the side window. Both cradled M-60 machine guns, pointed out and down, for the time being. Those machine guns would get a good workout during the next eight years.

Flying off a moving aircraft carrier in a helicopter was a real thrill. Disney would have charged two E-tickets for this ride. In the intense heat and humidity, the chopper had to work super hard to get adequate lift. While directly above the deck, air rushed downward from the revolving rotor blades, bounced off the deck back upward toward the blades, forcing them upward. This gave the chopper a powerful initial upward lift. But as the pilot maneuvered the aircraft, mostly sideways and slightly forward, we eventually slipped over the side of the flight deck and immediately lost the helpful updraft supplied by the deck. We lost lift and begin a quick dive towards the water. The dive gave us more speed, which gave us more lift. The 80-or-so-feet trip from the flight deck to the water took only a fraction of a second. If the pilot didn't do this just right we would end up in the water or he would stall the aircraft, with exactly the same result. In either case, it's not likely to end up being a fun time, especially with 75 pounds of sinkers on your back. The rotors finally caught enough air and took us quickly from wave top to an altitude of 1,000 feet where the air was cool and quiet. Our stomachs were in our throats. Out the side window I watched the carrier become smaller and smaller as it faded from my view. No going back now. Our next stop would be in a strange new country. I hoped the pilots could find the right country and put us down somewhere close to where the rest of the company was now residing. Two of the young marines sitting next to me lost what little breakfast they still had.

The first view from the air of the coastline of Vietnam was stunning. The brilliant white beaches provided high contrast with the light-green-colored farmlands and the deep, dense forests just beyond them. Majestic mountains loomed far in the distance, though only partially visible because of large, fluffy clouds that hid much of their ultimate definition. The terrain immediately below us, and stretching out in every direction, was dominated by small irregular rice paddies, chopped up in undefined, random plots. People were working most of them. They didn't seem to notice the noisy intruders overhead. An occasional river or stream darted through the countryside in irregular, winding patterns. Clusters of trees here and there housed small villages and most of the local population.

As we started our descent, we crossed Highway One, the area's only paved road. The road stretched north and south along the coast for hundreds of miles. I heard only the sounds of the engines and the roar of the wind pouring through the door. Nothing seemed out of order. Peaceful. Under control. If death and destruction were taking place somewhere below us it wasn't obvious from this vantage point, high above the landscape. Another change in the sound of the engine alerted us that we were accelerating our descent. The ground moved up towards us rapidly and the temperature began to rise. The chopper started changing direction frequently, as the pilot tried to avoid any chance of getting hit by ground fire and it became impossible to get oriented to features on the ground. We were supposed to land within a few hundred yards of someplace called Duc Lo. I caught sight of a village out the side door, just as the chopper sat down in what would become an all-too-familiar, very wet rice paddy. I hoped it was the right village.

The first step outside of the helicopter came fast. Twelve marines exiting a helicopter in a combat area looked something like one gigantic enema, I suppose. It was over fast. No future sitting inside the belly of that huge, green target. Let's get the hell out of here and on the ground where we can start doing some grunt stuff.

The rice paddy water came up and over the tops of our boots and we splashed around momentarily, confused by the rush of the wind and the water thrown from the rotor blades of our helicopter. We seemed to move in slow motion, as each footstep required an inordinate amount of energy. We stumbled in the general direction of the only village we could see in the vicinity, trying to locate someone or something that would give us our bearings. The choppers took little time in getting out of there once their loads were on the ground and out of the way. It was suddenly much quieter and each person went individually about the task of finding his unit.

The Skipper was easy to spot. He was surrounded by too many people, most of whom were operating and testing their radio sets, the communications glue for all combat units. The PRC-25, familiarly the Prick 25, was the workhorse of the communications network at the lower infantry echelons. They allowed the Skipper to be in constant contact with his four platoon commanders, the Battalion Commander, artillery units, air units and naval gunfire ships. All require individual radios and their separate operators. Wonderful technical stuff and very necessary in the constant fight to stay in contact with all of the units around and in support of us. Unfortunately the Prick-25 has a 10-foot-high aerial that waves high in the air like some crazy lightning rod. The one thing they always attract is enemy fire. It won't take Charlie long to figure out that the guy with all the radios is the boss. The more radios, the bigger the boss. This unfortunate fact of life gets more Purple Hearts for company grade officers than any other single factor in the war. It becomes a constant battle to keep the headquarter groups spread out enough to avoid giving away the location of the commander. Few hours will go by without hearing the cry "Don't bunch up. Keep spread out."

As I arrived at the southwest corner of the village where the Skipper was operating his command post, I sensed from the radio chatter that everything was more or less under control. The first two platoons had cleared the village, without incident. Nothing there but several old ladies and an old man. A few kids peeked around the corners of the grass huts but kept their distance from the marines moving around them. Off to the left of my position I could see what looked to be elements of H Company moving out across an open rice paddy. Through the rush of green humanity, I sighted Max helping some injured marine back to the rear. Probably a sprained ankle, as I hadn't yet heard any gunfire.

I moved away from the command post so as not to cause any further congestion. A few corpsmen and assorted clerks, members of my small staff, followed me wherever I went. As the Executive Officer, I'm like the Vice President. Not much to do unless somebody gets hurt. We found a small group of trees 50 yards away from the command post and waited for the Skipper to give the signal to move out. Eyeballs peered out from every helmet, searching and scanning in every direction, fully alert, and absorbing sights and sounds from the new and strange surroundings. Sweat was running from every pore and uniforms, only minutes ago so clean and starched, were dirty and wet. Cigarettes tasted like hell. The water in our canteens was warm and would stay that way for the next year.

In the distance, the sound of small arms fire could be faintly made out but seemed far enough away to be somehow nonthreatening. A small group of jet fighters lazily circled overhead, as air cover for the choppers. Just like we practiced it, so far.

Over my company command radio, I heard the Skipper give the order to saddle up and move out, as another wave of choppers began to hit the deck behind us, unloading the next units of the assault force. We'd been here half an hour and no resistance had been received. No shots fired. No bad guys. No Charlie. Maybe this wasn't going to be so bad after all. Probably heard we were coming and decided to get the hell out of the way.

We started moving quickly, in unison right from the beginning, without the need for urging or pushing. Everyone on their feet and in motion in one quick stroke. No one wanted to get left behind. No one wanted to get lost. We've got to move about three miles west and get dug in on a hill overlooking the village of Pac Bu by nightfall. Two hours ought to do it as long as we don't run into some unexpected Charlies or encounter some other unforeseen complication. As we moved out, we passed through the larger part of the village that served as a rest stop for our first minutes in country. It contained a dilapidated old church, a small building that was probably both a school and city hall, and a few dozen thatch-roofed hooches. This was home to maybe 300 people but today we saw no more than 20.

The old ladies ignored us, but the kids figured out, in quick fashion, that marines were a great source of candy, cigarettes and food. They had immediately learned to speak the few necessary words of English. The marines responded by using the three or four words of Vietnamese they'd been taught during our 17 days aboard ship. It was an instant love affair that would last through the years and one which would cause no small number of marines to fall victim to a well-placed grenade, thrown from the hand of a child. Charlie used any weapon he had, including the kids. I noticed my hands had finally stopped shaking.

I could see our lead platoons working their way past open paddies in three parallel columns along dikes that separated one rice paddy from another. Dikes offered the only consistent source of dry ground from point A to point B in most parts of this country. They also proved to be a fertile location for booby traps, the most feared and deadly weapon used by Charlie. A hundred thousand lost American limbs and organs would attest to that. Most of these booby traps hit more than one target because of our natural tendency to stand close to each other, gathering comfort from each other. Often a deadly idea.

"Don't bunch up."

"Keep your intervals."

"Spread out." The calls for safe procedures kept coming but were frequently ignored. It was just too natural to want to be close to your neighbor.

The cakewalk in the rice paddy turned to mayhem with the arrival of the first sounds of incoming rifle fire from close range. It was close but decidedly undefined. It was hard to pinpoint the exact location of the immediately understood threat. Our forward units seemed somehow to be participating by the looks of the sudden change in their tempo. People no longer followed well-defined paths. Some stood up. Some took refuge behind nearby trees. Movement seemed to speed up and slow down at the same time.

Within seconds radio traffic was at full speed. The Skipper wanted to know what the hell was happening. Whatever was going on, there was sufficient activity to bring each of us and all of our senses to a total state of alertness.

Most of the activity turned out to be a slight overreaction to the spotting of two or three stragglers from one of Charlie's main units, which was retreating from the advance of another marine unit moving forward on our far right flank. Our forward platoons caught them by surprise. Our guys opened up on them from a couple of hundred yards away and several hundred rounds of fire were put on the target. It should have taken two or three well-aimed rounds to get the job done.

At least one of the soldiers, clad in what appeared to be black pajamas, disappeared behind a distant dike and returned a few harmless but nonetheless tension-causing rifle shots before disappearing forever into his turf.

We eventually found one body but the rest seem to have slipped away into thin air. Where the hell did they go? Not a trace. No blood. No tracks.

Movement of our column stopped while the Skipper moved forward to get a firsthand look. He takes reports from the people most involved, ensures himself that they've done a good job of searching the area for bodies, and issues orders to move out again. We all relax a bit but a feeling of some disappointment spreads to each unit. We had reacted correctly and quickly. But the two Charlies that had disappeared bother us. Where were they? Would they pop up later to do some damage? How could they slip away so easily? This wasn't good.

We had put some incredible firepower into a few square feet of worthless ground. The fire had been well aimed, deadly and generally useless. We had killed one bad guy and a lot of rice. Not much to write home about. The corpse looked surprised. He had died instantly. He was different from us in several ways besides being dead. He had no helmet, no flak jacket or much ammo. Shower shoes were the heaviest thing he carried, besides his rifle. No food. These guys were traveling light.

For most of us, this was the first real experience with violent, swift death. The corpse had no name, no identity, no claim to us but as each of us walked by his mangled, dirty body, the thought of how easily this torn body could have been one of ours, lying stretched out in the mud, rushed quickly through our minds. He had been shot in the right ear and hadn't suffered, but the concept of such an instant, final ending was now physical and real. This could be one of us, any second. This would be many of us over the next eight years.

We realized for the first time, but not the last, that finding Charlie was not all we needed to do to kill him. He was smart, elusive and would require us all to learn more about him and his way of life if we were to do our assigned task and stay alive. Somehow the terrain seemed more friendly to him.

Our mini-battle was over in less than five minutes. It seemed much longer. It also seemed much shorter, not more than a few seconds. We had drawn our first blood. Made our first kill. Shot our first shots. Seen our first death, up close and personal.

We moved on, our composure somewhat shaken but also with just a hint of increased confidence and swagger. We knew now that we could respond and bring some misery to whoever decided to take us on. A small sample of what was to come, but a sample nonetheless, and we breathed a little easier knowing we had survived it.

We got no more than 125 yards further along our intended path when all hell broke loose about midway down the company column, on our left side. This time Charlie got off the first rounds and this time enjoyed the advantage of surprise. He placed well-aimed rounds into the midsection of our company. Some of our troops were caught out in the open. Marines drop. Blood flows. American blood this time.

"Corpsman! Corpsman!" came a call that would become all too familiar. "Corpsman! We need a corpsman up here!" Immediately two of these unarmed angels of mercy responded. They always seemed to be there, no matter the risk. Two hundred marines hit the deck and reacted to the incoming fire. Two Navy corpsmen stood and moved toward the sound of pain. They ignored the danger around them to get to their patients, quickly and without reservation. No hands-off medicine for these guys. No call-me-in-the-morning crap. They came when they were called. These guys made house calls.

The corpsmen all have the same name. Doc. After four wars this century, it would seem possible to come up with something more original than that but no other name seemed to fit as well. They take major harassment from the marines until somebody gets hurt, then everyone wants them for a buddy. Keeping a wounded marine alive until he can be med-evaced to a nearby hospital where real Docs close holes, remove stumps and administer the best emergency medical procedures known to man requires very special skills, and lots of raw courage. Corpsmen all seemed to have plenty of both. This war was made different from any other war in history by the helicopter. The birds got wounded to an operating table in minutes. A quarter of a million wounded did just fine. Fifty-eight thousand didn't make it in time. Without the helicopters and the corpsmen, another 100,000 probably wouldn't have made it either.

Our response to the incoming fire was more intense this time. Both of the forward two platoons were bringing the target under fire. There was a grenade explosion from time to time. I could hear squad leaders and platoon leaders yelling over the noise of the gunfire, moving people and pointing out new targets. It became an active, noisy place, a very noisy place.

The Skipper dispatched our rear platoon towards the trouble spot to bring more pressure on the target. People were pinned down along the main column but they continued to exchange small arms fire with the Charlies, who had taken refuge in a small cluster of trees about 100 yards forward and left of my position. The Captain couldn't get the artillery-fire unit to react to our situation right away and he got more than a bit hot under the collar.

"I need some HE at coordinates 574-355 and I need it now," I heard him yell into a headset which he had taken over, after failing to get any response through the operator. "Jumbo 3/9, where in the hell is my support?" he yelled a couple of seconds later, into the same headset.

The Artillery Liaison Officer was trying his best to get high explosives on the target, but was having the same basic problem as the Skipper. We needed the help and it was taking far too long. The target was too close to call in air cover.

One of the forward platoons finally managed to get someone to throw in a few well-placed rocket grenades from an M-79 grenade launcher, bringing clouds of dirt and smoke from the target area. Rifle fire continued from their side.

Our 3rd Platoon was now moving in carefully from the left side, taking advantage of Charlie's exposed flank. He was catching it from two sides now. The largest part of the force, perhaps 15 or 20 of them, made a mad dash further into the tree line and away from the fire we were delivering on their position. A few remaining Charlies either decided to slug it out or else they didn't see the marines coming on their flank. It's all over in one wild burst of automatic fire and a few well-placed hand grenades. They paid a high price for holding their positions. We had the first serious entries for our scorecard. Five marines needed medical attention. Twelve Charlies need a hole in the ground.

Body viewing was mandatory and horribly repulsive. The bodies had found completely unnatural positions. Legs and arms went off in crazy directions, making the remains appear like store dummies dropped off a fast-moving truck. Mud-caked bodies and bloodstained uniforms wrapped around deadly rifles that were now less menacing. This group looked much more like soldiers than the earlier VC we'd seen. They had packs, helmets and military insignias. These were North Vietnamese regulars.

I was now fully occupied with getting the wounded back to an area where the choppers could pick them up. The Skipper had his hands full reporting the results to Battalion Headquarters and trying to figure out how to get the show back on the road. We were now seriously behind our original schedule. The Battalion Commander wanted to know every detail and the Skipper couldn't get him off the radio. We didn't have many details to report. It would be days before Intelligence pieced enough of the details together to find out what units these dead bodies belonged to.

As word of our wounded started to spread through the company, I felt for the first time a sense of anger developing with the troops. Revenge enters our emotional makeup.

"Let's get some more of these bastards," I heard someone

whisper to his buddy, as if killing more of them would somehow make our wounded buddies feel better.

Before our emotions got a chance to calm down, things got exciting again towards the front of our main column. It started slowly and then suddenly accelerated into a full-fledged, all-out firefight. This time some of the supporting groups were starting to get into the action and I could hear, over the radio net, the 1st Platoon Commander request some mortar rounds out in front of his position. He was exchanging fire with 25 or 30 VC.

It took three or four minutes and several rounds to find the correct target. Once we have it properly located, the rest of the mortar section makes their sighting adjustments and moves in for the kill.

"Fire for effect," I heard the Platoon Commander shout in a loud and clear voice over the radio. "Let er rip, you're right on target," he added.

The mortar tubes, Max's platoon, now located a few hundred yards to our rear, let 15 or 20 rounds go all at once. The rounds landed in a tight pattern at the edge of a small cluster of trees just in front of our 1st Platoon.

"One more time, you're right on top of them," I hear the Platoon Leader yell. He gets his response immediately and bits of trees and dirt and smoke rise from the tree line. Now it's the Captain who wants to know what the hell is going on and rushes forward to have a look. Evidently the mortars, though very accurately placed, haven't done enough damage because the small arms fire continues at a furious pace. No letup in the activity.

The choppers for the wounded arrived a few hundred yards to our rear, but had to be called off temporarily because of the intense small arms fire they were receiving as they made their approach and because rounds continued arriving from overhead.

The forward units were starting to run out of ammo. Without waiting to be told, two of my clerks moved forward with a couple of cases of rifle ammunition we had been dragging along. I sent a runner back to the First Sergeant, instructing him to organize a detail to get some additional hardware up here from Battalion Supply. We were going through our ammunition at a lively pace.

Two of the wounded that had been assembled from our first firefight, a few minutes earlier, needed to get out of there quickly.

I was running out of hands to get everything done that needed doing.

The Battalion Commander was furiously trying to get the Skipper on the phone but he had outrun his radio operators and was temporarily unavailable. Our 1st Platoon Commander was reporting more casualties. He also wanted artillery support and more machine-gun ammo. The Captain arrived at his position with the artillery support radio in full operation and ready for action. Arty was now available. We were going to get to practice all the good stuff today.

I made a second radio request to Battalion for the needed ammo, grabbed a couple of boxes of machine-gun ammo, and started for the head of the column. It wasn't hard to find because of the ongoing noise. By the time I got there I was drenched in sweat and a little winded. I realized, sitting there behind a protective dike, that I was covered from head to foot with mud. I'd been crawling and moving on my stomach most of the way. No John Wayne stuff for me.

I handed off the ammo to a runner to get the remaining few yards up to the 1st Platoon Command Post and took a minute to catch my breath before we started to evacuate the new wounded, who had now been moved back towards my position.

The Skipper and the Artillery Forward Observer were 15 yards to my right engaged in an attempt to get the artillery fire on target. It takes longer than it should and at the same time our mortar people are now temporarily out of ammo, so the VC have a few minutes of uninterrupted pleasure.

The bad guys are in a tree line about 70 yards from my position. About half of our 1st Platoon is lying down in an exposed rice paddy, keeping their heads down and trying to locate a more protected location, behind one of the many dikes that provide the only cover in the space between them and Charlie. The other half of the platoon has found good firing positions from our own tree line and is doing the best it can to keep the exposed marines from getting chopped up by Charlie.

It was a fairly even standoff until the Skipper finally got the artillery on target. Once we got that accomplished, the exchange was over in a hurry. We poured in a quick 20 or 30 rounds on top of them. All enemy fire immediately ceased. For good measure, the

Skipper gave the entire area another pretty good going over. He halted the artillery fire for a minute and waited for a response but none came. He waited some more. The tree-lined area remained silent. No movement and no rifle fire.

Satisfied that the path to the far tree line might now be safe, the Skipper ordered forward the marines in the exposed paddy area. It took several minutes for a sizable group of them to traverse the remaining few yards as they now moved with newfound caution and care. In twos and threes they rushed forward a few yards at a time, threw themselves to the ground behind another dike and then provided cover for the next group of two or three. They alternated this series of movements, until they finally reached the tree line at the far side. It's the standard tactic for advancing over contested terrain where there is no cover.

Once in the tree line, they found that the ever-elusive Charlie had disappeared with only a few traces of his earlier presence. Spent cartridges and an occasional blood spot in the dirt were all that remained.

While other units were rushed forward, those of us toward the rear finally arranged a successful med-evac. It took four helicopters to retrieve the wounded, which now numbered 15. The same choppers also brought in a much-needed resupply of ammo. This exchange of bodies for ammo would be a scene repeated thousands of times over the next eight years. The choppers that flew to our rescue were a source of all things good and I doubt that any marine would ever entirely lose the special emotional sensation caused by the sounds of whirling rotor blades overhead.

The Skipper wanted to talk. As I moved forward toward his position I passed a few less seriously wounded marines. I couldn't force myself to look directly at the wounds even though most were superficial. Somehow I found it easier to focus on some other aspect of the person than the wound itself. It's as if ignoring the pain and blood would somehow make it less real. Once the wounded man is evacuated you don't have to deal with it anymore. The Company Command Post activity was moving at a frantic pace. The Battalion Commander wanted us to move out. He wanted information about the casualties, disposition of enemy forces, and how much toilet paper we had left. The Captain wanted the wounded evacuated, more ammo, and status reports from his staff.

He wanted the Colonel off his back. He wanted it fast. The Company Gunnery Sergeant and I started on some of the work details, while the major part of the company prepared to move out again. We were a full three hours behind our original schedule.

The Gunny was in full swing. He yelled and people moved. Not even the Captain could put fear into people the way the Gunny did. Better nose-to-nose with Charlie than the Gunny. It was his first shooting war too but you'd never know it from his confident demeanor. The 15 years of training he'd had in the Corps was paying off for him like it was for all of us. We were all starting to do things right. It was surprising how instinctive our moves as individuals and groups seemed to be. I guess it shouldn't have been such a surprise. The Corps had been doing it like this for nearly 200 years. I found myself watching the Gunny and wondering where the hell the Corps found these guys. He was everyplace.

It seemed like a strange time and place to realize that I'm essentially having what amounts to a fascinating experience. I'm starting to feel a deep sense of satisfaction and accomplishment. It felt good to see our company, and me as a part of it, getting the job done. Won't the folks back home be proud of us? We'd only been here a few hours but we'd already proved we could move, react, grunt, sweat and die. And kill. Just like the movies except for the lack of music. I coughed from the strong stench of death and gunpowder that filled the air. This was the real thing and I did OK. We all had. A few more days like this and old Charlie would definitely be on his way back to Hanoi.

The Colonel was having one of his fits. He screams at the Captain over the radio to move out but keeps talking so long and asking questions that the Captain doesn't have much time to do his job. No way to please this guy. I guess he had his problems too. K Company, on our right, had pushed a large group of Charlies back into a small village several hundred yards directly in front of us. It was urgent we get to them before they escape.

We started moving with more quickness and clarity than before. People stuck closer to the ground. They moved in quick, short steps. They covered each other's moves. This terrain and the trails we were following could have easily been booby-trapped, so the word comes down again.

"Don't bunch up."

"Keep spread out."

"Maintain your intervals." Something about human nature draws us closer together during times of increased fear.

There wasn't much activity in the village by the time we arrived. K Company had it pretty well under control. After a brief discussion between the Skipper and his counterpart from K Company we started a house-to-house search for the VC. They had been here only minutes before. Now we didn't find any. Where had they gone? Where we weren't.

The troops did find some small amounts of ammunition hidden under the floor of one of the bigger thatch-roofed houses in the village. Other items of little significance were found in other places in the village. None of the villagers had any knowledge of where this ammunition came from or who it belonged to. They don't know anybody named Charlie, for that matter. They don't know what village this is, or their own names. They don't know diddley-squat.

This village was definitely one of Charlie's hiding places, a fact that was verified some time later, when one of Battalion's South Vietnamese interpreters extracted a confession from one of the ladies from the local population. Nice guys, these interpreters. Crude and violent. They wanted information. They got it. It didn't seem to matter to them how they got it. They screamed, threatened and maimed. They made no friends with the local villagers. We had to keep a constant eye on them to maintain some semblance of civilized behavior. The Company Commander had to intervene to prevent one of them from removing some old lady's left ear with a not-so-sharp knife during his interrogation of her about Charlie. Are these people really on the same side? Nobody was sure on this day.

The 1st Platoon found an interesting underground passage behind one of the houses. The Skipper asked for volunteers to go explore this mysterious hole in the ground. I looked the other way and pretended to be heavily occupied with some other urgent program. Two young marines finally stepped forward. This was scary stuff, but the two marines slipped silently out of sight down a hole just large enough for each to get through. The opening led to a rather large-sized underground room. With the use of a flashlight they could determine several people had been living here.

Cooking and eating utensils were in evidence, as were several sleeping mats. Two tunnels large enough to stand up in led out of the main room in two directions at right angles to each other. A quick search of the room turned up no weapons, but the two marines seemed to think they could hear noises coming from one of the tunnels. Their voices became a little tense as they relayed information to those of us standing above them.

The Skipper ordered the interpreter down into the tunnel, but he wasn't anxious to join the two marines down there and tried to find other things to do and pretended he didn't understand what the Captain was trying to tell him. He was more interested in yelling at the ever-present kids from the village and in beating the hell out of an old lady who wouldn't answer his questions. He finally got in the tunnel, yelled a few well-chosen words in Vietnamese where the noises seemed to be coming from and quickly crawled back out.

Moments later, two extremely nervous and scared boys no more than 10 years old came scrambling out with hands held high over their heads, talking a mile a minute. They jabbered on in Vietnamese for a few seconds to the two marines, who now had them covered with rifles. I'm not sure which group was the most scared. The marines answered the boys in halting English, commanding them to get out of the tunnel and up out of the hole. Not much real communication going on here, but eventually the boys got the message and they came scurrying out of the small hole. The boys swore that they were the only ones down there. They hadn't heard of anyone named Charlie either.

No more noises could be detected in the tunnel. It was determined that this haven for Charlie should probably be destroyed, so we arranged for some explosives to be brought forward from Battalion Headquarters, now only a few hundred yards to our rear. By the time it got there, the rest of this village had been gone over and a few more small pieces of evidence were found to definitely determine that this was a place where Charlie liked to hang out.

The locals started to remember that Charlie came from time to time, forced the villagers to feed them and care for their wounded, then left. The villagers claimed they hated the VC and would prefer to be left alone. It was probably true. These people did not look all that interested in this shooting stuff and would probably like to get back to growing rice, raising kids and feeding their water buffalo.

A couple of explosives experts arrived with the stuff to shut down the tunnel. They scrambled down in the hole to set about placing the explosive materials in strategic places to tear it apart when we pushed the button. The tunnel was not part of the community anyway. It was definitely Charlie's home away from home.

As the TNT did its work, we all watched with interest as traces of smoke rose from more than 10 separate locations outside the village in various rice paddies surrounding it. This hole in the ground was quite a network of interconnected tunnels. The Skipper ordered people from the nearest units to rush to the locations where smoke was rising and to lob a few grenades down the holes. If someone was still hiding down there, the concussion would kill them, if the shrapnel didn't. We waited for sounds of activity to come from the main tunnel or any of the many other routes into or out of the elaborate system, but none came. We decided to get on with our mission above ground. Leave the cave exploration to someone else. It was bad enough going after Charlie when you could see him. Let him have those dungy, dark, mysterious holes in the ground.

We reached our main objective for the first day, three hours late but without further complication or delay. Just enough time to lay out our defensive position for the night, dig our holes and grab a cold can of ham and lima beans before the darkness sets in. A treeless, small, nobby hill just south of Duc Lo, and about two miles inland from the sea, will be our home for this night. Our first day had been filled with extraordinary, first-time experiences. I felt emotionally drained, physically spent and ready for some rest. But, on this night we would have very little time to relax or sleep. Internal alarm signals were set at the high.

The normal tasks of digging holes, laying out wire and positioning our main firepower was accomplished without the usual grumbling and unnecessary chatter. After the events of this day the troops needed very little pushing to motivate them. The hill was a rather easy position to defend, especially with two rifle companies. Heaven help Charlie or any stray animal that might venture into our position. Every trigger will have a finger on it.

The foxhole I shared with the First Sergeant is on the rear side of the hill facing away from Pac Bu. It was just big enough for one of us at a time to sleep while the other stood watch. This arrangement will become quite familiar to us. We had been told to meet with the Skipper about 2100 hours and as we stumbled across the top of the hill to his position, which was no more than 50 yards away, we got a little disoriented in the total darkness of this moonless night and it took us too long to get there. He had already started the meeting without us.

"Nice of you two to join us," he said, as the First Sergeant and I came fumbling into the gathered circle of people.

"Battalion believes there are still quite a number of VC out there tonight and they may try to make a run for it," he repeated for my benefit.

"I want at least 50 percent of everybody awake and alert at all times tonight and I'll be out there checking. You do the same," he continued.

"Any questions?" he offered.

"Password?" the Gunny asked.

"Yeah. 'Tennessee Waltz'," the Captain responded, slightly embarrassed that he had forgotten something so important. "Make sure everybody gets it," he added. I couldn't see clearly because of the complete darkness, but I could barely make out and identify the features of the people gathered around the Captain. Faces were tensed up. Jaws tightened. Not just another night in the boonies. Our first night on the ground in Vietnam and everyone had on their serious expression. After the Captain finished his instructions, I patted a couple of shoulders, mostly to cheer up my own spirits, before heading back across the hill to my spot in the dirt.

On the way back to our position the First Sergeant and I made some house calls. Nobody asleep yet. People were peering out into the darkness trying to get their night vision, searching for movement or noise that wasn't supposed to be there. Extra ammo and grenades were laid out in nice precise patterns, so they could be located and used without losing valuable time. Everyone seemed to have weathered the excitement of the first day. Most of them had put the events of the day out of their minds and were ready for the excitement of the first night. A few wanted to know if we had heard anything about their wounded buddies.

Getting comfortable in my foxhole was impossible. Muscles started to cramp after some time in the same position and there always seemed to be a small, sharp rock in exactly the same location where I was trying to position an elbow, knee or the cheek of my butt. The First Sergeant took the first watch. I stared up at the stars for a while, trying to relax enough to allow sleep to come. It was too early and there had been too much activity for that. It was extremely quiet. Every small sound could be heard. Even the tension could be heard, as hands gripped and regripped rifles.

Time goes by slowly and pictures of home drift in and out of my consciousness. When it came time for my watch at 2400, I wasn't certain if I'd slept or not. Probably did, but it didn't help much. It was time now to be fully on the alert and I didn't feel like being alert. I need to sleep now. Before I didn't. I'm not in sync with the war clock just yet.

The First Sergeant stretched out in the hole next to me and began to snore. Thanks a lot, Top. For the next three hours, myself and several hundred other marines on this hill fought the urge to close their eyes. In this darkness and quiet it became an almost impossible task. I tried to will my eyes open and constantly reminded myself of my responsibility to stay awake and alert. I changed positions, played with the dirt all around me and listened to the smallest of sounds. Time drug by. I told myself that next time I wouldn't waste my chance to sleep.

A burst of small arms fire was a welcome relief from the unbearably long dark night. It came from the other side of the hill and I judged that it was probably somewhere out in front of our 3rd Platoon's position. Radio silence was broken and on my radio set I could hear the Skipper ask the young lieutenant to explain the situation. They evidently had some confirmed movement out in front of their position and were receiving a small amount of incoming small arms fire. It was being returned pretty heavily by the sound of it.

Machine guns joined in, which is not by the book unless you are under full-scale attack. Once you've fired them, you've given away their position and hiding place. You also lose night vision. So wait to use the machine guns until the bad guys are right on top of you, then open up big time.

Based on what he heard of the situation, the Skipper ordered the young platoon commander to get the machine guns stopped. He then requested some artillery illumination rounds to light up the area so we could see what the hell was going on. If you've lost the ability to see in the dark, and given away your positions, might as well make it really bright.

Within a couple of minutes gigantic flares dropped from the sky just forward of our company position lighting the area to near-daylight levels, shocking the eyes and causing a slight disorientation. The First Sergeant and I, both now fully awake, made our way to the top of the hill and from a very prone position had a ringside seat for the action. As one parachute flare burned out and plummeted to earth another appeared out of the sky, keeping the area in full light and somehow making it more friendly.

Our 3rd Platoon ceased fire, hoping to get a fix on where the incoming was from, but no new fire was received. Whatever and whoever it was had disappeared just as suddenly as they had arrived. We waited and listened and waited and listened, watching the shadows move and looking for something more definite that could tell us where the bad guys were hiding. Nothing moved.

After a few more flares the Skipper called them off and we settled back into the intense and bitter darkness of the night, darker and heavier for our loss of night vision. It took some time for the silence to return to the area, as the radio nets were still going full blast and people were moving around the area checking things out. Everyone reporting to LBJ and down wanted to know what was happening. The Skipper made his reports for the next half hour even though there wasn't much to report. Yes, we did receive fire. No, we didn't see anyone. Increase the alert level to 100 percent for the remainder of the night. Who could sleep anyway.

The night passed without further incident except for the attack of B-52-sized mosquitoes just before dawn. The surrounding rice paddies produced the largest, most aggressive flying insects ever known to the human race. They seemed to thrive on American blood. I wondered if Charlie had a hand in training these monsters. It was possible, from time to time, to spot a marine without his rifle, his helmet or his flak jacket but after a few nights like this one, never without his insect repellent, neatly attached to his helmet for convenience. The repellent bottle became a permanent symbol of the war. It's on the statue honoring Vietnam Vets in Washington, D.C.

There would be many other nights at full alert during the next 12 months, none quite as well defined or as spooky as this one. Every movement and noise was somehow etched in permanent memory. No fuzziness, no missing segments. None of the many other nights could be the first one. There are many kinds of fear we had to come to grips with, but none quite like night fear. We had trained, constantly, at night so that we could learn to exploit it, use it to our advantage, but that was easier said than done. For the most part Charlie would own the night. He used it better. We fought it. We will continue to try but with little success. We turn the night over to Charlie and sometimes pay the price.

Once the first light of day appeared we sprang to life again. We filled the holes that served as our hotel rooms, grabbed a quick cup of intolerable instant coffee and hit the road in search of the elusive VC. Two days of hunting, stopping, digging in, and hunting some more proved fruitless. Charlie had disappeared, leaving little trace of his existence in the area. We swept through the area and then back through it again. Nothing but nearly empty villages, irate old ladies and persistent kids. No Charlie.

Our brief but intense first meeting with Charlie left scars on both sides. We had learned that we could operate as an effective combat unit. We had learned how to spill blood. We would never forget our first meeting with Charlie. There would be more. I was part of a Marine front-line fighting group. I had been training for this job and with this group for two and a half years. The training was over. This was the big show. As we moved towards a staging area that would be used to pick us up and move us to our new destination and home in Chu Lai, I couldn't help but ask, How did I get here?

2

Country's Freedom

Tolleson, Arizona, was a fine place to be a kid. The air was clear, the sky was big, the schools were closed all summer.

Summers spent in the heart of the Valley of the Sun were not always carefree days for a teenager growing up in the 1950s. There was work to do. Hard work. Teenagers were a big part of it. The work was a big part of us. Agriculture dominated the environment we lived in. The sun dominated everything. Social status was primarily determined by how much time you spent in the sun to earn a living. Kids often started serious work before they reached their teens. All of the known treasures of life, such as baseball mitts, spending money for dates, cars and pinball machine money, required some form of employment.

My parents were incredibly generous with whatever money they had, which most days was as close to zero as one ever wants to get. It wasn't a big thing not to have money. Nobody did. It didn't make you some kind of freak. There was almost always plenty of work to be found. Keeping out of the sun somehow was the key to survival and keeping one's place on the social scale. I had a strong enough back and the need for money was always there, but I had to acquire, over several years and many painful experiences, the willingness part of summer employment.

I was fired from several early jobs for horsing around while I was supposed to be working. It was very difficult for a 10-year-old to have the required concentration to go for eight or ten hours at a stretch without an occasional break for chasing butterflies or taking a few moments to hit dirt clods with a stick, to sharpen one's baseball skills, but most employers were intolerant of this deviant behavior. I lost a good-paying job as a grocery clerk for drinking too many free Cokes. I was removed as a phone answering service person, at a lumberyard, for playing hide and seek with two of my buddies during working hours. I was a complete failure in the workplace, before I turned 12. I turned a very profitable paper route into a financial disaster in about six months. Profits were plowed into candy bars and pinball machines at a frightening rate.

Rich, white farmers owned the fertile fields where world-class produce of every type and shape was grown. Stretching miles and miles in every direction from the center of the town, neatly kept fields and rows of various and sundry vegetables and melons grew to full size in the constant blazing sun and irrigation water, brought by canal from mountains lying many miles to the east. There were not-so-modest signs posted at the east and west entrances to the town proclaiming us to have 3,000 residents and announcing our boast: "Vegetable Capital of the World." Both claims were highly exaggerated, but there was some heavy-duty farming going on, in and around Tolleson. The land itself had been, for hundreds of centuries, barren, useless desert, home to a few lizards and snakes. Because huge amounts of mountain water had been transported overland via the irrigation canals, and crisscrossed the valley land-scape in awkward patterns, the land now produced mountains of lettuce, carrots, onions, cabbage, cantaloupes, watermelon and other assorted foodstuffs on a year-round basis. It was grown and harvested here and shipped to every corner of the world. There must have been good and bad years with the crops but to young eyes there seemed a constancy and permanence in this part of our lives. Each year brought more and different crops and always more jobs. There was work if you wanted or needed it. And we did.

Backbreaking work in the open fields, exposure to the unrelent-ing desert sun, where temperatures would have reached 110 to 115 degrees in the shade, if there had been any shade, which there wasn't, employed the Mexican population of our small town. Legal residents of the U.S.A. or not, the Mexican families brought with them to Tolleson a distinctive and interesting culture. They spoke a different language, ate different and very delicious foods, and participated not at all in the white-dominated town government or business community. They owned few stores, ran few businesses and held no governmental offices. They seldom owned their homes, made up about three quarters of the population of Tolleson, and shared very little in the economic wonders of the community. They worked the fields as families, kids six or seven years old working alongside their parents in 10- or 12-hour shifts, in the blistering hot Arizona sun, stooped to the ground in paralyzing, never-ending efforts to coax food from the soil. Dad kept most of the money and often spent a good share of it at the separate but equal tavern of his choice. A man had to have his beer. Mom worked the fields and kept food on the table for the normally large family. In good times there might be some meat to fill the tortillas. Beans were more usual. The warm, pleasant aroma of cooking beans and tortillas was always present in their homes. For us outsiders, it was always a treat to be asked to share some of this very different and wonderful-tasting food. In our house we treated racism more like an acquaintance than a friend.

Mexican kids grew up fast. They often slept three or four to a bed, ate when it was available, struggled with two languages, worked like an adult before they knew how to ride a bike. They had strict rules of conduct enforced harshly by both Dad and the parish priest. They rode in the backs of pickups when their dad was successful enough to afford one, wore hand-me-downs of every size and shape and had little time for the things of children. It was a stark life that encouraged premature aging, early parenthood and a lack of interest in educational achievement. There was no welfare for the farm workers, and no unemployment benefits. They didn't exist. Neither did disability insurance or health insurance. You worked or you didn't eat. You got hurt and that was your problem. There were no long-term unemployed. It wasn't possible. Vacation was a word that had very little meaning. When things got going at full speed in the summer, when harvesting had to be done, there was little time for any kind of leisure activity. There was no escape from the working of the dirt or the struggle to survive the torture of the suffocating heat. For the Mexican descendants of Tolleson it was too often a lifelong struggle.

I didn't completely escape either. One summer, when I was about 11, I was reluctantly dragged by my father to the potato fields. We had to be at work by 4:00 a.m., six days a week for seven or eight weeks. The morning wake-up came at some hour that was totally foreign to me. Pleading, crying and loud screams could not get me out of this morning madness. The day's work had to be done before the sun could turn the brown, dirt-lined potatoes to mush. I faked injury and serious illness. I invented excuses of every type and shape. But I went, not because my father was cruel or lacked understanding, but because he had tried the same excuses in his youth. They didn't work then either. I hated everything about the work but needed the money, since an ice-cold Coke cost a dime and a candy bar set you back a nickel. My dad needed the money too, so he drove a tractor that was used to pull up the potatoes from six or eight inches below the surface. I was part of the crew that put them in a sack. It was attached to the front of my waist and went between my legs and drug behind me, as we moved along the ground, stooping to reach for the objects of all this attention. When filled, the bags weighed 100 pounds. Pay was usually a quarter for each bag filled. I seldom made much money because of my unwillingness to move at a fast enough pace across the newly turned soil. I needed to stand up and stretch my aching back far too often. Talking to friends was more fun. Throwing a clod at some unsuspecting target, while the sun was still waiting to come up, was far more interesting and kept my mind off the pains and blisters that were developing.

In between such massive successes in the workplace, I screwed up a perfectly good paper route I had inherited from some older boy, but I did learn a lot about slow-paying customers and dead-beats. My customers learned about late deliveries and wet papers. I got walked out of a lumberyard by a union official who considered me a scab. And I badly mowed several thousand lawns, at a quarter each, and spent one full day as a cotton picker. Cotton picking exceeded all bounds of reasonability, as far as I was concerned. At the age of 16, it was not clear to me or any of those around me that I was going to be any great success in the workplace. Things just never seemed to go right and I had a certain aversion to getting too close to really hard work. There had to be better things in life.

Summers also provided plenty of leisure time for kids. We were free to have fun and explore our world, in the very best and simplest sense. We didn't have baby-sitters, we had 3,000 of them. Well, those big signs said 3,000, and who's to say otherwise? With our beat-up, one-speed bicycles for wings, we had complete access to our entire world and most of what we needed for entertainment. We roamed the town and all of its outlying areas, with few if any restrictions. We were seldom more than a few minutes away from home. We were also never far from some ball game or another. We tried every kind of game but in the summer, baseball was always easily tops. Baseball gloves were a necessity of life. New ones were rare; good, old ones a treasure. They were taken care of with great attention to detail. They were oiled and rubbed, hours on end. Everybody had a secret favorite formula to keep the leather alive one more season, one more game. On the very rare occasion when someone got a new glove, we spent days forming the pockets to perfection, by constant games of catch and by slamming a ball thrown from one hand into the glove on the other. Playing catch was serious business. We not only passed the time of day this way but used the opportunity to perfect the curveballs, drops and fast balls that we knew would be much-needed skills once we reached the big leagues.

By the end of each summer, I had a gigantic urge to get my nose back into an algebra book. There was no remorse for the coming of summer's end. Fall and the return to school was a relief beyond measure and it made the years at school such a pleasure and so rewarding. Like every other kid in Tolleson I had learned to work with my hands and back. I had learned to work hard. I was in no way unique. Tolleson didn't raise other kinds of kids. But probably I wasn't going to be a kid forever, and I didn't figure to spend the rest of my life in Tolleson, Arizona, either.

My mother did a lousy job of forging my birth certificate. Captain Simpson, the Commanding Officer of the Phoenix-based 4th Engineer Company, Marine Corps Reserve Center, started laughing when he saw the poor artwork. He knew that I was two weeks short of my 17th birthday. Before I reached that birthday, the Marine Corps would cancel a program that allowed me to attend boot camp during the summer of 1957 and return home for my last year of high school.

"Do you expect me to accept this birth certificate as proof you're old enough to join the Corps?" he asked me, as I did my best to stand at attention, not knowing exactly what that required.

"Yes, Sir, please," I begged.

"Is this the best forgery you could produce?"

"Yes, Sir."

"Bullshit."

"No, Sir."

"All right, sign your name in these three places," he said, pointing to the forms in front of him.

My hand was shaking badly but I managed not to misspell my name.

"Raise your right hand, and repeat after me," he instructed, with a slight grin across his usually stern face. I officially entered the Marine Corps in a very quiet, private ceremony, attended only by me and the Captain. Immediately after the ceremony, he and I walked out behind the Reserve Center complex and burned the phony birth certificate. He swore me to secrecy and then shook my hand. A less-than-auspicious start, maybe, but a start, nonetheless.

On May 27th, 1957, I joined three other high school students for a trip to San Diego, California, and an introduction to the U.S. Marine Corps. It was the first time in an airplane for all of us. Marine Corps Boot Camp was not going to be like a Boy Scout camp and we knew it. We had no real knowledge of what it would be like, but our youthful imaginations were working overtime. We had joined the toughest of the tough and this was the initiation. Could we measure up to their standards? Were we good enough to wear the sharp-looking uniforms? Would we be able to withstand the physical torture that we had all heard about? The same questions that thousands before us had asked. We were worried about the reputation Marine drill instructors had for being overly physical with recruits. We had nothing to worry about. Mostly. The Marines had suffered an extreme embarrassment the previous summer, when a DI at the Marine Corps Recruit Depot, Parris Island, South Carolina, led a platoon of recruits on a night march into a swampy area near the base. A quarter of the platoon never came back. Congress went on a rampage and the Marines initiated a new set of procedures devoted to showing the nation's moms and the congressional paymasters that recruits weren't unnecessarily abused as part of their recruit training. The Marines acknowledged some excesses had existed and vowed to change. None of us believed that things had changed. It was widely known that shutting down the Marine Corps was a top priority of the Kremlin.

"Get your ass in the back of the truck. Keep your mouths shut and no noise," came a quick set of instructions from the official greeter who failed to properly introduce himself, as he drove up to the curb in a green-colored van, with a large Marine Corps emblem on the side. "Welcome to the U.S. Marine Corps Recruit Depot, San Diego, California," he added, sounding less than sincere. We piled into the truck quickly and quietly, just as we had been instructed, and waited for the van to pull away from the curb. The trip to the base took less than five minutes and we all took a big deep breath as we passed through the main gate and into the world of the unknown. The van came to a halt and the back door opened.

"You have 15 minutes to eat," our driver yelled. "Get in the line there," he said, pointing to a building door a few feet away. "Report back to me right here when you're done and don't be late. I haven't got all day. Move out. Now!" came a stream of precision-stated orders we weren't really expecting. At the very end of the mess hall, we could see a person of obvious authority inspecting every tray being brought to the finish line of this 15-minute race with hunger. Any tray that wasn't completely empty didn't get accepted into the pile designated for cleaning. The holder of the tray was instructed to return to a nearby table and finish the remaining food. If it's on the tray, you eat it. Simple rule.

There was no way we were going to be able to follow the rule. We had eaten a big meal on the plane just minutes before. Human stomachs weren't built that way. The turkey drumstick, mashed potatoes and four pounds of vegetables looked up at us. I could imagine they were laughing at us. Revenge perhaps? We'd been on the base less than 10 minutes and we already had a dilemma on our hands. Mom wasn't there to help. Dad's not here right now, sorry. The guy inspecting the trays didn't seem to have a cooperative attitude. He was intent on maintaining his rules.

The turkey continued to laugh. How in the hell were we going to get by the authority figure near the dishwasher area? Maynard Tidmore eventually came up with a solution. Being 6'7" and 140 lbs., he could get noticed more easily than most kids.

"Can you please tell me, Sir, where the bathroom is?" The human barrier pointed at a door.

"Thank you very much," Maynard said, with dire scratches, hopping from foot to foot, making sure the barrier was paying attention to the asshole recruit who headed directly off toward a section of the building quite different from where the barrier had told him to go. The human barrier went after him with vigor, pointing out his stupidity and inability to carry out instructions and general worthlessness in a loud and clear fashion, several feet from his assigned post. The moment the barrier's back was turned and his attention focused completely on the designated asshole, we made a mad, desperate dash to the garbage can with our mostly full trays. It worked like a champ. By the time the barrier got back to his post, the trays were shiny clean and no one was the wiser. We had pulled one off. Knockout. TD. Grand Slam. It would be the last one we would pull off on the marine instructors for quite a while.

The next three days were a blur of activity. The inevitable and famed haircut, uniform and equipment issuance, at least 30 medical shots, dental checkups, forms to fill out by the hundreds and many other formalities necessary for starting recruit training. The Receiving Barracks was our home for this short-term assignment and was a favorite for all recruits. The schedule was sometimes hectic, with screaming khaki-clad marines at every corner and watching over us every minute. Other times, it was relatively quiet, as we waited for the next activity on the schedule. There was constant confusion and turmoil. People got in the wrong lines, and went to the wrong assignments. They attended the wrong meetings. It was hard not to get lost in the shuffle. Not knowing what was coming next was nerve-racking. We all took plenty of time to run our hands over the top of our heads, trying to get comfortable with the lack of hair. No more duck tails, no more curls, no more DAs, no more Wildroot Cream Oil Charlie.

At 0600 on our fourth day at the Recruit Depot, 50 of us were assigned to Platoon 347. We were lined up in three neat rows in front of the Receiving Barracks and as we stood quietly and rigidly at attention, we were introduced to our Drill Instructors, Technical Sergeant Dye, Sergeant Honda and Sergeant Householder.

TSgt. Dye walked slowly to the front of the uneven lines of recruits and faced us head on, quietly at first. Looking over another fresh group of American boyhood from beneath the dark brown campaign hat which was pulled low over his eyes, TSgt. Dye presented a snarling, pained expression, clearly meant to show his dissatisfaction over what he saw, and for the hard work that he knew was ahead of him before he had the opportunity to turn this mob into something the Marine Corps could accept.

He waited a few seconds to say anything at all. Just observing. The two younger DIs walked silently among their new charges. We tried not to notice the silence but couldn't help but let it affect our nerves. We knew it wouldn't last but after awhile we weren't so sure. Eyes that were supposed to look straight ahead at nothing in particular glanced quickly and carefully at the short, stocky mean-looking Marine specimen standing in front of us. He was impressive in his carefully starched and pressed uniform, with five stripes decorating each sleeve and three rows of medals poking out from his chest. The first sound to halt the silence came from TSgt. Dye, as it would frequently do, breaking the ice and relieving some of the tension.

"My name is Technical Sergeant Dye," he said in a hushed but confident tone, his voice a thrust of gravel, as if he had a bad sore throat. "I am the Senior Drill Instructor for this platoon," raising the pitch of his voice ever so slightly. "Sgt. Honda and Sgt. Householder are the two Junior Drill Instructors assigned to this herd," he continued, hands now on hips and feet spread slightly apart in a challenging stance. "When it is necessary for you to address us and only when it is necessary for you to address us, the first word out of your mouth and the last word out of your mouth will be 'Sir'," he instructed in a level that was now gathering emotional energy. "Is that absolutely clear?" he screamed.

"Yes, Sir," came the answer from 52 strained voices.

"You idiots aren't listening to me and that pisses me off. You'd better not piss me off again," he said, stating the obvious.

"I said the first word out of your mouth had better be 'Sir'," he repeated. "Now do you understand me?" he asked again.

"Sir, yes Sir," we tried again.

"That's better," he said in a slightly calmer voice, moving now to the inside of the formation.

He moved slowly through the ranks, examining each recruit that he came to with careful and penetrating eyes. The two junior drill instructors joined the fun and each picked a recruit to get nose to nose with.

"You lookin' at me, boy?" Sgt. Honda asked one of the recruits standing next to me.

"Sir, no Sir," came the correct response. It was not good enough for Sgt. Honda.

"You keep looking at me, boy, and I'm going to think you're queer," the Sergeant stated threateningly. "You queer, maggot?" he asked, generating a few snickers from the ranks.

"Sir, no Sir," came the indignant reply.

"Then you keep your eyes off me and keep them focused straight ahead," he ordered.

"Sir, yes Sir," came the answer.

On command from the drill instructors, we each picked up our newly issued belongings, which were completely contained in one large, green seabag and one unhandy silver water pail. We headed for a series of quonset huts located a few hundred yards away from the Receiving Barracks. These huts would be our home for most of the next 12 weeks. Boot camp training was now officially under way. Like millions of others before me, I had wanted this challenge. Marine Corps Boot Camp defined the term "toughness." Want to see how tough you are? Try the Marines. I was 6'2" and 145 lbs. and 17 years old. A stick that only slightly resembled a man's body. I wasn't world-hardened at all and had very little real physical strength. I could run all day. I had endurance. I had speed. What we hadn't counted on was that Marine training included an uncompromising demand for discipline and teamwork. Most of us could stand the physical part of the training. The few that weren't were weeded out, very quickly, and put in special programs to get their bodies prepared for the onslaught. None of us were ready for the level of discipline that TSgt. Dye would demand every minute of every day. The platoon was a mixture of tough ghetto kids, bikers, farmers and a large number who were here because some judge gave them a choice other than serving time in jail. It was not an especially high-IQ group. The Marine recruiters weren't too selective in that area, it appeared. In 12 weeks there would be no more street kids and farmers and jailbait, only trained, hardened marines, a team of marines, a team molded from personalities as diverse as all America. It wouldn't be easy.

The Marines had it down to a science. It involved eradicating the individual personality. Utterly. Without reservation. Without compromise. The eradicated part would be replaced with a new focus and a change in spirit, developed over almost 200 years of experience. It was newness that would mark us for life as marines, still individuals but with a new sense of union and collaboration.

We covered the last 250 yards to the new platoon area in a very painful duck walk. To make this experience special, we placed the shiny new pails on top of our heads and hoisted the heavy seabags on the back of our shoulders. Screams from the drill instructors came from every direction and in words that were impossible to understand with the pails covering our ears, but they were not words you associate with Boy Scout leaders. Nobody could navigate with a bucket over his head. We stumbled and fell and grabbed on to the nearest person. We hadn't made very good time but we probably provided a pretty good laugh for anyone watching. Legs cramped and sweat poured. There was certainly going to be some pain involved in getting through this next 12 weeks. More than any of us recognized. We strained and groaned to make it the last few feet to the front door of our new home.

"All right, maggots, this is home," TSgt. Dye announced. "On your feet and get those buckets off your stupid head," he bellowed into the ear of one recruit but meaning it for all of us. We were spread out over half an acre and the junior drill instructors were rounding up the stragglers and prodding others to keep going and finish the course. A very unorganized group that took some doing to get back together and into some semblance of order in front of our long row of quonset huts.

"You pukes think you want to be marines. The only way you can ever dream about being a marine is if I say you're a marine. As far as I'm concerned and from what I just saw none of you is gonna make it. You're the sorriest bunch of crap I've ever seen. I don't like you. I don't like any kind of civilians and you're about the sorriest bunch of civilian skuzz I've ever laid my eyes on. I'm going to personally see that none of you ever gets through this training. I'm going to make your life miserable. You're going to hate the day you ever thought about joining my Marine Corps," TSgt. Dye added, sounding like he meant every word. His crusty, sunbaked face never broke into a smile in the 12 weeks we knew him. His gravelly voice brought instant fear and attention. He seemed to be in a perpetual bad mood. He was scary. And tough. He made it abundantly clear that very first meeting that he was in charge. He never changed that posture. Even though both of the junior drill instructors were black belts in judo, any of us would rather have spent a day in a fight with either of them than 10 minutes in a fight with TSgt. Dye. He gave us an open invitation to go out behind the quonset huts and settle things with fists, any time we thought we were capable of kicking his butt. No challenge was ever offered or taken.

Since the Marines had cracked down on violence, TSgt. Dye had changed the openness of challenges to his recruits but I can't imagine even the largest, toughest of them taking up the challenge unless he had some sort of suicidal wish. The Sergeant wasn't very big really, but you could see that he fully filled out his uniform, in all the places where it counted most. For a man of 35 or so, in a world filled with kids, he gave no quarter or needed one. He was in magnificent shape, and did anything physical that we had to do, with great ease. He ran like a deer when he needed to. He could do push-ups all day long. He also appeared to have a mean streak, judging from the way he looked and talked to us. I don't think he was happy to be there. He wanted to be at war, fighting bad guys in some faraway place. Preferably killing them. Especially killing them.

For the 12 weeks of boot camp we were never more than a few feet away from a drill instructor. They supervised our every move. They assumed we knew nothing. They taught us everything. How to shave. How to shower. How to eat. No part of our life was left out. Every aspect of our life had to be modified. Old habits eliminated. Do it the Marine way.

Every minute of every day, from reveille at 0445 until taps at 2100, the DIs spent tearing down the individual. Teaching us to do things the Marine way. The only way. Increasing the discipline, building strength, learning unquestioned obedience to orders and teamwork. The first days of training concentrated on the basics.

"This is your left foot, shithead. Your other's the right foot."

"Chin in. Chest out."

"Left face. Ten-shun."

Corrections. Do it again. More corrections. Do it again.

It took some of us longer than others to catch on to the easy stuff. We went slow and repeated everything over and over again. We got instructions in how to tie our shoes, blow our nose, put on our shoes and of course how to stand at attention. We spent a lot of time standing at attention. And sitting at attention. And eating at attention. And sleeping at attention.

Haircuts came every five or six days. Physical training came every five or six hours. Lots of it. When we were not practicing our close order drill, we ran. The hot summer sun burned through our green drab uniforms and darkened the five square inches of exposed flesh around and beneath our headgear.

By the end of the first week we could understand most of the new terms we needed to know. We learned a Marine's General Orders, used to govern important guarding procedures. We learned to guard important things like washing racks and clotheslines. We took turns walking guard at night to watch for fires in the quonset huts.

We learned to distinguish our drill instructor's voice from the voice of the hundreds of other DIs on the base with and among the thousands of yet-to-be marines. We found this especially handy when we were introduced to the "Grinder," a 20-acre blacktopped plot, smack in the middle of the Recruit Depot.

The Grinder was the Recruit Depot's least favorite spot for recruits. Every recruit spent hundreds of long hot hours learning the fine art of precision drill on this blacktopped nightmare. Hot, nearly melting asphalt that radiated paralyzing heat up through the feet to the top of the head. Killing heat. Burning feet. We all came to hate this place. We marched and stood and practiced throwing rifles around in precision movements, while our feet pleaded with us to stop. Any time we saw an hour or two scheduled for the Grinder, our hearts sank. It was a place for pain. During any part of the day, every day but Sunday, at least 10 recruit platoons could be seen practicing close order drill there. The sounds from the many DIs counting cadence and yelling instructions were mixed together. They shouted instructions and orders necessary to teach the fundamentals of the marching drills and rifle movements and to keep one herd of recruits from running into another. Only the recruits could pick out the orders meant just for them. Like a calf in a large herd of cows, that could pick its mother's cry from all the others.

TSgt. Dye had one of the more colorful cadence-calling techniques of all the DIs at MCRD.

"Eih, high, hef, hight, hef," could be literally translated as "left, right, left, right, left."

"Hef holders, huh," was clearly "left shoulder, arms."

We came to know his every grunt. He made very sure of that. Each of the recruits got a private lesson at some time in the first few days, even though much of what we were being taught revolved around learning to work together as a team. TSgt. Dye made it very clear that each and every one of us would have to earn our own way onto the team. Every individual had to play with the team but at the same time earn his way onto the team with individual effort. No shortcuts, no marginal performance, no sneaking through. We were each going to have to prove to him that we could make it.

And we were going to have to prove we loved our rifles. Every marine is a rifleman. Marines do different jobs sometimes, but being proficient with the rifle is paramount to the life of each and every marine. It started in boot camp. The reason for the continuous existence of the Marine Corps is its ability to be able to put marine rifleman close to the enemy and to outshoot and kill them in the process, more cost-effectively than the Army, where the Army can't go, or won't go. Without that there would have been no Marine Corps. Congress had tried to eliminate the Corps several times but they could never find a better way to get the job done. Riflemen are the heart of the Corps. Every marine has to demonstrate his competence with the rifle, every year, no matter his lofty perch or job assignment. The first medal any marine ever wears on his chest is his rifle badge. All marines wear them. Pilots, cooks, generals and privates share this responsibility and love.

The Marines issued us our rifles one day during our third week of training. The serial number on mine was 19100863. The rifles were heavily covered with an oil-based preservative, called cosmoline, which all marines came to hate. It smelled like rotten baby barf and was impossible to get off the rifles' metal surfaces. We rubbed and scrubbed until our fingers bled to get that junk off of our rifles. We managed to do the impossible.

It was an M-1, which fired a .30-caliber cartridge, a .30-06, one good shot at a time. This the most powerful round on any standard infantry weapon. With a full clip of eight rounds that were hand-fed from the top of the rifle by a complicated finger and hand maneuver, it weighed nearly seven pounds. A competent rifleman could put seven of the eight shots into a heart-sized target at a quarter mile. The recoil gave you a very sore shoulder, and an aching right side. Southpaws learned the marine way was the right-handed way.

We had to learn to disassemble the rifle into its component parts and memorize the names of all of them. We had to assemble and disassemble the rifle with our eyes closed. We cleaned every component with soap over and over again, so that no DI would ever find a speck of dust. Screws, springs and all, an M-1 has 21 separate parts. They go together one and only one way. If you are not kind and loving to your rifle, we were instructed, some day it will not be kind and loving to you. Expect this to happen when the rifle to which you have been so faithless is the only friend between you and bad guys who really are trying to kill you.

"Trying to do what?"

"Sir, kill me, Sir."

"Do what, numb-nuts?"

"Sir, kill me, Sir."

We placed a light coat of oil on every working part. We practiced taking it apart in the dark. Putting it back together. Holding it. Protecting it from the rain. Cleaning it. Sleeping with it. Knowing the function of every working part.

We had to perfect the Manual of Arms, the techniques of handling the rifle while marching and inspecting the rifle. Port Arms, Inspection Arms, Order Arms, Left Shoulder Arms, and many other maneuvers with the rifle were practiced over and over again until the rifle became a more important part of you than the nose or the penis.

We practiced handling the rifle in the morning before breakfast. It continued, all day in front of the DIs and at night in the darkened hut, in our underwear. We made the wood soft, by applying linseed oil to the wooden parts for hours on end. We oiled the metal parts again and again. We crammed patches of cloth down the barrel, hoping to show the DIs a perfectly clean weapon. We applied toothbrushes to every nook and cranny. We wanted to show them how much we loved these rifles.

"This is my rifle. There are many like it, but this one is mine. My rifle is my best friend. It is my life. I must master it, as I master my life." We repeated the Rifleman's Creed often, day, night, anywhere, everywhere. We became one with the rifle. We made every move with our rifle. To be a marine meant always being in control of this instrument of death. We slaved to make this instrument behave as if it were part of our own body.

Most of us had never held a rifle before. Now we had to love one. It was a strange experience. It was a new love, a love none of us had experienced before, but all of us now knew was necessary to make this team.

I wasn't so sure I was going to make the team. I was trying, but it seemed like every time I turned around, something was going wrong. I wasn't a major screwup, like some of the others, who were often at odds with the DIs, and had generally bad attitudes. Or like Maynard Tidmore, my best friend since third grade, who because of his height drew so much attention from the DIs that he couldn't help getting caught doing something wrong more than his share of the time. I just seemed to be in the wrong place, at the wrong time, far too often. When we were supposed to move right, I moved left. My boots never seemed to shine enough. My rifle always seemed to have just a hint of rust someplace that caught the DI's eye. I'd get caught taking a small nap in some important class. The drill instructors got to know my name very early on and used it far too often. It was never good news when they started using your name. It was far better to establish anonymity and to stay lost in the crowd, blend in. Not me. They nailed me good and far too often for my comfort level. Sometimes, all of the pressure would get me down, until I saw how others handled it.

Maynard kept his sense of humor. "This shit ain't so hard," he whispered to me from his bunk, next to mine.

"I thought he was a little too tough on you today for turning the wrong way on that last drill," I answered, honestly.

"It wasn't so bad. Ain't no DI gonna get to me," he said. Maynard soon developed an ability to mimic the voice and mannerisms of TSgt. Dye and in the quiet of the room with only memories of home to keep sleep from coming, he'd whisper perfect imitations of TSgt. Dye chewing out one or the other of us.

"You shitbirds are really worthless. You better get squared away Recruit. You're a group of scum-sucking maggots. No way are you going to be in my Marine Corps," Maynard would spit out in exactly the same tone and sound of our Senior Drill Instructor. If he got us laughing too loud, as he was disposed to do most every night, there would be a certain visit from the DI on duty. Fifty quick push-ups or squat thrusts was the penalty and well worth the fun of goofing off for a few minutes. Maynard's end of the quonset hut was always good for at least a couple of close calls and an occasional large, heavy penalty. We learned to snicker very quietly. It didn't always work and when it didn't all hell would break loose. None of the DIs like to miss their few hours of sleep. Mess with their sleep and they were going to mess with your mind.

"You maggots not tired enough?" a voice would ring out, as the lights in the hut would come suddenly flashing on, breaking the darkness and bringing a shock to the senses. We would freeze in place, at attention, in our beds and pretend to be asleep. "Out of the sack, shitbirds," would come the command. "Assume the position and give me 50 big ones for the Corps. I want them counted out."

We would hit the deck and give the DI his required push-ups, not really having to strain too much, but wishing we hadn't laughed so loudly and hoping 50 would be enough to appease him. It usually was. Those quiet moments after lights-out, no matter the danger, allowed us to keep a little of our sanity and keep our minds off how much time we still had to do in this place.

These moments also offered the only real time we had to meet our neighbors, whom we lived with but didn't know, other than as a name. We found out soon enough that kids from Saginaw, Michigan, or Firebaugh, California, or Tolleson, Arizona, weren't really that different. We had come to the door of the Marine Corps from many different places and for many different reasons but now we all faced the same challenges and we were going to have to do it together, as a team. TSgt. Dye didn't discriminate.

The recruit training process slowly yielded results, through constant practice and techniques the Marines had been utilizing for decades. We got minor rewards for good teamwork, massive punishment for individual screwups.

"Do it together, people," came a familiar cry from the DIs. "Get with it, you shitbirds. You look like a mob, people."

Stand in line, march in line, shave in line, eat in line. We ate three huge meals a day and it all took less than 15 minutes of actual eating time. We all benefited from the high-starch, high-protein

diets. Some of the recruits had probably never had so many
balanced meals in their lives. We didn't know exactly what was
happening to us. We were learning to respond-together. To work-
together. To survive-together. We attended five or six lectures a day
on subjects near and dear to the Marines. History, tradition and
organization. We did it all. Together. Some would call it brainwash-
ing. More like personality washing. Gung Ho, Chinese for Work
Together, was one of the Marines' favorite mottoes. Semper Fidelis,
Latin for Always Faithful, another. Teamwork. Loyalty to the team.

In combat it was indispensable. It saved lives. It won battles.
That's what the Marines cared about. We were far from combat but
each day was preparation for it. Good preparation. Essential preparation. We had started this thing and one way or another we were
going to have to finish it. But only if TSgt. Dye said so.

By the time we got to the rifle range, about five weeks into
training, the DIs had eliminated most of the individualism from
each of us and they were now filling that void with Marine concepts,
like teamwork, pride and toughness. We could now march in
formation without having five or six people going the wrong
direction. Most of the time we could move rifles from a right-
shoulder position to a left-shoulder position with four sharp,
distinct slaps of hands on wood, in complete unison. Quite a
sensation, when it happened just right. We were starting to sense
the progress towards becoming marines and we enjoyed each small
success.

We even got a little rest and relaxation on Sundays. We were
encouraged to attend church. I didn't need much encouragement.
I had always gone to church at home, but this was extra special.
The Base Chapel was cool and silent and refreshing. No DIs to
harass. No punishments to absorb. We all went because it was a real
break in the organized chaos of our normal routine. I went because
I wanted to. I needed to. A chance to be alone with my thoughts,
my God and my prayers. I developed some new prayers during this
summer. I needed every one of them answered just to make it
through the next seven days. The prayers were answered. As always.

The time had come for us to learn about the business end of a
rifle. Three intense weeks of total concentration on the techniques
of delivering a well-aimed bullet on a distant target. A very new

experience for all of us. And the Marines had their own special way of doing it, worked out in 190 years of practice in thousands of live firing situations and under life-and-death situations. The Marines took this experience very seriously. Special instructors at every turn. Experts in aiming. Experts in breathing. Experts in correct body position. They knew every important technique. They insisted we learn every important technique. Their way.

We practiced firing rifles without real bullets for two entire weeks. The exercise was called Snapping In. Hours after long hours in the hot summer sun of Camp Mathews, home of the Marine Corps Rifle Range, 25 miles north of San Diego, we learned about shooting a rifle while standing, kneeling, sitting and lying. One bullet at a time. Or a clip of eight at a time. We learned to do it in the most awfully contorted positions possible for a human body.

"Squeeze the trigger, shithead."

"Let the explosion be a surprise."

"Don't jerk it, stupid."

"Pull straight back, slowly."

"Hold it steady."

"Quit moving."

"Keep the front sight in focus and centered on the back sight."

"Don't squeeze unless you can see the black of the bull's-eye on top of the front sight."

"Don't tense up."

"Steady."

Nonstop rifle firing instructions. We now had so many instructors and instructions there was never a moment of peace. Our entire attention was being focused on real bullets and eventually on a qualification firing to top off this three-week portion of training. Time to find out if we could fire real bullets at real targets. The pressure was on to demonstrate a level of skill with this weapon. Pity the poor recruit who didn't qualify.

Pity the DI who had too many recruits who didn't qualify. Five platoons were firing at one time. The DIs with the best rifle range record got three days of liberty. All the other DIs walked the 25 miles back to San Diego with the recruits. Lots of money was bet on the results of the qualification shoot. Lots of competitive pressure but at the same time they wanted us to relax and concentrate on shooting well-aimed bullets, so they let up a bit on the general harassment. It didn't help me much.

While suffering from a really bad case of the Asian flu and a 103-degree temperature which threatened to wipe me out and wash me out of the entire program and send me prematurely back to Tolleson, I had the misfortune to fall sound asleep while practicing the prone firing position one very hot day on the Snapping In range. I was trying to concentrate on the practice session but lying there in the sand and the blazing hot sun, very sick and exhausted from the temperature, I couldn't resist the urge to close my eyes to find some needed relief. I awoke from the sleep with the foot of one very large instructor placed squarely on the back of my head, pushing my face ever so rudely into the hot sand. I remained in this position, feeling the sand grind through my lips and into my mouth as the instructor gathered the platoon around the two of us to deliver a lecture about paying attention and staying alert.

"Guess what I got here?" he asked my gathered friends and fellow inmates. "This shitbird thinks he can learn to fire this here rifle in his sleep," he went on. "Anybody here agree with him?" he asked, ready to kill somebody if he got a positive answer. "This here maggot has shown me that you recruits ain't paying attention. We're going to stay two extra hours tonight, just so you maggots learn a lesson about how serious this practice is," he finished.

His boot was boring a hole in my head and I was starting to choke from the dirt that was clogging my breathing passages. I knew better than to move but I was starting to panic. I couldn't get my breath. The lecture droned on. Everybody was having a good giggle at my expense. I wasn't giggling. In addition to the extra Snapping In practice, the platoon did an extra 50 push-ups before lights-out that night because of my misfortune. Popular me. I was taking some of the pressure off of Maynard, the favorite "pick on" target of the DIs. Maynard loved the fact that the DIs had to look up over a foot to look him in the eye. They would often get something to stand on so they could get nose-to-nose with him. Their taunts only added to his often overhealthy sense of humor. He took all they had to offer and asked for more. I think he secretly hated the fact that I was screwing up so often and diverting some of their attention from him to me.

A couple of days later I did it again. I got caught committing the unpardonable sin of sitting on my rack during the workday. The DI who caught me figured that since I loved the rack so much I should have it with me wherever I went for a couple of days. I dragged it to the chow hall. To the range. Around the platoon formation twice for every letter received at mail call. The entire camp got a big laugh out of this one. I struggled everywhere with my metal bed, mattress and all. What a sight. What a mess. What a marine.

The third week at Camp Mathews signaled the start of the big show. Four days of live firing practice, a rehearsal day and the final day when the qualification scores would be recorded.

"Ready on the right. Ready on the left. All ready on the firing line. Watch your targets. Commence firing." The Range NCO announced these instructions over the loudspeaker system every morning and every afternoon. We now had live ammo. We fired in the morning and pulled targets for the other shooters in the afternoon. At night we worked on our firing positions and prayed. It took some adjustments to accommodate the real thing. When the noise of rifles started going off all around you, it was hard not to flinch. Flinches meant bullets going off in wild directions and bringing up a big white flag, called Maggie's Drawers, indicating a complete miss on the target and soliciting a lot of sudden, unwanted attention from the instructors.

"Concentrate, you shitbird."

"What the hell are you flinching for?"

"Squeeze, asshole."

The noise was incredible. The pressure was worse. I was doing about average and was confident with everything except the "off hand" or standing position, at 200 yards. Overconfident as it turned out.

On qualification day I dropped a quick 12 points in my least favorite position, another 10 in the sitting rapid fire exercise. A 60-point loss would mean disqualification, an empty chest at graduation, no shooting badge. Dishonor. Big time harassment for the rest of boot camp. I dropped 10 more points in the 300-yard sitting and kneeling slow fire and another 17 in the rapid fire prone position from the same location, when my entire group of 10 shots clustered nicely was a good foot left of the target's center. I needed

39 out of 50 from the last event at the 500-yard line. Very possible but not a cinch.

The walk back to the 500-yard line was long and gave me time to think too much. My hands were shaking more and more. I was starting to panic. So were the DIs. We had five guys in trouble. I was one of them. The entire instructor staff now surrounded the five lucky recruits.

Encouragement, threats and last-minute lessons all wrapped up in one. My breathing got shorter and harder to find. My eyes watered and my hand would not stand still. I couldn't get the sights on the rifle to hold steady on the target. I tried to take my time.

I did take my time, thanks to an instructor talking me through this nightmare. The scores came up just as slowly. I squeezed off each round. Four. Four. Five. Three.

"Don't jerk, asshole, squeeze the trigger," came whispers from an instructor, now operating six inches from my left ear.

"You can do it."

Five. Four. Five.

"Three more good ones, Private."

"Take your time."

More encouragement now.

Two.

"Squeeze, don't jerk," he said, pleading rather than instructing.

Most of the other shooters had successfully finished now and were putting their own personal celebrations on hold pending the final outcome. They all gathered around the remaining shooters, doing their best to help us aim and squeeze, via ESP.

Five.

One bullet left. I had to hit somewhere on the target to make it. A stupid lousy two. I loaded the last bullet with a hand that couldn't disguise its trembling. There were only two or three of us left on the firing line and it suddenly got quiet. I could hear my own breathing as I settled in for the last shot.

The explosion came as a complete surprise, a good sign. As I stood up and began getting out of my special shooting gear I said a small prayer. "Please let it be somewhere on the target, Lord, please," I said silently.

The jokers in the target area took their sweet time. Either they were trying to give me a heart attack or they were searching for a small hole in the target and couldn't find one. The DIs were going crazy. Two guys hadn't made it. They couldn't stand another "nonqual."

The target was raised at about a quarter the normal speed. Or was life in slow motion just now? Would we glimpse Maggie's Drawers? They took their time.

A black disc. A four. I came about three feet off the ground. I had passed. An instructor actually hugged me.

One night after a particularly good week of drilling and test scores, we got our one and only night off during the 12 weeks of boot camp. A movie. No popcorn, but a little relaxation. We were treated to one of 1957's best films, *The DI*, starring Jack Webb, an overly romantic but popular picture about our favorite subject, Marine Corps Boot Camp. Wonderful. We got to watch Jack Webb yell at recruits all night long, on our one night out. We only had to sit at attention the first half of the movie. TSgt. Dye eased up a little for the second half. Maybe he thought the movie was punishment enough.

The rigors of recruit training could no longer faze. No amount of physical training, and there was still lots of it, could exhaust us, the way it had a few weeks earlier. Duck-walking around the barracks, even balancing a footlocker on our head, a favorite exercise of TSgt. Dye, would only bring laughter and howls now. It didn't hurt anymore. We asked for more, and got it.

Our six-mile morning run would end up with us trying to run up the DIs back at the finish line. We had been melded into a group of willing Marine fodder. It felt good. We were so proud of ourselves and how good we had become. We laughed more now and the laughter and pride were almost tolerated by the DIs.

Graduation was a grand spectacle only the Marines could produce. Pomp and ceremony flowing from every corner. Speeches. A band. A parade. And the Marine Corps Hymn. From that day forward we would all be known as marines. Never ex-marines. Just marines. We had pulled it off. Only a few million people in the history of the world had completed this training. Only a few million would ever dare it.

3

Almost an Officer and a Gentleman

Flagstaff, Arizona, is one of the Earth's great natural treasures. The air is thin and crystal clear. The smell of pine trees is sweet, strong and inescapable. In winter, snow covers the town in a thick, fluffy white blanket, sometimes as deep as 10 feet. Summers are gloriously cool and refreshing to visitors from the desert areas that surround it in every direction. Majestic mountains explode from the landscape and dominate the view from every angle. Several American Indian tribes made these mountains holy shrines long before the white man arrived in this part of the world. At an altitude of 7,000 feet, you have to work at taking a breath, but the work is worth it. Cleaner air probably doesn't exist anywhere.

Arizona State College at Flagstaff nestled softly into a mountain paradise in northern Arizona. It had fondly adopted the nickname of the Friendly College in the Pines, and was just exactly that, a nearly perfect place to expand your horizons and mind, without a lot of interruptions from the hustle and bustle of modern life. The town of Flagstaff held few attractions for students. Classrooms, dorms and the Student Activity Center dominated our world. Students were uniformly poor and as the saying goes, didn't know the difference. Friendships by the dozens were formed quickly and lasted a lifetime. We were joined together by a common struggle with dangling participles, complicated chemical formulas, and quickly forgotten child developmental theories. Winter came early and stayed late at this altitude. For most of the students, including myself, this was a foreign climate. Most of us were children of the desert. The shock of 10 feet of snow every year was stunning. For most of the school year moving from one building to another was something of an endurance contest. The weather dominated our life and kept us prisoners to campus much of the year. Real privacy was nearly impossible to find. We were drawn together, in a very special way, in all of our common daily functions.

The entire student body shared three meals a day in one cafeteria at the center of campus. We had one small library and a handful of dorms housing less than 2,000 students. It was total immersion in college life. Sporting events and dances were always well attended. Romances were never secret for very long. Dating was simple, cheap and easy. Nobody had the money or the opportunity to do anything too complicated. Coffee dates at the Student Union, studying together at the library or rare trips to a downtown movie, usually Dutch Treat, were the norm. Sex, or what little of it that took place, was practiced in cars parked in whatever out-of-the-way place could be found. The car was, more often than not, borrowed. A heavy snow covering on the car usually provided the needed security from unwanted onlookers, and a sufficient illusion of privacy. Or, at least, boys thought so.

We had a good time. Not always of course. Sometimes we played football. Playing football for Coach Max Spilsbury was not a trivial matter. He had taken a failing football program at Arizona State College at Flagstaff, Arizona, from the edge of extinction to small-college prominence in three years. He kept it there on the strength of his will and personality. Most high schools had bigger budgets. Most high schools had more assistant coaches. He had taken 25 scholarships and a few hard-nosed kids from small Arizona towns and turned them into a team. He loved tough guys and street fighters. To be his kind of guy you had to throw your body around with total disregard for pain or injury. I wasn't one of his favorites from the beginning. That profile didn't fit me at all. But if you had some football skills you might get one of the scholarships. I needed one of those in the worst way. We had lots of tough guys and lots of skilled players and a few that were both, all fighting for a shot at the prospect of an expense-paid trip through college. It was a competitive dogfight and Max was the leader of the pack.

Max had grown up on a working cattle ranch in northern Mexico. He loved to fight and he loved anyone who shared this special and crazy love. His high school coach finally shamed this

troublemaker and rebel onto a football field, by challenging him to
a fight. It was love at first sight for Max and the coach. Football and
Max were made for each other. Legalized brawling appealed to this
rugged 14-year-old. He was soon the star of the team and the terror
of the league, not by skill, which took years to develop, but by his
unique style of play, which was much more basic. He loved to hit
and be hit. He was strong, fast and totally fearless. World War II
provided a short respite from battles on the gridiron. He enlisted
in the U.S. Marines the day after he graduated from high school
and immediately volunteered for the Marines' roughest outfit,
Edson's Raiders. Specially trained to fight in small units, behind
enemy lines, the Raiders were the toughest of the tough. Getting
selected was extremely difficult. Surviving once selected was even
tougher. The dropout rate in training was very high and so were
the casualties. Congress poked into their training methods because
of the high rate of fatalities. They practiced with real knives and
live ammunition. They recruited all the crazies and malcontents
they could find. They didn't want conformists or people interested
in surviving this war. They asked for volunteers to go on a suicide
mission and conducted their training accordingly.

Lt. Col. Charles Edson's dream was to create a small, fast-
moving strike force, capable of working independently for long
periods of time behind enemy lines. His standards were high and
not many measured up to his demands for aggression, strength and
endurance. Killing was taught in every combat form. Knives and
hands were the favorite weapons. Silent death was their trademark.
Max made his childhood training in Mexico pay off. Although the
training prepared Max for combat of the most brutal and deadly
kind, his time in action lasted a total of approximately one and a
half minutes. He and his unit made an amphibious landing on the
island of Tinian, later to become famous for its airfield, from which
the B-29 *Enola Gay* made its historic flight over Hiroshima. They
were part of a night landing party that came from the sea in small
rubber boats discharged from a submarine. Max's first steps ashore
placed him directly in the line of fire from a Japanese machine-gun
emplacement. Two well-aimed rounds found their way through
each leg, smashing, for eternity, both of his knees.

A little more than a year later, and with the help of some strong
surgical wire, his legs were put back together and Max returned to

his true love, football. He put the pain aside. Walking without the use of functional knees would always be uncomfortable and extremely painful. Playing football again an impossible dream? Not for Max. Somehow, he found the courage to walk out onto the football practice field at the University of Arizona. College football provided yet another outlet for his love of contact and combat. He played end, on both offense and defense, even though he couldn't run the 40 in 10 seconds and his pass-catching skills were almost as dreadful. The recognition of Max as an authentic All-American was strictly a tribute to his unrelenting and persistent ability to knock people on their butt. His mission during each game was to destroy anyone with the wrong-colored uniform. He went about his mission with a sense of purpose that amazed and inspired his teammates and coaches. The University of Arizona Wildcat football team became his next venue for legalized violence.

I found myself asking Max for permission to try out for a scholarship by putting my body on the line during spring football practice of my sophomore year.

"What makes you think you can play on my team?" he asked me.

"I was pretty good in high school," I answered.

"This isn't high school, but if you really want to give it a shot, be my guest," he offered, with a slight smile.

"Thanks, Coach, I'll try my best."

"You probably won't last more than a few days anyway," he said. Max felt that to play football well, you had to be able to endure pain, and to endure pain, you had to practice having pain. No amount of physical contact in practice was sufficient to achieve perfection at hitting and being hit.

I was the designated fifth team quarterback, right from the beginning. There were only five candidates. As the last man for the position with the most competition, it was very difficult to be too studly. Most of the first week of practice I spent on the sidelines as an interested bystander. As a fifth teamer, I didn't get much playing time. For one thing there weren't five teams. There were about 70 bodies, sweating, snarling and smacking each other in hopes of getting one of the 45 team positions or better yet, one of the 25 scholarships. Some of the veterans were sure to make it. Bobby "T.T." Ramos was one of the several can't-miss types. As an offensive fullback, his 5'10", 210 lb. frame was a perfect size for what was required of the position. He was a punishing blocker and an even tougher runner. He was quick but not especially fast. He went down hard. As a defensive back, he destroyed people. A tough Mexican kid from Globe, Arizona, one of the state's toughest mining towns, T.T. had run with gangs all his life. He was never far from a fight and certainly never walked away from one. T.T. was clearly one of Max's favorites and deserved Max's admiration for his performance on the field. Max called him the toughest man he ever knew. He once played a game on a broken leg. He went through an entire season on a knee that required massive surgery. Pain seemed to be a stranger.

I'd seen a drunk cowboy with a large knife challenge T.T. to step outside at an all-night restaurant. Cowboys in Flagstaff loved to fight, but none of us had ever seen one with a weapon. Fists were the normal choice. T.T. took the guy on, straight ahead, with little or no regard for the knife. No funny stuff, no dancing and no defense against the knife but his hands and body. The cowboy placed three or four permanent scars on T.T.'s upper chest before T.T. got in close enough to grab the knife. During the entire encounter, including the knife-slashing, T.T. never lost the smile on his face. It was a cold smile, not caused by nerves but from the pleasure coming from within. Once he finally got inside the arc of the knife his hands moved in a blur. The cowboy's head almost came apart, on the second right hand that reached the middle of his face. I don't think he ever saw the hands. Within seconds the fight was over. T.T. didn't stop right away but the cowboy did. After making sure the cowboy would remember this night for several weeks, T.T. pushed the bloody body under a pickup truck, broke the knife in two, and put his foot through the hat which now lay on the asphalt near the half-dead body. He went back into the restaurant to finish his cheeseburger. After our meal, we convinced T.T. to go get some stitches at the campus infirmary. On the way to the car, T.T. reached under the truck and drug the still-silent body out into the open. He then proceeded to step on both of the cowboy's hands until all the fingers were broken. Not many people messed with T.T. after that, cowboys included.

There were other major and minor T.T.'s on the team, and it took some adjustments for me to feel as if I belonged to a group to whom fights and violence was such a natural part of their being. It wasn't a natural part of me. But surviving Max's training camps and endless practice sessions drew us together in a very special way. The other players learned to tolerate and maybe even like this sissy quarterback, especially when he showed he could throw deep.

By the midpoint of spring practice, I had moved up to fourth string, more or less. The old feel started to return. Passes started finding hands instead of grass or air. Handoffs got to the correct hands. We had no more than 20 running plays and few pass patterns, so learning the system wasn't much of a problem. Max liked to keep things simple. Pads seemed to find their rightful place on my body and I could now run and move with some semblance of grace. One guy in front of me quit and I moved up another notch. Getting absolutely flattened once in a while began to feel normal. Max even smiled at me one day after I hit a halfback in full stride out in the flat. With 10 days to go in spring practice, I found myself taking snaps with the second team offense against the first team defense. It was mostly a mismatch. I became pretty adept at eating grass. One of us on the second team, who never seemed to despair at the prospect of the constant butt-kicking, was our center and spiritual leader, Ron Boatwright. Boat and I had played as teammates one year at Tolleson and two years as archrivals when he moved to Agua Fria. At 5'10" and 215 he was a bit small for a college lineman, but he never knew that. He was also slow. The guy ahead of Boat on the depth chart was six inches taller and 50 pounds heavier. And quick. Big and quick enough to be drafted later the next year, in the fourth round, by the San Francisco 49ers. Boat's only weapon to fight this monster on a daily basis was his absolute refusal to give up. He was all that stood between me and the fourth round draft choice, who was trying to take off my head on each play. In the huddle I looked eyeball to eyeball at Boat, before calling the next play.

"Run up the middle, will you? I want to get that big bastard on the ground," he announced, knowing the probability of that happening was slim.

"How about a 21 trap?" I asked.

"Love it," he said, spitting out a little more blood.

Our common bond as second stringers was our shared underdog role. Closeness grew quickly. My roommate, Dusty Everman, who was perhaps the squad's best athlete, broke open on a deep pattern, and before I was leveled by some unseen defensive end I let the ball fly with all I had. Dusty caught it in full stride about 30 yards down the field. He went 50 more yards on his own, unmolested into the endzone. A few minutes later, when we got the ball back again, I hit Dusty for a couple of additional short passes. And then I hit Charlie Bowers on a swing pass in the flat and we scored again. Eighty yards in four plays. Max went into a rage.

"What kind of defense is this?" he bellowed. "I've seen better girls' teams than this. No rush. No coverage. This rookie quarterback is making you guys look sick. At this rate we'll be lucky to win a game next year. Let's do it again and this time let's see some football, girls," he screamed at the defense. "Try it again offense, let's see if you can do it again to these sissies," he said, looking straight at me. The second team lined up on our own 20-yard line, to see if the first-team defense could stop us. The more Max yelled, the better our plays seemed to work. With four days to go in spring practice the first-string offense had me as its quarterback. Reporters started asking me questions. I gave absolutely dumb answers. The scholarship was in the bag. I had a way to get through college. I needed to find something to do with my life after graduation.

On a blazing hot and muggy day in the summer of 1959 I drug myself off a long and mostly boring flight aboard what must have been the last of the four-engine prop-driven planes still serving Washington, D.C. Twelve hours in the air from Phoenix to our Nation's Capital, with stops in St. Louis and Louisville, had provided me with an unforgettable first impression of the length and breadth of the country I was preparing to serve. I was traveling across the country to experience the unique world of the selection, training and development of future officers for the U.S. Marine Corps. I was hot. I was tired. I was alone. I was small-town. And I was scared.

In one of my life's many unexplained turn of events, a book titled *Battle Cry*, by Leon Uris, had found its way into my hands when I was 16 and a high school junior. I read the book seven times in the first two months I owned it. I have read it more than 20 times since then. I digested the book and its characters. I memorized many of the segments, without realizing I had done so.

The novel is about the Marines in World War II. I identified instantly and completely with the events and the characters. I wanted desperately to be Danny Forrester, the story's central character.

I wanted to be a local football hero, which I wasn't, a surviving war hero, which I wasn't, and come home to marry my high school sweetheart, which I didn't have. Most of all I wanted to be a marine. Danny Forrester was everything I was not. Three of my buddies and I enlisted in the Marine Corps Reserve in Phoenix a few weeks after I first opened the book.

My initial Marine experience, during the three months of boot camp training between my junior and senior years of high school, had been one of the best things that ever happened to me. In many other ways it had also been a huge failure. Survive was about all I did. A not insignificant part of the exercise. I did not distinguish myself as a marine during that first attempt.

How I expected to be a leader of marines I'll never know, but one bright morning in early 1958, in the middle of the Student Union, during my first semester at ASC, Flagstaff, I ran into two poster-perfect marines, standing near a rundown old cardboard table, containing a picture of another poster-perfect Marine specimen beckoning young college men to serve with the finest, as a second lieutenant in the U.S. Marine Corps.

One look at those dress blues, which fit the two recruiting officers so perfectly, and I was a goner. I had enlisted in the Platoon Leaders Class before the first of our many cups of coffee together had cooled down enough to drink. Maybe it was the Danny Forrester in me who enlisted. I'll never know for sure but one thing was absolutely certain. I hadn't lost the desire or the need to be a marine. I had to be one. I had to wear one of those blue uniforms. Nothing was going to stop me.

I must have been the easiest quota ever met by the two Marine recruiters, Capt. Robert Foster and First Lieutenant William Lynch. They were on the campus only two days but they caught two of us, myself and Don Price, a fellow freshman, who was to remain a lifelong friend and a lifelong marine.

"How intense is the Platoon Leaders training?" Don asked Captain Foster. "Anything like boot camp?"

"It's a little different than boot camp but more emphasis on developing leadership skills," the Captain answered, without any tone of concern. "If you made it through boot camp, you should be able to handle it. As long as you want it," he said, with a slight warning in his tone.

"What should we do to get ready?" I asked.

"Get your ass in shape," Lt. Lynch responded, with a strong sense of insistence.

Don and I spent every waking hour with the two officers while they were in Flagstaff. We met them for breakfast, lunch and dinner and at every break from the classroom routine. We asked incessant questions about the Corps and what our training and life in the Corps would be like. They glorified it immensely and lied through their teeth about how good it was going to be for both of us.

Don Price had spent the two previous years on active duty in the Marine Corps, as an enlisted man, and knew more about the action than I did, but still the mystery and imagery of becoming an officer in the Marine Corps was beyond his total comprehension. Don had come to college for only one purpose, to fulfill the requirement for commissioning in the Corps. The Marines applied this requirement to all applicants for commissioned service. Get your degree or get out. We shared a dream of becoming the best officers the Marines ever saw. We also talked a lot about being good servants of our country. We were highly motivated and blindly patriotic.

Getting accepted as a candidate for commissioned service was one thing. Making it through the 12 weeks of intensive screening was another. The first half of those 12 weeks was scheduled for the summer between my freshman and sophomore years in college at a Marine outpost near Quantico, Virginia, 35 miles south of Washington, D.C. It was worlds away from Tolleson, Arizona, but Leon Uris called.

Camp Upsher was, without question, the low-rent district of Marine Corps Schools, Marine Corps Base, Quantico, Va. Established during World War II, it was built on a smallish clearing 15 miles from the main base and was carved out of dense Virginia woodlands and forest, miles from the nearest civilized area. One rundown wooden structure served as the mess hall. All remaining buildings were tin-covered quonset huts, positioned in neatly arranged rows, a rectangular array of concrete and tin that could just as easily serve as a prison or a POW camp. It had all the hominess of Sing Sing and drill instructors to boot. It smelled of sweat, dirty socks and old mattresses. It was of course just the kind of place the Marines needed to convert some snotty-nosed kids into something that might resemble marine officer material.

The Marines had six weeks to get a good look at us and to see if under extremely adverse conditions we had elements of our personality and makeup that somehow marked us as leaders of men. In particular, they had six weeks to answer the question of whether or not they were going to allow you to eventually become a platoon leader.

A marine infantry platoon contained 40 marines. Were they going to let me stand in front of 40 marines and if necessary lead them into combat? One thing was certain: The Marines were going to take one very hard look before they decided. What I was completely surprised about was the extent they would go to get you to decide to drop out of the program if they didn't think you had the right stuff. I had survived Marine Corps Boot Camp two years earlier and since that was widely considered to be demanding training, I was sure this six weeks was going to be tough but tolerable. I was far too confident.

I was making small talk with my seatmate on the bus, a guy from the University of Washington, when we arrived from Washington, D.C. through the gates of Camp Upsher at about 2:00 a.m. I'm not sure what I expected, but as the bus pulled to a halt, I was shocked into the full realization that something important was about to happen to me and my body.

Drill instructors appeared from everywhere screaming at the top of their lungs, at everyone and nobody in particular.

"Get out of the bus. Get out. Get out. Now. You're taking too long girls," came a stream of commands from the front of the bus.

"Here we go," I said to my seatmate.

"It's too late at night for this shit," he said, grabbing his small bag and heading for the front of the bus.

"I haven't got all night, maggots. Move. Move it. Give me three lines, right here," came a further set of screams from a voice I could hear but from a face I couldn't quite make out in the dark.

"Not wasting any time, are they?" I said to a nameless person standing next to me in the line we had formed.

"Knock off the noise, college boys. Quickly. Quickly. Move it, people," the voice of authority advanced, cutting off all conversations in the ranks.

Roll was called and apparently everyone on the invitation list had made it to the party. We were evidently the last of the group to arrive. We were also late, which pleased the drill instructors no end, since they were missing their sleep.

One small group of us was moved together through the darkness and into a nearby quonset hut that was already partially occupied. Each of us somehow found an empty mattress on one of the bunk beds, which fully occupied the inside of the hut. We made a bit of noise as we struggled through this task without the benefit of a light of any kind. Voices in the night reminded us that some of the people had arrived earlier and were trying to sleep and that we should shut the hell up. I crawled up on a top bunk and tried to get comfortable on the sheetless, pillowless mattress. Though tired from the long trip and the late hour, rest didn't come easy. It was still hot as hell, even though it was almost daylight, and every thread of clothing seemed to stick to my body. Was I really ready for all of this? I'd better be.

Reveille exploded on us at 4:00 a.m., now 0400. A sudden burst of bright lights and two very loud marine sergeant types made it utterly clear that the time had come to officially enter the day-to-day activities of the Junior Platoon Leaders Class. I'd forgotten how much fun it was to have all this help getting up in the morning.

The two sergeants were everywhere, pushing, shoving, yelling, kicking and herding this group through the shower area and to the mess hall. It seemed to thrill them enormously. By 1000 we had been fed, given the haircut, put into uniforms of no particular size, formed into our final units and introduced to our permanent drill instructors and our Platoon Commander.

Second Lieutenant Bill Uren looked like an older-brother type. He spoke rather softly and with a slight stutter. No problem here. Sergeant Barnes was not much older and obviously rather new to this drill instructor stuff. He seemed a bit ill at ease and unsure of himself. He appeared a bit overweight and probably slightly out of shape. No problem here.

Staff Sergeant John Crowe, on the other hand, was something

else again. Tall and slightly built, he looked and acted every bit the part of a seasoned and well-trained Senior Marine Drill Instructor. A 15-year Marine veteran, on loan from the Marine Corps Recruit Depot in Parris Island, South Carolina, he knew how to bring fear into every part of your being, in an instant, by a mere glance or movement in your direction. This guy was to be avoided, whenever possible. He made it very clear that to obtain a commission in the U.S. Marines you were going to have to go through him and he also made it abundantly clear that he had no intention of letting anyone the least bit undeserving through his clutches. He meant every word and proved it true from that first morning and every subsequent moment, until our final bus ride home six weeks later.

The pace of the training started quickly and it stayed that way. It caught me by surprise. It devastated others. Five of the 50 starters dropped out in the first two days. Quitting was encouraged and easy to do. Raise your hand and you were immediately removed from the training activities, placed in a special hut, asked to sign a few papers and within 48 hours, you were on your way home without penalty, and returned to normal draft status. Just like it was before we signed up. Weeding out officer candidates was the main objective of every exercise. Every hour of the day included requests, demands, by the instructors to quit.

"Please quit. Being a marine officer is too hard. Please quit. Please quit now. Make it easy on yourself, do it now. Don't wait because it gets harder. If you want to quit, do it now. You'll never make it. You haven't got what it takes. I'll personally see you don't make it. Make it easy on yourself. Do it now. So-and-so is already on his way home and he was better than you are. Don't kid yourself, you can't make it. Quit before it really gets tough." The pleas came from the instructors on a regular basis.

The training did get tougher and so did the weather. It was suffocating. Arizona summers could never compare. Ninety degrees and 90 percent humidity. Sweat glands seemed to work overtime. Nothing was ever dry. Sleep was impossible. The quonset huts trapped what air there was in a stale and motionless state. Nights, the only period during the training which contained some time for personal thoughts and relief from the constant strain of the daily grind, seemed to never end. Mornings found sheets and bodies soaked with sweat.

Mornings started with a quick three-mile run in the predawn darkness, usually led by Lt. Uren, who ran like a deer. The run felt wonderful as the cool damp air of the predawn morning rushed by our sweating bodies and gave them momentary relief, for the one and only time during the day. The relief was temporary and by the end of the run a sweat had developed that would not stop. Even a cold shower couldn't stop the flow. Then the sun came up and it began to get hot.

By the end of the first week we started to get into a routine that would seem more or less comfortable. Morning runs, forgettable meals, physical training of every sort and torture, classes, more runs, rifle drills, eat again, more classes, more running and then more classes. Then run some more.

SSgt. Crowe proved to be ever so efficient at every aspect of our training. He led calisthenics, ran us everywhere, kept us awake during the class with a jab of his swagger stick, and never seemed to look the worse for wear. He looked organized, cool and in control. We always looked haggard, hot and tired. He pushed and we followed. He also had a mean streak.

He introduced us to what certainly was the favorite part of his unique program, an exercise he called Thump Call. As a veteran of Marine Boot Camp, I knew most of the drill instructor's tricks, but this one was new. Thump Call usually took place right after evening meal, and before we settled in for an evening of study, boot polishing and rifle cleaning.

"You pissed me off today, Candidate," SSgt. Crowe announced, as he stepped in front of a candidate a few feet from me. "I don't like having you piss me off, Candidate. What will it take for you to stop pissing me off?" he asked, knowing full well there was no acceptable answer. "Do you think it's OK for you to piss me off?"

"Sir, no, Sir," came a sharp reply, from a concerned sounding candidate.

"But you did it anyway, didn't you?" he questioned. "You shouldn't do that," he said. "I'm going to show you why. Tighten your stomach muscles. Are they tight?" he asked in a louder voice.

"Sir, yes, Sir," came a strained reply.

"Good. I'm going to give you a thump. Are you ready?" he asked, increasing the tension in the quonset hut.

"Sir, yes, Sir," even more strained now.

The sound of the blow echoed through the quonset hut. So did the sound of the wind being forced out of the target's body.

He then proceeded from one candidate to another and delivered a single, hard right-hand jab to the midsection of the young man in front of him. Sometimes he gave a reason for the blow. He would cite some failure or another during the day but normally he just explained that surely some mistake must have taken place and since he missed it, he didn't want us to think we had gotten away with anything.

The blow itself hurt pretty good, especially if you were close to first in line. As we got in better condition and we became more prepared for the punishment, the blows did less and less damage and the more courageous of us would ask for seconds, just to show him we could take it. In any event the daily offering of thumps finally came to an end with about a week to go when he sprained his wrist delivering one of his best. We knew we had it made after that.

Every American college, it seemed, was represented in the candidate class. Everything from Harvard to Arizona State College at Flagstaff. We had jocks and scholars, rich kids and poor kids, overachievers and superpatriots. Accents and slang from every corner of our great country, were in full abundance and were the source of a never-ending series of jokes and constant, good-natured ribbing. The drab green uniforms which we all wore were a great leveler. No matter the background or amount of money one had, on the drill field or bayonet course it didn't make much difference. Everyone had an equal chance to screw up.

Friendships were made rather swiftly and casually. Survival depended not only on our individual efforts, but also on relentless teamwork. It was us against the system and the instructors, who were trying to force us out. If you couldn't get things done as a group and work together as a team, there was no way you were going to become a Marine officer, or any other kind of marine.

SSgt. Crowe didn't much care about where you were from or what kind of car you drove. He cared a lot about whether you could perform the rifle command of "Inspection Arms" with some degree of sharpness and without dropping the rifle. He was also big on shined shoes.

I had very little time to worry about where I stood on the social ladder within this group, but in the beginning I must admit that on occasion, I did feel a slight twinge of jealousy or two when there was a minute to socialize and I found myself among some group from the Ivy League or some other elite-sounding group of institutions. I tried not to make Flagstaff sound all that good.

I was also just a bit surprised to find out that not only could I compete against this cream of the American crop, but from time to time I could even excel. My confidence increased with each successful romp through the obstacle course or at the end of another of those eye-opening three-mile runs. By the end of the second week we were settled into the routine of things and the fact that more than 20 percent of the starting class had dropped out gave me a bit of confidence. It was beginning to feel like I belonged here.

After the completion of those first two weeks, we got a day and a half of liberty, Saturday noon to Sunday evening with nothing to do but figure out how to let off a little steam. In a great Marine tradition, we headed straight for Washington, D.C., home of the legendary eight girls to every guy. We found a reasonably priced hotel that would look the other way when 12 guys moved into one room with two small beds. We didn't plan on sleeping very much. We had to go entertain eight women, or maybe 28 women. There was no way, was there, all those women could resist such wonderful examples of American manhood? But they did. It wasn't a very pretty sight either. We blamed it on the haircuts. Since Washington, D.C., was one of the few places in the world with a drinking age of 18, we consoled ourselves with what was for most of us our first legal beers.

We awoke on Sunday morning stiff and sore from a night sleeping on the floor and with our first legal hangovers. Six of us rented a limo for the day, and proceeded to treat ourselves to a firsthand lesson in American history. Despite the previous night's failures, we managed to have a good time, as we jumped from one spectacular historical sight to another. It was difficult to absorb so much in just one day, but we tried. We visited the White House, Congress, 25 statues and the Smithsonian, all at a record-breaking pace. No time for details, rush through and take a few snapshots, and then on our way to the next excitement. We managed to spend a little more time at the Tomb of the Unknown Soldier and the Lincoln Memorial, the clear favorites of the entire group. On subsequent weekends we would always come back to those two. It took no effort to enjoy one's sense of Americanism when looking into the penetrating eyes of old Abe. Our country was truly blessed.

Monday morning came early and with a horrible sense of reality. The sound of the recorded bugle call over the camp-wide microphone and sound system made it ever so clear that it was again time to get on with this selection and weeding-out process. Lt. Uren decided to have us go for a five-mile run this morning just to clear out the cobwebs brought on by the weekend festivities. By 0600 we were on our way to another hot and muggy day of training that held no particular distinction. More of the now familiar grind. Uniforms were already dark from the sweat. More classes on Marine history, leadership and field training with bayonets and a couple of quick trips over the obstacle course, sandwiched in between the constant practice in formation marching and rifle drills. Scorecards were kept on a daily basis. Every movement and response was being recorded for some unknown purpose. Failures were pointed out immediately and with great clarity, in front of all of your contemporaries.

"Come on shithead, why don't you quit?"

"Make yourself and the Marine Corps happy at the same time."

"You can't make it, you never will."

"You're wasting your time and mine."

Such was the daily challenge by the drill instructors. We also faced an internal and more personal challenge. Could we last? Could we survive and still have enough energy at the end of the day to stand up straight and look like good officer material?

Each morning, as we prepared for yet another day of training, my inner voice expressed serious doubts. Each evening after another day of tortuous training in the unbending heat, and after Thump Call, I found myself still standing. Each day also seemed to find one more bed empty, as another candidate gave in to the constant pressure from the drill instructors. I was making it. Fewer screwups each day. It seemed my determination to continue could control the desire to quit. I was surprised. I think the Marine Corps was too.

In the fourth week of training we continued our uncompromising schedule, with one unpleasant surprise, saved for the end of this part of the program. The Marines scheduled a 15-mile forced march for us, through the backwoods and hills of rural Virginia. Full uniform and equipment, including helmets and rifles. This was just part of the load we would be required to carry, on this six-hour trek through the dirt, mud and swamplike areas that surrounded Camp Upsher. The psychological buildup was intense. The drill instructors billed it as the ultimate drop-out mechanism. If quitting was ever on your mind it would happen here, somewhere on the trail leading out and back from nowhere to nowhere. The pace would be gauged on insuring the largest fallout possible.

The Company Commander, Captain Mike Armstrong, took his position at the head of the column of 200 men who would attempt this little walk. Capt. Armstrong was seldom seen during the training we had received up until now, so we weren't exactly sure what to expect from him. He was no Superman. Five feet seven, maximum, and slightly built. He may have been the smallest of all the men in that marching column. We were younger, bigger and stronger. This march probably wasn't going to be that bad after all, if this little runt was going to be at the head of the column. How could he hurt us?

By midway through the 15 miles we began to understand. We were inhaling water at every break. The Captain took none. Our uniforms looked like limp, wet washcloths. He still had every crease in place. Sweat had turned our uniforms a dark green. He had a slight spot that was barely visible under his arms. At break time, we collapsed beside the trail and unloaded our gear as quickly as possible. He stayed on his feet the whole time, helmet neatly in place. He moved among the troops, checking for possible heat exhaustion or stroke. He made sure we all took plenty of water and we all had begun frequently refilling our canteens. I never saw the Captain open his canteen.

"Everyone take two salt tablets, now," the Captain repeated as he moved down the column, now sprawled along the wooded trail. "Everybody got plenty of water?" he asked, stopping from time to time to check on the condition of one of the more tired-looking candidates.

"How does he manage to look so cool?" I asked my buddy C.P., as the Captain walked by us.

"Practice, I guess," he answered.

"I don't like this practice shit," I said.

"What the hell else you got to do today?" he asked unsympathetically.

"On your feet. Let's get moving," the Captain ordered, as he moved back to the front of the column.

The little bastard had to take two steps to our one but he was keeping up a very rapid pace and looked as fresh at the end as he did at the beginning. At about the eighth or ninth mile this pace began to extract its toll on the ranks. One by one, someone would go down to the heat and loss of water, from which we were all suffering. Trainers riding in jeeps at the end of the column would pick up the bodies, get them cooled off, watered down and drive them back to Camp Upsher. There were five such vehicles, and they were kept very busy.

Step after step we moved forward, urging each other to hang on and be tough. Before the afternoon sun reached its peak, we began to choke on dust as the red Virginia clay dried out and began to swirl with each gust of wind that blew across our path. I was making it but I was hurting. The helmet was driving my spinal column down into an extremely uncomfortable position and the straps of the pack and rifle seemed to be ripping holes in my shoulders. Cramps seemed to come and go. I was gulping down water and salt tablets at every opportunity. It would be very easy to sit down and be picked up by the jeeps for a nice leisurely ride back to camp.

Stubbornness, pride and fear of failing in front of your friends kept us on our feet and moving forward. And also the growing desire to walk that little shit at the head of the column right into the ground. Why not create a little competition? Let's walk right over the top of him. Let's make him ride the jeep home. It kept us going. We were starting to develop a deeper sense of how hard this was really going to be. No wonder marines feel so much pride in being a part of this organization. It wasn't easy and you had to earn your way onto the team. Nobody would be given anything. Each person had to find the strength and desire in his own person and apply it with great care in every situation. You couldn't fake it. Nobody could do it for you and what was being asked of us was something very special. This was not fun.

This was man's business and there I was standing at the finish, feeling very good about myself and my ability to withstand whatever was to be given out. Less than half the starters had made it. Some went down voluntarily, losing the battle of the mind. Others merely collapsed in a heap, unaware for several minutes that they weren't still on their feet. What we soon learned was that this was just the warm-up. Next week we would go 20 miles and the last week of training would require a 25-mile torture test. Could I continue to hold out? Would I still want to get on my feet after 25 miles in the 90-degree, 90-percent humidity? Would they drop me, too?

Once or twice a week, a Social Club was opened for us, so that we could enjoy a beer or two before the lights went out. The night after our first big march was mercifully one of them. Not only did the beer taste especially refreshing on this particular night but we were also feeling a very natural high from the completion of this major obstacle and we were in a mood to celebrate and do it together, as a unit.

It didn't matter much that the Club itself was about as glamorous as a high school locker room. We were off that trail and free of packs, helmets and rifles. The beer was cold. The three broken-down tables and five plastic chairs for 200 candidates provided all the ambience we needed for our relaxing night on the town. The march survivors gloated and the quitters complained. The beer flowed too freely and tasted ever so good. We had put in a good day's work and I was beat to a pulp. I felt good.

I was clearly, at 19, in a transition phase from boyhood to manhood and this challenge couldn't have come at a more opportune time. I was being stretched and pushed in a way that I could never have done by myself. The Corps was doing the pushing and somewhat to my surprise I was measuring up. I was doing manly things, with a little help from my friends. Marine green started to feel especially comfortable on my shoulders. I was alone and far from home but this really did feel right.

Just about the time we who were left began to feel we were going to make it without any more pain, the training was stepped up. The harassment intensified. Even going to bed at night became an opportunity for the instructors to create more havoc. Bed Drills became a constant occurrence. We would all stand at attention in front of our respective beds, then we would be ordered to face to the right and begin marching around the room in a circular fashion until the instructor called the formation to a halt, turned out the lights and ordered everyone back into his own bed. Thirty or so bodies crashed randomly into each other in a wild attempt to find the way back to our original positions. If it couldn't be accomplished in three or four seconds, we got to try it again. Sometimes the exercise was tried with 60-pound footlockers perched upon our heads. When the instructors got tired of this they'd try Thump Call.

My personal favorite was the Fire Drill, where everyone had to alternate getting under their beds then back into their beds, then under again, as fast as possible, whenever the drill instructor yelled "Fire Drill." It was quite a sight and usually quite a mess before it ended. They wanted very badly to let us know that the test wasn't over until the test was over. Don't get cocky. Every day is a new challenge and until you've passed them all you aren't through with us. Until we're through with you, you aren't through with us. You'll never be through. You'll never make it as a marine. Do yourself a favor. They wanted to observe us function in a state of near exhaustion, stripped of energy and dignity. Could we still function and possibly lead others? Every time we expected them to let up and give us a break, they added to the pressure instead.

The promise of one more weekend in Washington, D.C., kept our spirits raised. The naive anticipation of somehow finding that elusive, lonely secretary, who needed a little weekend companionship, kept us focused on making it through the constant screening out process. No secretaries came forward. Our shaved heads were a dead giveaway and held responsible. We approached the weekend this time with less resistance to the tourist routines and got a little more rest. We had two weeks to go. No need to get too tired.

Van Sandt, my bunkmate and best friend during this short phase of my life, proved a good tour guide. His two years at West Point had ended in failure but it did provide him with a better perspective about the historical sights in Washington, D.C., than did my upbringing in Tolleson. After his West Point failure, he had restarted his educational pursuits at Cal. Poly, San Luis Obispo. He joined the Corps to please his father, a serving colonel in the Air Force. C.P. was dead cool. A bit older and wiser than most of us, his two years at the Point had prepared him for all the harassment the Marines could hand out. It also helped that C.P. was a avid surfer and physical stud of the first magnitude. He was totally confident and set very tough standards.

"Hey, Johnson, you're making it hard on all of us by falling behind on the morning run," C.P. said to another candidate, as we sat on our footlockers, applying our 13th coat of polish to our boots.

"I do OK for the first two miles," answered the target of C.P.'s scorn. "After that my legs start to cramp. I can't help it," he said, rather apologetically.

"Maybe you ought to quit," C.P. offered, sounding more like a demand than a request.

"I'll make it tomorrow," Johnson answered.

"You'd better," C.P. said, as if he were a voice with some special authority.

C.P. didn't tolerate bellyaching or complaining of any sort from other candidates, even his friends. If you couldn't take it, get out, was his motto. He ran more than one candidate out of the program. So eventually he won the trophy for best candidate of the summer. Perhaps any summer. He breezed through most of the physical stuff and never opened a book. The rest of us pored over the books night after night and struggled through the repeated trips over the obstacle course. We strained and he laughed, never quite taking himself or the Marines very seriously. It seemed so easy for him and almost unfair for the rest of us.

I was pretty sure I could make it through the last two weeks but I needed to draw a lot of strength from C.P., as he pushed himself and all the rest of us. We had big hurdles to get over and I knew that somehow, someplace on the trail, I was going to have to look at him and steal some of his confidence, determination and strength. Thump Call had now become a great lark and I was enjoying all the other routine screening drills. We were close. Failure at this point was just too unthinkable. I decided to stay close to C.P. If all else failed, maybe he'd drag me across the finish line. I had to make it, somehow.

Capt. Armstrong once again headed up the march column. Two files of men stretching nearly half a mile through the Base Main Gate and out into the unfriendly backwoods of northern Virginia.

Each man in the column was preparing mentally for this assault on nothing in particular as we passed through the gate.

Our platoon, headed by Lt. Uren, was to bring up the rear, the most hated position in any marching column. We'd be running much of the day to keep the gaps closed. No matter what speed the front of the column went, gaps would develop up and down the column and the rear units would have to run to keep up, as the gaps opened and closed, in an accordionlike fashion. One of life's great mysteries. Why did the rear end of a column have to run to keep up with a column front that never breaks stride? Run, stop, run, stop! It was maddening, and with all our equipment pressing and pulling at every muscle, we were in for a long day. We were breathing hard by the time we had traversed the first 500 yards. C.P. had a slight grin across his face, a clear signal that he was ready. Lt. Uren, who would always turn slightly redfaced during any period of extreme physical activity, was already a light scarlet. He looked like the sun was getting to him but kept a very smooth pace during all of the marches and always finished with energy to spare. His pace would be slowed temporarily, some nine years later, when a Vietnamese land mine took his right leg.

SSgt. Crowe was growling constantly, at no one in particular. He had a really rough time on the first hike and wasn't destined to finish this one or the next one either. It didn't do much to improve his disposition. I think he hated life, in general. He had nothing much in life except the home he had found in the Marines. Two years later, after a night with too many beers and too many war stories, he put a loaded .45-caliber pistol in his mouth and pulled the trigger. One too many hikes or one too many snotty-nosed recruits. This particular day, we just tried to stay out of his way, a feat that was easier said than done. He wanted to share his misery and worked very hard to bring it, in abundance, to each of us. Double thumps for anyone who dropped out was his promise and reward. He was one of the first casualties that day. Too much beer the night before, we suspected. Those of us who made it got to perform Thump Call on him that night, at his insistence.

Being last in the column put us right in front of the ambulance team, so we all got a firsthand look at all the dropouts. There were more this time than the week before because of the increased distance and because somehow the weather conditions were even more brutal. Blisters which hadn't quite healed from the week before reopened early. Cramps became a constant battle and of course the ever-present threat of heat exhaustion or heatstroke was always just around the next bend. We all hoped these wonderful conditions, if they had to strike, would strike the other guy. Please not me.

We trudged ahead, step by step and hill by hill, shoulders aching and heads throbbing from the constant pressure of the stupid helmet. Breaks never seemed to arrive soon enough and when they did, they never brought the hoped-for relief. The heat didn't stop and neither did the sweating or the pain. Blisters hurt more, somehow, when we stopped. All too soon, we would be back on our feet, doing one more segment of this 20-mile walk through the woods.

I was fully aware that I was being tested in a new and very special way. My limits were being explored. I had to reach for resources that I didn't know for sure were there. Quitting seemed very near at times. Who the hell needed this anyway? Why volunteer for this kind of pain? Lots of people, good people, were quitting. Why not me? Who would know? There had to be an end to this stuff. Would the end find me on my feet, standing tall? At the 10-mile mark, I wasn't all that sure.

Somehow, it did end. Triumphantly. Gloriously. And painfully. For some of us. Only one-third of the starting group stumbled across the finish line. Both drill instructors came home in the ambulance. It was a mess but we had made it. A cold shower, a few very cold beers and removal of that stupid helmet and pack made the whole world wonderful once again.

The pain was soon behind us but not forgotten. The survivors were exuberant. And confident. Bring on the next one, we can do anything. The commission now looked more real. Would being a marine always have moments like this? This wasn't bad at all. Nothing I had ever done had ever given me so much enjoyment. Could pain really spawn such a thrill?

One last furious week and it was over. The 25-mile march was more of the same. The guys who could cut it, did. Those that couldn't, didn't.

Graduation was a low-key affair by Marine standards. Nothing spectacular except the smallness of the group. No fancy uniforms, just the green utility fatigues we had lived in for the last six weeks. A modest parade at best. No guests, no parents, just a small celebration with people who were strangers six weeks ago, and close friends now. One-third of the original group stood for the parade. We had a two-thirds dropout rate. It had been brutal. The survivors felt very proud of having made it through. We had one ceremonial Thump Call by SSgt. Crowe, as he passed out our individual diplomas. Lt. Uren gave us a nice firm and sincere handshake. I had been rated in the top 10 percent of the survivors of the first half of Officers Candidate School. Maybe I did have something to contribute. I had competed, successfully, against some pretty heavy-duty competition, from the best the U.S.A. had to offer. Why should I stop now?

4

On the Land

Coach Spilsbury was ready. He had already been at it for a week, working with the freshman and other football squad "walk-ons." He loved this part. Lots of blood and lost teeth. His screening process for the new guys was very intricate. Twice a day he took his old steel-backed chair and moved it to the center of the football field, took half of the candidates and formed a single line starting 10 yards to his left. The other half formed a line 10 yards to his right. He sat in the chair, his coach's whistle at the ready. Every few seconds he blew the whistle. At the sound of the whistle the first person in each line charged forward into a violent collision with his counterpart from the other line. The two combatants would slam into each other until somebody was on top and the clear winner of the mini-battle. If he was satisfied with the contact and aggressive nature displayed by the two participants, he'd blow his whistle to end that particular contest and the two survivors moved to the back of their opposite lines. If he didn't like the action for any reason, the two candidates got back into line at the front and went at it again.

This procedure often resulted in matchups with small wide receivers facing much larger defensive-tackle types, but it made no difference to Max. He wanted to see who did and who did not want to hit, and keep on hitting. Unabridged aggressiveness was awarded with a chance to try out for the final varsity squad. A lack of aggressiveness meant a quick trip home, or at least back to the dormitory, regardless of the other football skills that may or may not have been present. It was an excellent test for a love of contact

78

and a willingness to bleed. Football skills could be evaluated later. He wanted to test a person's character first. After three or four hours a day of this for the better part of a week, the real gladiator types emerged. Seldom did more than eight or nine guys survive from the 40 or 50 who started the program. That's all Max wanted to work with anyway. He loved this stuff and he loved the survivors. It was his favorite time of the year. My junior year at Arizona State College was about to begin.

We were loaded with talent. Seven guys who walked out on the field that fall day would play in the NFL or the new younger version, the AFL. Two of them, Rex Mirich, a 300-pound lineman, and Mike Mercer, our all-purpose kicker, would play more than 10 years of professional football each. Not bad for a tiny school, in a tiny conference, located smack dab in the middle of nowhere in particular. We were in good shape before the arrival of the outlaws, much better with them. Mike the kicker, Charlie Bowers and Gino Persetti, the outlaws, arrived the previous semester as transfers from Hardin-Simmons University. All three had mysterious football pasts. None of them would give a really direct answer to questions about their football history. After a while we knew not to ask questions. We might lose them as part of the team if the wrong answers came out. All three of them had evidently been asked to leave Texas by college officials who took a dim view of some activity or other. Charlie played three years as a halfback with the New York Titans (later the Jets) before an automobile accident took his life. Gino was better, until he tore up a knee. These three gave us several new offensive weapons and the ability to put some serious points on the scoreboard.

Mickey Alzoa, the competition Max was so delighted to have for me, had transferred during the summer. He had played some for us the preceding two years. The previous semester he had packed up his bag and moved to North East Oklahoma after a squabble with Max about how many passes we should throw every game. He never played a down at the Oklahoma school, never was there during a football season. His transfer back to ASC during the summer was against even the very loose NAIA eligibility rules, but who checked? Toss in a few guys fresh out of military football programs, a few junior college transfers, and it made for an active, talented squad. The team had won eight and lost two the year before, and expectations for this year ran high.

To Max it was a simple game. We didn't have a screen pass or a draw play in our repertoire. We practiced sweeps and off-tackle running plays over and over and over again. Quarterbacks got to throw a few passes at the end of each practice. Sissy time. We usually didn't even do it under full contact conditions. We had one target on each of the three or four pass plays in our selection, so none of the quarterbacks really developed the ability to look at the second or third receiver in a pattern. There weren't any. We dropped back and threw the ball. Not much mystery involved. Passing was not really an integral part of our offense. It didn't involve hitting enough people, so Max could never really take it too seriously.

Mickey had a great sense of humor and kept everyone pretty loose on the field. He barely hid a strong, competitive nature. He and I stayed pretty close friends during the intense competition for the quarterback job, mostly as a response to the common harassment we were both getting from Max.

"I've told you a hundred times Van Zanten, don't try to run a 21 Trap against an Oklahoma Wide Tackle Six defense. Audible to something off tackle. Pay attention. It's your job," Coach Spilsbury screamed at me, during one of our longer afternoon practices.

"Sorry, Coach, I thought they were in a straight up six," I apologized.

"Sorry doesn't cut it. Read it," he shouted.

"They were in a straight six until just before the snap," Mickey whispered to me after the coach had walked away. "They shifted after you had already set up. Nobody could audible out of that," he added. "Don't sweat it."

"Thanks," I said, aware that he and I were the only two of the 50 people on the field who believed my call had been correct, after what the Coach had yelled.

At the end of every practice session, Max liked to get our attention with a string of 100-yard wind sprints. At 7,000-feet altitude, these runs through the grass were especially brutal. After a three-hour hitting session, legs and lungs were screaming for relief. The rule Max applied for these practice-ending sprints was that they went on until at least three guys started to vomit. This could take seven or eight trips down the field. The big linemen usually were the first to let go. They could barf in great style if they'd prepared for the moment properly. This proper preparation consisted of the correct selection and consumption of colorful fruit juices. Grape juice was considered the best because of its dark color but orange juice was also a popular choice. Taken in large enough quantities before practice, the juice could induce vomiting after only three or four of the 100-yard sprints. The big guys perfected a form of projectile vomiting. The colors were spectacular. But distance was the ultimate challenge and they went at it with great enthusiasm. Rex Mirich, our 300-pounder, still holds the unofficial record at something over 20 feet. The deep purple stream had to be seen to be believed. As soon as one guy got going, it became contagious. Often times an orange juice man and a grape juice man could get together for a little mixing. This produced an especially colorful spray. Max always made a big show about being cheated out of his sprints, but rules were rules.

"Hey, Coach, look at this one," Rex said, as he let a stream of grape juice go.

"You guys make me sick," the Coach announced. "Get out of here. Back on the field at two sharp."

To keep my academic progress on schedule, I had to surround myself with upper-division courses. Three advanced math classes, one physics class, first-year Russian and American Literature added up to 18 semester hours. Max thought I was crazy but didn't interfere with my decision on classes even though physics lab cut into one hour of practice each Tuesday. I'd have to remain focused on the books or it'd be all over.

The school administration discovered, to their embarrassment, that there was not enough dormitory space for all the men who wanted to attend ASC in the fall of 1960. A handful of nails and some 3/8" plywood were used to close off one end of one wing of North Hall, a girls' dorm, to allow 30 young men refuge from the winter cold, in what had to be one of the most unusual arrangements of that day and age.

In another major administrative blunder, they picked three seniors to be dorm supervisors for the 30 guys caught up in this situation. One was my roommate Dusty. I went along with the group of seniors as extra baggage. Dusty and the other two guys were members of the school's BMOC organization, the Chain Gang, 13 secretly selected campus leaders and the occasional odd-ball. The Chain Gang was responsible for teaching and maintaining tradition throughout the campus. They wore distinguished-looking orange sweaters and carried large leather paddles to announce their presence and enforce their rules. They struck fear into the hearts of all freshmen, especially those who couldn't remember the school fight song or forgot to wear their beanies. Grab your ankles and take a swat with the leather paddle. It made for great school spirit. Everyone knew the fight song. Many swats were delivered on any given day during the beginning of each school year. We didn't do much to distinguish ourselves as dorm supervisors. We occupied our time trying to listen through the thin plywood panel for sounds and conversations from the female side.

"Do you think they'd mind if we put in an extra window here?" I asked Dusty, as we surveyed the wall that stood between us and the female world on the other side.

"Maybe some one-way glass would be OK," he answered.

"Nah, they'd figure that out. How about a real small one? Where's the ice pick?" I asked seriously. The ice pick worked wonders for viewing the activity on the far side, but we got caught soon after it had been installed. Too much giggling from our side. The girls learned early on to escalate the frustration. They knocked on the wall to get our attention and then whispered unidentifiable sexually oriented messages behind well-disguised voices. This was dirty pool. They perfected the technique and practiced it at odd times of the day and night. We tried to retaliate but with far poorer results until we unleashed our secret weapon, Junior Vargas. Half Italian and half Mexican, he had looks that could challenge any movie star, then or since. In addition to his good looks, he was also Mr. Nice Guy, very popular with everybody including the teachers and staff, and utterly in control of his world.

Once the girls on the other side of the wall discovered that he lived in our section of the dorm, the teasing stopped and the serious stuff started. All of the frustration switched to their side of the plywood. Mr. Cool played hard to get. We tried to get him to encourage more activity through, around or over the wall. He didn't cooperate at first.

"Junior, Junior, where are you?" came the call several times of day.

"Junior, I've got my jammies on and I want to say good night."

"Junior, please give me a kiss good night, I know you're there." The soft, teasing female voices drove me crazy. Not even once did I hear a voice call "Bill, Bill," through the wall. It wasn't fair. Junior remained largely disinterested, only rarely joining in the fun.

After several months, the pressure became too much for the voices. They began to use the ice picks. Some of the more ardent Junior admirers learned that they could crawl out a window on their side of the wall, inch down a narrow pathway behind a large hedge near the outside wall of the structure and enter our apartment through a window that I always left open for such emergencies. In an age of complete separation of the sexes, this was pretty exciting stuff. How did one entertain a group of pajama-clad girls? We did the best we could. We had invented coed dorms. However, we couldn't tell the world about it or we would have been expelled and have never been given the credit we so richly deserved. I think a small plaque would be in order, somewhere near that window, and a mention in the National Register of Historic Places. Meanwhile the other male residents in this unusual dormitory arrangement ran amok and were totally unsupervised. We expected to be thrown out at any time. It never happened. Another administration blunder.

"You want to go up there and tell them to quiet down?" Junior asked me, in response to some really loud noises coming from a party in the room directly above us.

"Nah, they never complain when we're making noise," I said, hoping to sound fair.

"Yeah, but we're supposed to be monitoring and controlling this kind of stuff," he said, talking about his job responsibilities for the first time all year.

"Who cares?" I answered, with my best illustration of runaway apathy.

Like many of our mutual friends, Junior wanted to be a high school teacher and coach. He also wanted to see a little bit of the world before he settled down, but wasn't certain just how to go about that. I tried for months to convince him that a three-year stint as a Marine officer might give him the outlet he was looking for. He eventually took the bait. Immediately after graduation he took off for Officers Candidate School at Quantico. He hated it. He hated me for getting him involved in it. He struggled through his first year while I was still in my last year at Flagstaff. I met him later after he had spent two years in the Corps and by that time he had learned to tolerate life as a marine. Another year later, I met him in Okinawa and he had started to really like some parts of it but he still held a grudge against me and the successful job I did recruiting him.

In 1968, during the Tet offensive, and seven years after leaving Flagstaff, Captain Jay R. Vargas was involved in one of the most furious battles of the war. He wasn't even supposed to be there. He had come to Vietnam this time as a wounded, recovering marine, supposedly out of action for a while. He was supposed to be in Okinawa. He snuck his way into the country and quite by accident found himself in charge of a rifle company that had lost its commander. The company had been all but wiped out. Junior kept things together for more than two days. He had only a handful of marines left when reinforcements arrived. He was awarded the Congressional Medal of Honor for his actions. Always a little slow of foot, he also collected five Purple Hearts. Another handful of various medals he picked up along the way made him the most decorated marine of the Vietnam War. Eventually his anger at me subsided and he settled down to a brilliant career in the Marines. He's still cool.

One stormy night in April at about 2:00 a.m. I had a visit from my three roommates dressed in their bright orange sweaters. The 13 current members of the Chain Gang had slipped out into the night to the various men's dorms and drug back 10 half naked, half asleep, totally frightened recruits to the home team locker room of the main gym for the initiation ceremony into the most prestigious organization on campus. The rites were rumored to be brutal. The long leather paddles which they carried gave credence to the rumor. I was one of the first of the newcomers to arrive, and watched with horrified interest as one by one my soon-to-be fraternity brothers were pulled, kicking and screaming, into a position near me on one of the benches in the dimly lit room. We knew that the vote had to have been unanimous or we wouldn't be here. The yelling, crazy people in the orange sweaters really didn't hate us, even though paddles slammed into metal lockers, caving in doors and causing huge dents in places where no dents had existed. If one of the paddles could do so much damage to a steel cabinet, what was it going to do to a bare ass?

"Blood tonight. We're going to have blood tonight," screamed one of the Chain Gang members, who I couldn't recognize.

"Pain. Pain. Wait until you feel the heat of this paddle," screamed another.

"New meat. I want some new meat. I've been waiting all year for this," screamed another.

They kept us locked in the darkened room and in suspense for the better part of an hour, alternating between leaving us alone to face our private fears and further demonstrations of how much damage one of these leather paddles could do to a wall or wall locker. I was the third victim. As I was led out, I was given a nice long look at the two very red and bloody butts that had preceded me in line. It was not a pleasant sight. I dropped my trousers on cue and bent over a gymnastic side horse that had been placed strategically in the middle of the basketball court. Every muscle I had seemed to be twitching, especially those in and around my very exposed rear end. The noise from the screaming 13 filled the gym.

"Van Zanten's gonna bleed," came a shout from the group going into a frenzy. It sounded like Junior, but I couldn't be sure.

"Let's get some blood flowing," I heard requested through the uproar that was engulfing the gym.

"Hey, Van, hold on tight. After the first one, the pain ain't so bad," said one of the new members, who had already completed his rite of initiation. He lied. Without warning the gym turned grimly silent. Then suddenly I heard the sounds of footsteps approaching, slowly at first and then faster, from across the floor. The pain nearly blinded me as the first paddle found its main target and quickly wrapped its way around the side of my lower body. How could I not be ready for this? I let out an uncontrollable scream and grabbed tighter to the horse. Whoever the swinger was let out a grunt from the effort he had put into it. It hurt real bad.

It got worse. Mercifully the next 12 came in very quick order and suddenly the screaming and yelling came back to deafening levels. It was over. I staggered with some help to an upright position, the pain exploding inside my head, and found my place in line alongside the other two finished products. The damage was inspected by all of the participants. The bleeding from my wounds was evidently below normal and the participants vowed to do better with the next subject.

We stood in line suffering our pain and with our pants down until all 10 of the newcomers were through with the ritual. Slowly the pain subsided and the realization of these early-morning events started to sink in. This was the ultimate climax to a really good year. I was now an official Big Man On Campus. What price we often pay for acceptance. I had arrived and it felt good.

The 10 graduating seniors gave the 10 newcomers their orange sweaters to wear the rest of the night and all day the following day, to announce to the campus the identity of the newly selected members of the organization responsible for upholding and continuing the multitude of campus traditions. How and why we got selected remained a mystery and a subject for much discussion on the campus for several days to come. Many popular guys and some thought-to-be-obvious choices were not included. The new group included one black guy, two with Mexican names and seven gringos.

My senior year our football team was "rebuilding." It was a new experience for Max, who started sending in the plays from the sideline with alternating linemen. The plays were generally lousy calls, often out of rhythm for what was going on out on the field. In my mind the whole concept was wrong. I might have been the only college quarterback in the country to have his plays called for him. Paul Brown had tried it on Otto Graham, the great quarterback of the Cleveland Browns, but it just wasn't a widespread practice and I hated it. The other players hated it. They started to ridicule the play selection and had less confidence in what we were trying to do. I was having trouble controlling the huddle.

"What idiot play did you bring this time?" someone would yell at the messenger lineman.

"OK, knock it off," I would try to insist.

"The last one didn't work," another player would inject.

"Slot left, X–25, slant."

"Slot left, X–25, slant, on one," I would pass on to the attentive huddle, with all the enthusiasm I could muster.

"Oh, shit, they're been in a five-man line all day, we can't run that." A typical response.

"Shut up and run the play," somebody else would offer.

"Stick it." A frequent reply.

When I brought up the subject of who was going to call plays the rest of the season with the coach. Max as usual had his opinion and wasn't much interested in mine. "Young man, I get paid to run this team and you get paid to do what I say," he told me in a voice that didn't try to disguise his anger.

"But, Coach, I can call the plays too and the guys hate having to wait for the play to get in."

"I'm not going to discuss this anymore, Van Zanten. I don't need a smart-mouthed know-it-all out there running my team. I need a player who can follow orders to the letter and the question is are you a player or do you figure on doing my job instead?" he asked with a sarcastic grin on his face.

"I'll play, Coach, but I still don't like it," I said, heading for the door of his office, underneath the small, cold stadium.

"If you don't like it, don't do it," he said, making sure I knew who was going to decide this issue. Max was not a happy camper. Our practices got longer and contact scrimmages were increased. The coach and I hardly spoke. He thought I was a smartass. I thought he was an old fogey. He was more right than I was. Warming up for the fourth game against the University of Red-lands, he walked up behind me as I limbered up my dead arm. We were one win and two losses on the season.

"If you think you can play better, I'm going to let you call the plays today," he whispered, so that only he and I could hear.

"Right, Coach," I said, trying not to grin too widely.

"Screw up and I'm going to have Daly in there," he added for effect.

Redlands had a weird defensive system. They ran something that looked to me like a 5-2-4 setup, two linebackers on the outside and four defensive backs. The five defensive linemen lined up in a very strange way, a nose guard playing over the center, two tackles who played outside our offensive tackles and two defensive ends very wide. Their scouting report must have told them we went wide on every play. They were heavily stacked outside. The middle looked like the Grand Canyon. After we ran the fourth consecutive play over left guard and into the void, Lanny Westbrook, our 170 lb. left guard, began announcing to the defense as we came up to the line of scrimmage that the play was coming through his position once again.

"Better get some more guys over here," he would shout as he was preparing to take his stance.

"I'm gonna block this guy over here," he would yell, pointing to the outside linebacker.

We ran that exact play 36 times. They wouldn't change their defense. And I wouldn't change my mind. We won 27–7 to even up our record at 2–2. Max was furious.

"Did you forget the plays, Van Zanten?" he shouted out as the team was reviewing the game films.

"We do have more than one play, Van Zanten, what were you thinking of? Why didn't you try something else?" I thought we had played a pretty good game and winning wasn't so bad either. Max was right too. We couldn't run one play all year. But we called plays differently. I wanted to take advantage of their defensive weaknesses. He wanted to call plays that would make defenses react to us, and make the enemy play our game.

He won the argument, of course, and called all the plays in a fifth-game loss. I was miserable. The team was miserable. Coach was miserable. On Monday he called me into his office.

"Saturday's game was about as bad a game as I've ever seen one of my teams play," he scolded. "What's wrong out there?" he probed. "Do you like this game?" he asked, sounding like he was about to dump some bad news on me.

"It's not fun when you're calling the plays," I said, surprising myself.

"Why don't you quit then," he challenged.

I looked hard and long at him, wondering what the hell he was trying to do. Don't be a dope. Five more games and it's all over. Quit, and you lose your scholarship. What are you going to use for money? Tell him the truth. Go through the motions. I was very uncomfortable. I'm still not sure whether I just chickened out or acted on my convictions. Maybe both.

"I have to tell you Coach, I'm really not enjoying being a

quarterback with somebody else calling the plays," I said with a shaking voice. "I guess I'd better give it up," I added, handing him my paid-for meal ticket with a hand that was covered with fresh sweat. He accepted the resignation without further comment, feeling certain that he had rid the team of a troublemaker not fully committed to the excellence he demanded.

I was the talk of the campus for a couple of days. Then it was over. Everybody forgot about it. I became a janitor in the Student Union building and took out a student loan to pay for room and tuition and things were once again possible and the path to graduation quite clear. I was just another hardworking student. I floated through my classes, having to sweat only my Advanced Russian Language Studies, which was turning into its own special kind of nightmare. A year earlier the program had been introduced for the first time and attracted 35 students. Three of us had survived and persisted. I had to complete the course to complete my graduation requirements. The Russian professor was trying to kill us. If I didn't pass, I'd have to start over again on some new course of study. Another year or more of school might be involved.

In the spring, spirits always rose with the temperature and promise of the end of winter and the 10-foot snowdrifts. Bathing suits and short-sleeved shirts found their way out of the closet and as soon as the air temperature got above 60 degrees, afternoons and weekends were spent in Oak Creek Canyon and in the waters of Slide Rock. The red-stained canyon walls, carved majestically out of the stratified rock formations, provided a startling backdrop for this special corner of Arizona. We used our special little corner of the world for an outdoor, springtime playroom. The high desert trees filled the landscape and completed the bursting color scheme on our favorite real-life canvas. The creek water was shockingly cold and fresh, the sun hot and glorious and very much appreciated after months of hiding behind cloud-filled skies and living in a snow-lined campus for most of the year.

Second Lieutenant Don Price came home from the Marines to graduate with his class. He had made it through college in three and a half years and had gone directly into the Corps. He had been a Marine officer for several months when graduation came around. Don and I had been close friends because of our shared love for and participation in the Corps. He was a townie, living with his mom a few blocks from campus, and arrived in Flagstaff at the beginning of the final week. I couldn't get enough Marine talk. I had very little interest or real need to study to get through finals, except Russian. No break for the seniors from that professor. He was going right down to the last day. He also informed me, with about three weeks to go, that if I didn't attend every single class remaining on the schedule, I would be a dead man. Flunk time. I only half believed him but made a serious effort to at least sit in on all the classes. Three people survived this four-semester horror show of a class from the 35 starters, and now the guy was threatening to flunk all of us. Chicken do-do.

The night before the last class, Price and I stayed up all night long talking about our futures with the Corps. He was full of advice for how to get through the last part of Officers Candidate School and the subsequent six-month Basic Infantry Officers School, which he had just finished.

I sucked it all in. I couldn't get enough. I was scared I wouldn't make it and scared I wouldn't get the chance. I just couldn't wait and I couldn't stop talking about it. We finally exhausted ourselves by eight o'clock on the morning of the last day of Russian class, the only remaining class I had to attend. It started at 9:30. I arrived back in my dorm room at 8:30 and layed down for a 30–minute nap, which I desperately needed after an all-night session of talking and considerable beer drinking. Bill Epperson shook me awake at 9:25.

"Wake up, idiot, you're going to miss Russian class," he yelled at me.

"I'm not going, I'm too tired," I answered. "He won't flunk me," I said, trying to sound confident and totally unable to get my eyes open. "I passed the final," I lied.

"Get stuffed," he yelled again, jerking me to my feet.

"I wanna sleep man," I said, hoping he would leave me alone.

"No way," came his serious reply. He pushed and shoved me across campus to the classroom where the class was being held. Bill walked me to the door and made sure I went inside. The other two students informed me that the professor had just walked over to the administration office to take my name off the graduation list. Wonderful. Let's don't make this thing too easy. Let's go right down to the wire and screw it up.

The professor arrived back in the classroom about five minutes later and did a double take at me sitting there in the front row, all nice and attentive. He excused himself for another 10 minutes and, true to his word, notified the administration that I had passed all requirements for the course. Everything in its place. All courses completed. I had a sheepskin. B.A. Mathematics. Minors in Physics and Russian Studies. All earned on the up and up. It couldn't be taken away.

5

From the Halls and to the Shores

The first face I saw when I stepped off the plane in Baltimore was a familiar one. Standing near the exit was my old friend, Lt. Don Price. I was off on a whole new episode in my life and it was exciting to be on my way. I walked confidently and happily towards Don.

"Pick up your baggage, shut your mouth, and get on the bus parked at exit five," he said, catching me totally by surprise.

"Yes Sir," I replied, rather meekly. This wasn't a very warm welcome. This is my new life and even my friends won't talk to me? We arrived at our location sometime in the middle of the night, a very hot and humid night in the middle of July 1962. It was too dark and too late to do anything but find somewhere to lie down and close our eyes for the few minutes before the customary early-morning Marine Corps start. We lined up to get a pillow and an unnecessary blanket in one of the empty barracks near where the bus had let us off a few minutes earlier. I was standing at attention, waiting my turn, and caught sight of Don walking smartly down the center of the hall. As he drew even with me, he unloaded a sharp, quick, very hard forearm shot to my right shoulder. I was stunned. My shoulder went numb and my knees buckled.

"Keep this line straight and I don't want to hear any more noise," the Lieutenant shouted, scaring sleepy candidates half to death.

"What the hell did you do?" the candidate standing behind me asked, after Don had left.

"Nothing that I know of," I replied, not mentioning that the mad bomber was one of my best friends.

"I didn't think officers were allowed to hit you," he whispered, hoping he hadn't seen something that was now going to be part of his life.

By the end of the second week I was beat. The hills surrounding Mainside Quantico had provided our instructors with a never-ending source of misery. One of the hills was our post-breakfast source of fun, each morning. It started steep and got steeper. Before we reached the top, half the company would be lying beside the jungle-lined trail. Knowing that it was coming early the next day kept us from sleeping well the night before. None of us wanted to die by having our lungs explode.

Don met me in downtown Quantico on my first day off. It was just slightly against the rules for him to be fraternizing with a mere officer candidate but he did it, despite the rules. Thirty more days and I could join the club. Wear the gold bars. He couldn't imagine doing anything else. I couldn't think of anything else either.

Two major changes in the rules which now applied to our training made this session different from my experience in boot camp or Junior PLCs. One was caused by the deaths of some officer candidates during a hot spell in the summer of 1960. Now when the weather got bad enough, hard physical training would be temporarily halted for fear that others might surrender to heat-stroke and die. This meant that almost every day an alarm would be sounded somewhere on the base and we would head for the barracks for an impromptu lecture, out of the direct sunlight. The other change was that if a candidate decided to quit the program, he was obligated to serve two years as an enlisted marine. This meant even the most miserable candidate tried to avoid dropping out. Discouraging dropouts probably didn't serve the Marine Corps very well. Too many marginal people hung on. Dropping out didn't end the misery, but just delayed it. Even so, we had 25 percent attrition. The training and the overall selection process still remained hard enough. No real incompetents made it this far anyhow.

I was not completely stupid and reported for training in pretty good condition. I had very little problem keeping up with what they wanted us to do. I got good grades in all aspects of training and was appointed as the Parade Adjutant for the graduation ceremony. I had finished fifth in the class of 600 people who completed their officer training. Twenty-five of the 600 would be commissioned immediately after the graduation ceremony and move on to active duty as second lieutenants the very next day. Most of the rest headed home to finish the last year of their college work.

We were fitted for uniforms of brown, green and blue. We tried on swords and hats and overcoats and gloves and shoes, all part of an officer's official wardrobe. We were each presented a bill for approximately $2,000, representing about nine full month's pay. Each day we would try on these gleaming, beautiful uniforms, have them altered to perfection and then climb back into the grubby green utility fatigues used by all candidates and head back to the barracks to be yelled at, screamed at and pounded on for another day.

The Parade Adjutant role required that I use much of what I had learned over the years from my many drill instructors. I had to yell orders in a crisp, loud, military fashion to the parade elements more than 500 yards away. I had to march alone and smartly to the center of the parade field, position myself in front of hundreds of people, salute smartly, execute several movements and report to the Parade Commander the status and readiness on the parade troops. I had a small memorized script. I did it all rather successfully, although my heart was in my mouth the entire time and my hands were dripping with a constant stream of freshly produced sweat.

Don Price was there at the parade's conclusion to take a salute and offer a strong handshake. I had done it. The next day some major general was scheduled to pin a pair of gold bars on my collar and I would be off on a new career. An adult career. A unique career.

On September 1, 1962, I became Second Lieutenant William Van Zanten, USMC. In front of a handful of family and friends, 25 of us walked proudly into a new life. Moments later, I chased a young enlisted man down the street to get my first salute and make the somewhat surprised young marine a silver dollar richer. The Officer's Club and living quarters at the Bachelor Officer's Quarters took some getting used to. I had to learn to quit referring to all marines as "Sir." Salutes came as a surprise, returning them a constant pleasure. Then it slowed down. Hurry up and wait.

Becoming a marine officer is only the first step in a long road to serving in an operating marine field unit. After commissioning, you have to be intensely trained and acquire basic skills for performing the required duties. It starts with infantry skills. All marine officers are first and foremost infantry officers. Whether they later became tank officers, or supply officers, or communications officers, or intelligence officers or any number of the specialties which are required to run an integrated Corps, we all had to first learn the skills of an infantry platoon commander.

The Basic School (TBS) was the academy where these skills were passed on to the young, uninitiated second lieutenants. Stuck deep in the middle of the thick, densely wooded Virginia countryside, six miles from Mainside Quantico, it was a self-contained facility that provided all of the necessary ingredients and facilities to teach us about the responsibilities and pleasures of leading a marine infantry platoon. Six months of intense lessons on weapons and tactics and communications. More lessons on leadership and character development. The program demonstrated to all of us the importance the Marine Corps placed on the art and science of infantry and amphibious operations.

Most of us in this Basic School class were obligated to serve three years on active duty. The first six months, or more, of that enlistment would be dedicated to preparation and learning. No second lieutenant could step out in front of a platoon of marines without first being given a very well thought-out and executed master's degree program in infantry platoon management.

"Gentlemen, during the next six months we will concentrate on learning and teaching only two things," said our first instructor on our first day in a loud, clear, Marine voice that caught all of our attentions and brought the auditorium to a hushed silence.

"Number one, is to get the job done." Simple enough, I thought, as the instructor raised his index finger in the air high above his head.

"Number two is to take care of the troops," he added, as he added another finger to the pose, above his head.

"That's all it takes, gentlemen," he said very seriously, taking his time and making eye contact with several in the audience. "Let me repeat that," he said, now prowling the front of the class, completely in control.

"Get the job done," he screamed at the top of his lungs,

bringing all 250 of us an inch or two out of our seats. "Take care of the troops," he followed, in a hushed voice. "In that order," he added, repeating it again two or three times as he moved up the aisle into the middle of the class, all eyes focused on him now.

What was he going to do next? All of us wondered as he walked up and down the auditorium steps, in slow, measured paces.

"Write it down. Write it in big letters so you never forget it or the order in which they occur," he said, stopping to make sure everyone was taking him seriously.

"As a platoon commander, you will be given many, many difficult orders. Tough orders, perhaps even deadly orders. You cannot, never, ever, fail to carry out those orders. That is our heritage, our tradition, our reason to exist. We cannot compromise on our standards, or accept less than perfection in this area," he said, his voice now low and calm.

"The Marines do it better and more often and with more dedication than any other fighting force in the history of this world."

By now the adrenaline was flowing in every vein in the room. A first-rate pregame speech. Let's rush out and lead a platoon somewhere.

"Is this clear, gentlemen?"

"Sir, yes, Sir," came an immediate response from all 250 pumped-up marines in the audience.

"That's a pathetic response, gentlemen. If you're going to lead my marines, I want some enthusiasm for the task," he said in a scolding fashion.

"Let me ask you again. Is that first rule absolutely clear?"

"Sir, yes, Sir," a response so loud this time that the walls almost came down.

"That's better."

"Rule two is just as simple," he said in a low, firm voice from behind the dais, at the front of the room. "Take care of the troops. Write it down. Now," he said as 250 pencils went to work.

"Remember, you are Marine officers now. You are different."

"Army officers are not referred to as soldiers."

"Navy officers are never called sailors."

"Air Force officers are never called airmen."

"Marine officers are called marines, first, last and foremost."

"You will be responsible for all the marines under your command. You don't eat until they eat," he stated, very strongly now. "You don't sleep until they sleep. They are your total responsibility. They are the treasure of the Corps. We are nothing without them. You are nothing unless they agree to follow you. You have to earn that privilege. It must not be abused."

By now we were exhausted. If we weren't already on active duty we would have enlisted right there. No question in anybody's mind about whether or not the right decision had been made in bringing us to this place, at this time.

"You will take care of my marines or I'll come looking for you," he promised, in a very matter-of-fact statement.

The next six months were serious stuff. Uncomplicated but very serious. Supervising and managing the affairs of 40 marines that made up a marine rifle platoon. Getting ready to lead men in combat was serious business. a big load for young men, most of whom, like me, were no more than 22 or 23 years old.

And combat was not far from our minds. The Cuban missile crisis was two months old. The country had been at the brink of the unimaginable: nuclear war. Marine rifle platoons had filled and still filled the many Navy ships that still surrounded Cuba, as we were sitting in class in Quantico. America had been at peace for nearly 10 years but none of us expected that situation to go on indefinitely. The presence in the front row of the auditorium of three young lieutenants from the Marine Corps of the Republic of South Vietnam, already at war, was a gentle reminder that armed conflict was one of the world's oldest habits. It gave the training a quiet sense of realism.

My roommate for this six-month cruise was Eddie Taber, a small but very strong and fast black kid from UCLA. Black second lieutenants were a rarity. So was Eddie. Living in the South for the first time while being an officer in a Corps that was almost completely lily-white made Eddie quite unique. Eddie knew he was unique but he didn't spend much time dwelling on it. He went about his job just like the rest of us, except that his job was done a little better. He let his actions in the field, in the classroom and in his uniform do all the talking.

The Marines wanted more black officers but kept the obstacles to their admission extremely high. No average blacks allowed. No average anybody allowed. Eddie wasn't average at anything. Neither were the other two black guys who helped make up our 250-man company.

Eddie had stayed an extra year at UCLA to get his master's degree in History. He was married and had a beautiful young daughter. He lived away from our dormitory with his family most of the time. His bed, in my room, was always empty and remained ready for inspection at all times. His part of the closet was only partially filled and always in impeccable order. He showed up every morning, ready for action and with a big warm smile on his face. Eddie didn't seem to mind that he was something special. He never asked for or got any special favors.

His wife, Mary, was a beautiful person, who often welcomed me to their modest home, near Mainside Quantico. She found out that my favorite food was a well-made taco. The Marine cooks didn't do tacos and I was constantly homesick for Mexican dishes I had grown up with in Arizona. Mary was an expert. She went out of her way to set a place for me at her kitchen table every 10 days or so and would fill my plate with wonderfully prepared Mexican food. Eddie poured the beer. They were a happy family and they made me feel welcome. Mary quickly settled in to the demanding job of being a Marine wife. In some ways it's harder than being the marine.

A large number of the officers we were serving with had never known a black person in such an up-close and personal way. Some didn't like it and treated Eddie like a nonperson. Eddie didn't indicate that he noticed. Four miles from the base, restaurants and bars often had signs that said *Whites Only*. Eddie didn't indicate he noticed that either. I'm sure he did. Eddie was always in trouble. Our room was never clean enough during the spot inspections that came on an infrequent basis. He was never there and not at all responsible for the mess, but his name was on the door and he shared in the blame that should have been all mine. Those unsatisfactory inspection reports probably kept him from being Company Honor Man. He could do more push-ups, run faster and study harder than anyone else in the company.

He also changed lives. Months after Basic School had been under way, at a platoon picnic, the owner of the house we had rented for the bash asked my best buddy, Ron Walker, from

Savannah, Georgia, to ask Eddie and Mary to leave the premises. No blacks allowed. Ron, who was a redneck born and bred, and proud of it, looked at the guy in total disbelief and promised, without hesitation, to burn down the house if anything was said to either Eddie or Mary. I think he meant it. The picnic went on without further disturbances. Probably not a position Ron would have taken a few months earlier.

The next time I saw Eddie after Basic School was several years later somewhere in the middle of a jungle clearing in Vietnam. He was a highly decorated captain, serving, at that moment, as an aide-de-camp to Lt. General Lewis Walt, the highest-ranking marine in Vietnam. The General and Eddie stepped off an incoming helicopter in sparkling clean and pressed uniforms with spit-shined boots and shining brass. My unit was in the midst of a small firefight. Not the best time to have generals running around. The General walked over to the Battalion Commander and started a discussion. Eddie spotted me and walked over to where I was standing, in my dirty, wet and crumpled state. I saluted smartly in deference to his superior rank.

"Why don't you clean up this place before you get me in trouble again," he suggested. "You never change, Van Zanten, always a mess," he added, wrapping me in a bear hug. "Great to see you."

Basic School was run at quite a modest pace, compared to any training I had ever been through. Lots of eight-to-five stuff and a glorious five-day week. For the first time in my life, and for most of my friends, there was time off and money in our pockets. Not much really, but some, an uptick from any time in my life. Time on my hands, money in my pocket, a beat-up old car and a normal, not too stressful job. And we were living in the middle of the densest female population in the world. Who could ask for anything more? We studied hard but the classes were not terribly demanding. Tactics classes were a large part of the curriculum but nobody knew why. Every tactical maneuver for the infantry fire team, the squad, the platoon and the company involved the same basic thrust. Straight ahead. No feints. No envelopments. Nothing cute. Hi-diddle-diddle-right-up-the-middle. Find the bad guys and go after them. Straight up. No holding back. No reservations. Basics first. Get the job done.

We spent two weeks in wonderful Virginia Beach learning about amphibious operations. Up and down those dreadful nets that provided exit from a large Navy ship and entrance to a small wooden landing boat. These small boats bobbed up and down next to the larger vessel, making the trip up and down the nets extremely nasty, especially when you carried 75 pounds, plus weapons and ammo. Timing had to be just right. So did the confidence. Jump or leap at the wrong time and you could drown, unless you were crushed between the two vessels first. It came to much the same thing in the end.

We had fun too. Too much sometimes, according to the Base Commander at Little Creek Naval Station, in Virginia Beach. The Admiral objected to us stealing his dog. The dog loved our dormitory and all the attention he got from 250 lieutenants. The Admiral wasn't so impressed. No sense of humor. We gave the dog back, took our punishment from the Admiral and continued to learn how to operate with the Navy in our quest to be "Soldiers of the Sea," as we were called by the French.

We also learned about weapons and vehicles and artillery and supply and Navy ships. Amphibious operations and helicopters and communications. And history and tradition and military law. And leadership. In classes, in the field and in daily practice. We took turns being in platoon and company command billets. Company commander one day. Lowest private the next. Squad leader the following week. We were all equals but with different jobs on different days. If leading a platoon of marines was going to be difficult, leading a platoon of your peers was ridiculous. Fifty comedians trying to make your life impossible. One such funnyman rented a huge Cadillac convertible for his first tour as company commander. In the middle of a February, on a very cold morning, he arrived to take command sitting atop the backseat of the open car. A friend served as the driver. He looked like Eisenhower reviewing the troops. We were extremely entertained. The instructor staff were not.

Competition for the final standings in the graduating class at TBS was keen. This was a competitive group and filled with highly dedicated people. Several were gunning for the top spot. I was having too much fun to put in that much effort and there was just too much talent to get close to the top. I was fast but they were faster. I was smart enough but there were a bunch that were smarter.

Earlier I had been assigned as the Platoon Leader for an exercise in night combat operations. I was to lead the platoon in an attack against an aggressor force, located about two miles up a large fire break in the forest area not too far from TBS.

As we arrived in the jumping-off area, I gathered my three squad leaders together to discuss our attack plan. The situation appeared to require something pretty straightforward. Up the fire break, one squad on each side of the cleared area, moving as quietly as possible. Shortly before reaching the target area, we would gather all three squads for a frontal attack. Lots of yelling and shouting during the attack. Take a few prisoners. Have a few laughs and get back to TBS by midnight. No sweat.

I decided to conduct a small rehearsal with the platoon before we started the real thing. Unknown to me was that the area I had selected for the rehearsal, an area which looked very much like the real target area, was where training classes on the employment of concertina wire were routinely held. As we started, darkness set in. The front of the column started to run into barbed-wire obstacles. They had been cleverly deployed to make the area impenetrable, and hold intruders in a killing zone.

I was called forward toward the source of the trouble, followed closely by the Instructor, who was going to grade our platoon performance and mine, as Platoon Commander, on this exercise. We held our conference by soft whispering, silently developing alternative plans and directions to extract ourselves from this mess. Whatever movement we tried led us deeper into the maze of wire. We crossed ice-cold streams with waist-high water that took our breath away and soaked our equipment, making it less than useful and very uncomfortable. We'd find more wire. We went around in circles. We got nowhere. The complaining started. And the noise increased. Nobody bothered whispering again. A small defending force would have annihilated the platoon. They probably would have saved the officer for last, because such inept stupidity is a rare and precious gift.

"What a mess, what an idiot," came calls from my buddies in the back row.

"It's too damn cold out here for this shit," came another.

"Knock it off you guys, we'll be out of here soon," I responded, hoping somehow they would quiet down and that the Captain who was grading this exercise would notice my firmness and forget my mistakes. We returned to TBS at 0400, a beat-up, wet, tired mob, completely out of control the entire night. We eventually got out of the wire, hours behind schedule, and went after the aggressors. We made so much noise in our approach they ambushed us three times before it was all over. The Captain was very impressed. "Well, you got off the trucks OK," he opened. "After that it was pretty crappy."

At the end of Basic School we went through an interview ritual that helped decide which occupational specialty each of us would be assigned. I opted for and got infantry. The Marine first team. I applied for and got a regular commission, the key to making this a lifelong career. I was no longer a reserve officer. I was a permanent member of the establishment. This was my team. A place to hang my helmet for the next four years. This life seemed to fit me well. I liked getting up in the morning, ready to face the many challenges of being a marine. The harder the better.

We had a Mess Night that showed us how to have a really good drunk while dressed impeccably in our handsome dress blue uniforms. Chesty Puller, the most famous and heroic marine of all time, was the featured speaker and guest of honor. A living legend, a retired general, he was obviously thrilled to be back among the troops. We each shook hands with mouths agape and hearts aflutter. Chesty's exploits were all too familiar to every one of us. He couldn't be human too.

Graduation was conducted in our dress whites. A grand show, 250 ice-cream-vendor impersonators in one small auditorium. Lots of parents and friends. My folks were there, awestruck by the pageantry and the military bearing of their wayward son. I got top grades in leadership which put me in the top 10 percent of the class despite my other shortcomings. In Yalie terminology, this would be Phi Beta Kappa, but not quite Summa Cum Laude. Academics had pulled me down a little. I hadn't bothered to study very much. But despite my disastrous trip through the concertina wire when I had been acting Platoon Commander, I had finished with very high grades in leadership. Forty-nine of the 50 guys in our platoon had ranked me best in the platoon. One misguided soul ranked me second.

I was ready for the Fleet Marine Force. The real Marine Corps. So were most of the other 250 marines who filled the auditorium with flashing silver and brass and spit-shined everything. The six months had flashed by. Friends made. Romances started and finished. I was married to the Corps now. I had a clean, crisp set of orders to join the 3rd Battalion, 1st Marine Regiment, 1st Marine Division, an infantry battalion that would be heading for Okinawa and other parts of the mysterious Orient on or about September 15, 1963.

I had two weeks to get to Camp Pendleton and then an intense training period called "lock on," which would last eight weeks, prior to embarking on a Navy ship for faraway places and strange new lands.

Me and my ugly 1955 Buick headed west. La-La Land, south. Four of us with the same set of orders decided to find a house together in San Clemente, a few miles from the home of the 1st Marine Regiment. A new career. A set of gold bars on my collar. A very unusual haircut and some very shiny shoes. I even had a little money in my pocket.

The Fleet Marine Force is a serious place. Not much time for having fun in the California sun. This was the real thing. War practice and preparation was everywhere. Our battalion was at the center of activity. We had eight weeks to become a battle-ready unit. A new battalion commander, four new company commanders, 27 new second lieutenants and 500 crisp, new marine riflemen. A new team. Eight weeks to become a good team.

I lost a flip of the coin and became the Weapons Platoon Commander of Lima Company, 3/1, second choice but not a bad one. I had to concentrate on machine guns and bazookas. Lima Company, like all marine rifle companies in the Corps, was made up of three rifle platoons and one weapons platoon for support. A weapons platoon had three squads of M-60 machine guns and three squads of rocket launchers, sometimes called bazookas. Each squad of machine guns had two of these fast-firing, 7.62mm weapons and eight well-trained marines to operate, protect and supply the guns with a constant source of ammo, fed to it in long bandoliers. The squads were often attached to one of the rifle platoons during combat operation but it was my job to ensure that they could properly perform their intended mission of providing a very large amount of firepower on a target in a short period of time. We had been taught in TBS that the machine gun was primarily a defensive weapon. Properly deployed in a defensive posture, the machine gun would be the main protection against advancing troops, guarding the most likely avenues of approach. They needed to be hidden carefully and liked a field of fire that was long and unobstructed. They also needed to be well protected, and performed best in pairs. Members of the squad all knew how to fire the weapon but most were involved in guarding its nest and in keeping it supplied with the necessary ammo, until somebody got hurt. Then everybody started playing musical machine guns. As their Platoon Commander I had to make sure they knew how to keep the gun firing and operational in every kind of environment and condition. The gun was mechanically rather simple and very reliable provided it was kept clean and well oiled, not such an easy task when you're out in the boonies doing grunt stuff.

The other half of my empire consisted of three squads of 3.5" rocket launchers. Their mission was to provide the company with light antitank or antibunker capability. Each squad had two of the long, clumsy, pipelike tubes and eight people to carry the foot-long rockets that provided the firepower. These squads were also often operated as attachments to the rifle platoons and were also used primarily in a defensive role. The back-loaded rockets could penetrate several inches of armor plating or nearly two feet of concrete from a range of 200 yards or less. They required a great deal of good teamwork to load, aim and fire in a timely and accurate fashion and were extremely vulnerable to enemy fire because of their size and shape. They were easy to spot and easy to knock out. This weapon would prove to be of only marginal value to the rifle company in the jungles of Vietnam and would be replaced shortly after the start of the war with a much more effective and easy-to-use 60mm mortar. The battalion still kept control of the more powerful and accurate 81mm mortar, a capable, leftover weapon from World War II, but at the rifle company level, up close and personal, the smaller 60mm was easier to carry and faster to get into action. Never mind the long range capability or the bigger load, when we used the 60mm we needed it fast and close. But for now we trained often and hard in the art of destroying tanks and other large metal objects that the grunts needed to be protected against.

The two types of weapons gave the rifle company commander an extra arsenal of potent firepower. Firepower that was critical to achieve the results he would want in either an offensive or defensive operation.

We worked together to fine-tune the way we employed the weapons and we practiced continually on improving our effectiveness with each of them. Once we went in the field my squads would be spread to the winds in support of the different parts of the company commander's missions, often out of sight and out of control, but still my responsibility. I had to trust and believe in the capabilities of each of the squads that would be sent to support the other elements of the company. I now owned six of these machines of destruction and 54 hard-charging marines. My marines. Twenty-five or so had just started to shave. A half dozen corporals and sergeants about my age and a platoon sergeant with a dozen years in the Corps made up the personnel assigned to my platoon, 54 sets of eyes on me, measuring me, wondering. What kind of guy was this? They'd find out some of it, soon enough.

We didn't waste much time talking about how to put together an infantry battalion. We just did it. Morning, noon and night. We started with the basics and never let up. Everyone had to know their job. We made sure they did. Over and over again. For the first time in my Marine experience I was the teacher, not the student. My enthusiasm was impossible to restrain. The young marines responded well too. They were excited about our upcoming adventure and trip to the Far East, as well. I ran them hard, up the steep hills of Camp Pendleton and through the sand dunes that marked the western boundary of the base and led to the beautiful Pacific Ocean. During one three-mile run, as part of a fitness test, I set too fast a pace and put several of them on the side of the road gasping for air and temporarily out. Another time, one went down hard and only mouth-to-mouth resuscitation kept him alive until we got him to the Base Hospital. I had to learn how to pace our activity and be more observant about everyone's condition during training.

Get the job done and take care of the troops. A simple concept.

The responsibilities were immense. So were the privileges. This platoon was mine. I was father, brother and warden. And every 30 days or so we got a check for nearly $250. We managed to scare off most of the local womanhood with our bald heads and farmer suntans. We started work at 0530 and often worked through the night. Captain Morgan, my Company Commander, drove us hard. He drove himself hard. It was his rifle company and it was going to be done his way, the Old Corps way. He didn't garner much love and affection. He didn't want any. What he wanted was unquestioning obedience and professionalism. His four young platoon commanders gave it, sometimes with tongue well in cheek. If he asked for one more unnecessary inspection, we pleaded for two. If he wanted a three mile run, we begged for six. He never knew we were pulling his leg. Second lieutenants were his least favorite people in the world, though the list of usual suspects ran from civilians to communists. I had my own agenda for my platoon and for myself. I truly wanted to be ready, each day and each night, to push my marines a little closer toward having the skills they must have to get their job done. I wanted them to be the best platoon in the company and the best weapons platoon in the battalion. They seemed to want it too. The Marines had spent a lot of money preparing me for this job. It wasn't a wasted investment.

Then one day, no more practice. We were off to the 3rd Marine Division, located on the island of Okinawa, made famous by the last deadly World War II battle. We climbed aboard an MSTS (Military Sea Transport System) ship in San Diego and headed off into the sunset. I packed all of my belongings in one seabag and one footlocker. I hadn't accumulated a lot of "things." What would it be like on this dot in the Pacific Ocean? Two hundred square miles of rock. Geographically insignificant. Historically tragic and important. Twenty-five thousand Americans died to capture this poor imitation of civilization.

During the second week on the island, Captain Morgan volunteered me to fill a crappy job at 3rd Marine Regimental Headquarters. I became the Embarkation Officer for the 3rd Marines, a job any self-respecting second lieutenant would work very hard to avoid. I had to leave the company for six months. Leave the troops. It didn't make any sense. Why me? I was doomed.

Being an embarkation officer didn't involve much work unless someone needed embarking. The Regiment didn't. I played on the base basketball team. We played poker almost every night or watched movies that were years out of date.

I was in the mess tent near the top of Mount Fuji, Japan, one of our main training areas, having frozen eggs and greasy bacon, when I heard that John Kennedy, our Commander-in-Chief, had been assassinated. We had no TV or radio and it took days for the details to eventually get to us by way of the *Stars and Stripes* newspaper. We canceled all operations for three days. We held a memorial service in a small, dark, green tent, with a mud floor and simple, wooden benches. It was eerie. We had no feeling for what had happened. Or why. Or what was going to happen next. Lee Harvey Oswald and Jack Ruby were names that wouldn't come to our attention until weeks later. All we knew was that somebody had killed our President. Was it a random event or the start of a war? We had no way of knowing. Life had been turned upside down. Something important had been taken from us. John Kennedy had been an inspiration to all of us, a hero, larger than life. He made people believe in service and sacrifice. He made us proud of what we were doing. We lowered our flags.

The 3rd Division invaded Taiwan three months later.

I was in charge of getting the 3rd Marine Regiment loaded on the assigned eight ships in a manner that would allow us to be off-loaded in the required order, so that as each unit hit the beach, it was in the prescribed place and with the assigned equipment. The Division Embarkation Officer wanted me to load the regiment on seven ships. After three or four sleepless nights of trying to accomplish this objective with paper models of ships and equipment, I told him I just couldn't find a way to do it. He said I could. I said it couldn't be done. He said it would be done. The dialogue went on like this for several days. The Regimental Commander finally tired of the argument and my lack of progress, ordered me into a jeep and we headed for Division Headquarters, where for the first time in my career I found myself going eyeball to eyeball with a gentleman who had two shiny stars on his collar. The Division Commander.

"The Major says you've got plenty of ships to get the job done, young man," the General shouted, as the Colonel and I came to attention in front of his desk.

"I've tried, Sir, but I just can't make all of the equipment fit on the seven ships that have been assigned to me," I answered, hoping that I hadn't made some stupid mistake.

"Are you absolutely sure, Lieutenant?" he asked, eyes drilling right through me.

"Sir, yes, Sir," I answered, as loudly and as confidently as I could muster. My hands shook slightly as the General and the Division Embarkation Officer discussed some of the ways I could have messed up and what to do about it.

"Lieutenant, you'd better be right or I'm going to be mighty angry," the General said, his attention now focused back on me. "I'm sending the Major back to Camp Schwab to see if you've made some stupid mistake, or if not, what's needed. I really can't spare the Major but you've given me little choice. Don't you dare be wrong."

"Aye, aye, Sir," I managed, as I did a swift about-face and got the hell out of there. It took 12 hours for the Major to agree we needed another ship. When he announced that to the Colonel, a hint of a smile came across his face. I had dodged a huge bullet. We went on a three-week, all-expense-paid sea cruise and romp through southern Taiwan. Rocks and desert and cactus. We didn't see anything of the cities or the people. Just mountains and dirt roads and marines. I got to pin on my new silver bars indicating my promotion to First Lieutenant. And better yet I was told that when we returned to Okinawa, I was going back to Charlie Company. My sentence at Regimental Headquarters had been served. I was getting a parole.

Having a command again proved invigorating. Even Captain Morgan's ravings couldn't take the smile off my face. We had about three months to get ready for the really big show, a two-month tour as the Special Landing Force (SLF) for the 7th Fleet, the end of our overseas assignment. We were scheduled to be the ready unit for the entire Western Pacific, ready for trouble anywhere from Korea to Australia. We did the normal Marine stuff to hone our skills and get our bodies ready. Somebody had the bright idea to conduct a march around the north end of the island, a grand total of 150 miles in six days. None of us had ever tried that.

Captain Morgan was a good walker, tall and thin, with long legs that ate up the landscape at a furious pace. We scrambled along, as best we could, frequently running to keep up. By the end of the second day, half the feet on the trail were breaking down. Open, bloody blisters were everywhere. The corpsmen had to send back for an emergency supply of bandages. The two most miserable-looking pieces of foot meat belonged to the Captain. He should have quit. The Company Corpsman tried to force him to do exactly that. The Battalion Commander ordered him to quit. He wouldn't stop. As long as he was on his feet, nobody else was about to quit either. Mile after mile he moved ahead, through the most remote and inaccessible parts of the island. He refused to limp. Our oldest marine, the Company First Sergeant, sprained an ankle the third day and needed a cane to stay on his feet. He couldn't keep up with the speed of the column but he wouldn't quit either, so he walked by himself most of the time.

On we went, through villages that were untouched by the civilized world. No running water. No electricity. People living in concert with nature, not too different from what their ancestors had been doing for hundreds of years, or maybe thousands of years. Dusty roads made for oxen and carts, not jeeps or trucks. People stared at the crazy green men that passed through their world and out again, without making real contact.

The First Sergeant got up a couple of hours early on the last day so he could get a head start on the last leg of the trip. He wanted to march through the gates of Camp Schwab with the main column. He didn't quite make it. Captain Morgan led us through about 1400 hours, 25 miles since we had started the day, and 150 miles since we had started the march, six days earlier. We stopped just outside the gate to collect ourselves, straighten our equipment and to celebrate our success. We were the first company in the battalion to go through the gates. We ran the last half mile, in formation, counting cadence at the top of our lungs. We wanted to let the entire regiment know we were back, and back first. The First Sergeant came limping in three hours later, pulling on his cane and gritting his teeth. We made a welcoming line for him at the finish. He took the last few steps amid a chorus of cheers and applause that gave everyone including that gritty old man of 40 or so a lift in spirit and a rush of pride. I was not sure what exactly we had accomplished by this madness but finishing sure felt good. Nobody had failed to finish the course. Fourteen people had to be hospitalized after crossing the finish line, including the Captain and the First Sergeant. Dozens of us would have stopped somewhere along that 150-mile trail except that we just couldn't go down while Captain Morgan wouldn't. He had kept all 200 of us on our feet. One step at a time and eventually the journey is over. The job done. Just stay on your feet. You can give a lot more than you might imagine.

Then a few torpedo boats from North Vietnam fired on a U.S. Navy vessel, the *C. Turner Joy*. Or they didn't. The entire 7th Fleet and all Marine West Pacific units went on full alert. One of our nation's historical low points was beginning. Our battalion got aboard a group of Navy ships in a hurry. Our return to the U.S.A. was put on indefinite hold. Now our home was a Navy APA, the scum of the Amphibious Fleet. Twelve-high sleeping cots for the troops. Six-high for the officers. Too little fresh water. Too little food and too much sun.

For the next 57 days we sailed in a circle, a few miles off the coast of Haiphong Harbor. Around and around, day after day, waiting for something to happen. Waiting for orders. Being miserable. It was steaming. Living conditions were intolerable. The ship's Captain was an angel. He allowed us to dress in bathing suits and skivvies, our only relief from the constant beating of the sun and the suffocating humidity. We were allowed showers every three days. With water rationing, even that brought little relief. Too many marines. Too few facilities. There was a rumor an hour about our mission. We were landing. Then we weren't. We were going home. And then not. Movie tonight. No movies this cruise. We went around and around and counted the days in disbelief. Boredom mounted on boredom, except for the days when we decided to invade North Vietnam.

Twice we loaded into LCPs (Landing Craft, Personnel), wooden caskets that powered their way through the sea, each delivering 10 or 15 marines to a designated beach, provided they made it that far. We climbed down the nets from the side of the APA and headed for a beachhead in Hanoi Harbor. Make a landing. Establish a defensive perimeter and wait for further orders. Pounding through the open sea in our wooden boxes, most of the passengers sat silently, with heads bowed, waiting for the sound of unfriendly fire or for the ramp of the front of the boat to go down so we could hit the beach. Neither happened. With about half of the eight-mile trip to go, the fleet of wooden monsters turned gently and returned to our large, steel home and we climbed back up the nets. Just another drill? Nobody knew. We tried to take it in stride. After all, we were a veteran Marine outfit. Ready for whatever we were called on to do. We were called on to sail around in circles.

Lyndon Johnson was now in a race for the presidency against my man, Barry Goldwater. It was the wrong time to start a shooting war. He had to get elected first, by promising not to go to war. He made it on the peace ticket against the warmonger from Arizona. Tens of thousands of marines and soldiers would die under that leadership.

After nearly two months of this nonsense, we made our way back to Okinawa, grabbed our stuff and sailed off for the U.S.A., suntanned and homesick. Time for some home cooking and the California beach life. Girls and steaks and football. On my third day back I purchased a magnificent, shiny new 1965 Mustang, my first new car. And what a car it was! It was the first Mustang the dealership had ever received and my car never got as far as the showroom. Racing red. Stunningly beautiful. People would come from every corner of a gas station to look it over. I had never had a thing that anybody else envied. This was it. A mad machine. New car. House on the beach in San Clemente. Bachelor heaven for me and three of my marine friends. Another four lieutenants had the house next door. Luxurious beach houses. Surf and sand and San Clemente. By day we patrolled the hills and sands of Camp Pendleton, putting together a new battalion, the 3rd Battalion, 7th Marines. One third of the battalion consisted of people like me, who had just returned from the tour in the Far East. The rest were new. New bosses. New jobs. Same profession. Same hills.

On weekends we partied and lived the beach life. Where we got the energy I'll never know. Each weekend started with a promise to get some rest from the workweek, which the Marines provided. The rest never came. Friday nights started with a sparkling clean garbage can placed strategically near the front door of our house on the beach. We filled it with ice. Visitors filled it with liquids. Wine and beer and gin and lemonade. Whatever was available and cheap. Paper cups were provided. A plunger was used to stir the concoction. The garbage can got filled quickly and because of the large number of visitors it stayed full, though many hands drew many containers from the icy water. Saturday morning often found 10 or 12 people lying in various parts of the house or in the yard, near the beach. Last year, months before, civilian friends, and especially girls, were nonexistent. Here we had more than we could keep track of. People came and went and slept and had breakfast without bothering to introduce themselves. It was glitzy and stimulating and pulsating. By Sunday night, each of us would swear to never party again. Slow down. Rest a bit. Get some much-needed sleep. Each Friday we broke the promise. Every Monday morning at 0430, we prayed for rest.

There were also bad times. My sister, Patty, two years younger than I, was lost at sea. Gone. No more. She and her husband, Denny, had recently moved to Pago Pago, American Samoa, to teach school. It was their way to get away from Tolleson and find a little adventure. They loved the people and the place and the job. A thatch-roofed hut on the beach provided their permanent shelter. Inquisitive and friendly natives provided their students. They built a catamaran to provide some fun and entertainment. On its maiden voyage the catamaran was swept out to sea by a violent and strange storm. They were never seen again.

I took some leave and flew to Samoa. I rode a Coast Guard cutter for two days, searching every possible location where they might have ended up, in a perpetual seasick state. I commandeered an incredibly large and luxurious airplane from a band of congressmen who were screwing off in Samoa during a congressional break. We searched and searched. Hundreds of square miles of ocean. Too much open sea. No clues. No trace. They were both gone. Death had struck close to home.

Patty had been a pest while we grew up together, always interfering with my fun. I had to act civilized and protective around her. Like all little sisters, she was a nuisance. Sure, she had been pretty and bright and friendly and popular. Sure, she was sensitive and supportive to her big brother. Sure, she was caring and dedicated and reverent and deeply religious. Sure, she had a pure soul. Sure, she was anxious to serve other people. And teach. And live in crazy places. And sure, she was head over heels in love with her new husband and gloriously happy. Sure, she was a human and a family treasure. She was still a pest. I missed her, terribly. I couldn't comprehend why such a treasure had to be taken at such an early stage in life.

All too soon it was back to the beach and parties and life in the Corps. But perhaps, a bit more serious now. Up the mountains. Down the mountains. On ships. Off ships. Shoot, fire and move. Work hard and have a good time. Life went on.

By March 1965 I had been selected by the Marines for two years of Russian Language School before assignment to the Joint Command Headquarters in Berlin as a military spy. I also decided to get married. I had met a young, pretty schoolteacher from Laguna Beach. It was all over. Death to bachelorhood. A July wedding was planned and then off to Washington, D.C. and Germany.

"You and Georgia still planning on getting married?" my room-mate George McGillivry asked me, one night after work in early May 1965.

"Yeah, probably July 24th," I answered.

"If you want to get married, I'd suggest you do it this week-end," he said, with a face devoid of any special meaning.

"What are you talking about?" I replied, slightly bewildered.

"Just what I said," he continued. "If you want to get married, do it this weekend," he repeated, rather matter-of-factly. George was on the 7th Marine Regimental Staff. He knew what was going on. Rumors had been strong for several weeks that Lyndon Johnson was going to send the Marines to Vietnam. Maybe George knew something about what Lyndon had in mind.

"George, are we shipping out?" I asked.

"If I knew, it would be Top Secret, and I couldn't tell you," he responded. I had my answer. We were going. And soon. George was too serious about this. He wouldn't kid a guy. Georgia and I were married, three days later, in a big, formal, church wedding at the Camp Pendleton Chapel in full white dress uniforms, raised swords, beautiful bridesmaids, handsome attendants and lots of family. Marines can move fast when they have to. We had two or three hours for a honeymoon. One day to look for a place to live and move in. No dishes, not one utensil. No furniture. It was a little hurried. We had to adjust. And adjust fast. We borrowed from friends and our new landlord and set up home in the midst of the chaos that was now going on every minute down at Camp Pendleton.

Getting our battalion ready to deploy required a round-the-clock effort. I was a married man. I was also a man on the way to war. Five days later we were gone.

6

Right and Freedom

We spent a few days back aboard the USS *Iwo Jima* after OPERATION STARLITE while the Marine Corps decided where to drop us on a more permanent basis. Initial intelligence reports indicated that the operation had been a clear victory for the good guys. The hard-core North Vietnamese troops had been hurt real bad. What remained of their fighting force had scattered to the wind, not to be found again until much later in the war. Their attempt to capture Chu Lai City, an insignificant coastal town, had blown up on them. They had wanted to make a point with the South Vietnamese government and the local people, but marines from Okinawa, Hawaii and Camp Pendleton spoiled their party. We beat them to the punch. Surely this nonsense would soon be over and we could get back to our life in the real world.

From this time forward we could now claim to be combat veterans, even though few of us really believed we had been severely tested. We had only been ashore a few days. We had, by all accounts, received only a few casualties. We had taken on the best of the bad guys and had made them pay very dearly for their efforts. Surely, they wouldn't want to continue taking this kind of a beating. At this pace, our presence here certainly wouldn't be required for very long. The U.S.A. had flexed its muscles, the Marines had landed, the good guys were here and would as usual prevail. Wouldn't we? If Charlie still had any doubts, we'd just have to show him once again. We decided to declare victory.

Our chests stuck out a little more than normal during our trips to the ship's wardroom, where we were treated more respectfully

115

now by the Navy officers. Be careful guys, you're looking at a combat veteran, a cold, hard, killing machine. We've been bloodied. It's tough out there. We know. You can't imagine what it's like being in combat.

We wanted to be pampered a little and by Navy standards it sort of worked out that way. If we felt like a hamburger at 2:00 a.m., we got one. If we wanted laundry done, it came back in three hours instead of three days. Somehow, meals were bigger and loaded with more good meat and potatoes than usual. Was this a coincidence or were they trying to tell us that they knew we had done a good job? Who cared? We accepted the newly found hospitality without complaint. The troops got treated well too, and the flight deck was now open for us at all hours to catch some fresh air or to do some much-needed running. We were fully aware of the negatives involved in our recent experience, even though we didn't necessarily want to face them straight on. We talked little of our wounds. In a strange way, we didn't realize we had anything to worry about.

We should have been frightened beyond description. Our battalion had lost 27 marines to wounds and death. This was about 1½ percent of the troops aboard this floating war machine. Anyone could live with those odds. One in a hundred. No problem. What we didn't calculate, of course, was that over the course of a full year of combat, this projected to a 100 percent casualty rate. Those kind of numbers had no meaning, even in our wildest imagination. No one expected a full year of action.

What we also did not, at least openly, discuss at great length was a more telling statistic, one that struck closer to home. Our battalion, like all battalions in the Corps, had 27 lieutenants on the payroll. In four days we had lost two of our 27. We had lost 8 percent of our company-grade officers in four days. This should have been extremely concerning. Dale Rutherford had taken a bullet between the eyes. Very dead. Phil Avila caught a bullet in his left leg. He lived. The leg didn't. A surgeon tried but failed to save it during a 10 hour surgery at a military hospital in the Philippines. Phil would be fitted for an artificial limb to replace his lost leg within a few days of OPERATION STARLITE. Dale and Phil were part of an eight-man group of lieutenants that I lived with prior to leaving for Vietnam. There had been eight of us who shared two adjoining houses on a beautiful sand-lined beach a mile north of San Clemente. Serious bachelor pads. Serious bachelors. Of the eight occupants, two of us were now out of action in a very painful and deadly way. Twenty-five percent of our little fraternity in San Clemente was now dead or maimed for life. Twenty-five percent in four days. This had better be a statistical blip.

Max, Tom and I shared a room one deck below the hangar deck and well away from the noise of helicopters taking off and landing, and the other activity normal to carrier operations. The room was spacious and comfortable and hot. We spent a lot of time there writing letters and taking things easy.

"It's a good thing that little bastard couldn't shoot straight," Max said, describing an experience he had when one of the bad guys took a shot at him from close range. "This Texan's ass might be on the way home by now if he'd been a better shot."

"Charlie doesn't want to kill any Texans," Tom pointed out. "Their only chance of winning is if we end up with all Texans on our side."

"Screw you. Weren't for Texans we wouldn't have no Corps," Max retorted.

"We'd have a different Corps, that's for sure," I said.

"You're just jealous," he answered. Tom and I had seen all the action we wanted to, but hadn't had any particularly personal close calls like the one Max experienced.

The three of us caught up on letter writing, played cribbage for hours on end, and talked about how big a shithead the Colonel was turning out to be. And we talked about going home. We had spent the very best part of the last two years sitting on some Navy ship or another. It was getting old. Home sounded good. War sounded like hot, dirty work. Let's get it over quickly. The real world is calling. Let's finish the job and go home. We did not know that the "failed" North Vietnamese efforts successfully destroyed what committed elements of the ARVN had existed, eliminating any aggressive tendencies it may have possessed. No sweat. The Marines are here. It'll be over in no time now. Then back to the world. Home.

The Marines picked the city of Chu Lai for our new home. The 3rd Battalion, 7th Marine Regiment was assigned the primary responsibility for providing overall perimeter security on the south and southwest sector of the temporary airstrip under construction, just south of the city. We traded the comfort of the aircraft carrier for the rice paddies and hills of northern South Vietnam. Our landing in Vietnam, by helicopter this time, went without incident. No bullets and no bad guys to greet us. We quickly set about establishing operating positions and started normal routines associated with long-term living in the field. We conducted patrols, listened to and gave situational briefings, dug holes, strung barbed wire, read mail, filled in recently dug holes, and argued about the merits of the various selections of C rations, now our only consistent supply of food. We listened to the radio and dug some more holes. Within days boredom became a big part of our existence and a constant source of problems. Nights were long and often provided for little sleep. We signed peace treaties with the bugs and mosquitoes every night. They broke the cease-fire agreements with great regularity. We sent daily patrols to every village within five miles. We searched and searched for signs of Charlie. He didn't show up very often and we found very few signs of him anywhere.

We operated under fairly strict rules of engagement. Since significant local populations surrounded us in every direction, we were not allowed to engage in exchanging bullets with Charlie unless we were under heavy fire. Charlie occasionally fired a few rifle shots at one of our passing patrols from inside the friendly confines of a nearby village. We weren't allowed to return fire unless Charlie persisted. Charlie turned out to be persistent, but not stupid. He liked our rules of engagement.

We tried to make friends with the local villagers, a cause that was made much easier if we didn't repeatedly blow them to pieces. We try to track down the snipers but they fade into the background and are impossible to find once we arrive on the scene from where they took some shots at us. We mill around for a few hours, looking for hidden weapons or ammunition and searching the tunnels that are a part of each village, but frequently come up empty-handed. We give the kids more gum than they've had in their entire life and the corpsmen take care of minor aches and pains by administering a little first aid to anyone who has the courage to be seen with the American invaders.

Sometimes the villagers pay the price for accepting our assistance. Charlie tries to subtly explain to these ignorant farmers that fraternizing with the marines is not a good idea. They hang one or two of the guilty parties from a nearby tree to provide a clear message. Occasionally they decapitate one of the village elders and prominently display the mangled head on a fence post near the village gate. The message is clear. A war for the hearts and minds is being fought. The farmers are caught in the cross fire. They are dead in the middle.

As our presence in the area becomes more routine, Charlie carefully maps our tendencies and makes sure we have more booby traps and land mines to contend with on each of our daily jaunts through the countryside. These wonderful little weapons take their toll. We start to lose people to a war of attrition, making the rice paddies safe for democracy.

We didn't get many results from all of these efforts and management got a little antsy. Battalion Headquarters wanted every detail whenever we did have something to report. Get a confirmed kill and you'd get more attention than you'd really like. Get too many people hurt and you're on the carpet. It started to become a game of numbers and paperwork.

The troops, mindful of Charlie's little tricks, learned to walk like careful cats, each foot delicately placed, eyes searching every inch of space in any location that might contain one of his favorite toys. The best could spot a booby trap 10 yards away and disarm it on the move. The troops put in their 20-hour days with few complaints and ignored the corporate bullshit coming down from Battalion. We plowed through the rice paddies and the local villages in our never-ending daily search for Charlie. Most of the time Charlie chose to hide. When he felt like fighting, he picked his targets carefully. We supplied convenient targets. We continued to try our best to flush him. It turned into a very monotonous way of life. The hot sun and unfriendly environment was wearing us down. Faces were drawn and burnt by the constant exposure to the harsh sun. The troops went about their jobs with little fuss and their sense of humor remained undiminished. They frequently lifted my spirits and broke the boredom that permeated our souls. They were doing their job, one day at a time.

Battalion Headquarters started to take on a semblance of permanency. A Chow Hall was erected using local labor and lumber scavenged from some Seabee unit located down near the beach, about two miles east of our main position. Sleeping tents and 16-holers, with a full line of piss tubes, were lined up in neat, orderly rows, just behind the operations tent. In the hills, a few miles away, we slept on the ground when we slept at all, and buried our shit.

Max was now the Platoon Commander for our 81mm Mortar Platoon and got assigned the collateral duty of running the chow hall. More importantly, he was put in charge of the beer supply. It was the world's smallest stockpile but he put his whole heart into guarding it. Supply lines for really important stuff, like beer, hadn't been set up yet. In a really good month the troops got one beer and two Cokes. Of course, we did get all the warm chlorinated water we wanted. Max was probably the only guy in the battalion who could be trusted with this project. He counted every beer and kept incredibly accurate financial records. He made sure everything was done to ensure that the beer was being distributed in a fair and equitable manner, and that every penny was accounted for. He also proved to be a tough negotiator when the time came to exchange Marine money for Navy beer. It must have had something to do with the experiences he had in college, begging and pleading his way through classes and looking for free handouts of food. Even his old buddies couldn't coax him into breaking the rules over one lousy beer.

"Don't you come around here looking like some sick dog, trying to get my beer," he told me once, as I was trying to sweet-talk him out of something more than my share.

"Come on, buddy, I haven't had a cold beer in weeks. I've been working hard. How about helping out an old friend?" I asked, hoping to solicit at least some sympathy.

"You ain't anything special Van Zanten, friend or not. We ain't got much and you're not getting any extra," he insisted, firmly.

"Thanks, pal," I said, as I walked away, hoping to toss a little guilt his way.

Max was stuck in Battalion Headquarters full-time now, and consequently got little time out on patrol with the rest of us, and he hated it. When he shared a meal with me, which wasn't often, he bugged me to death for details of what was going on during our daily patrols. He was afraid he was going to miss all the action.

"You finding any trace of Charlie out there?" he asked.

"About once a week we stumble across some lone sniper. That's it," I answered.

"We came all this way to fight one stinking sniper a week?" he asked, knowing the answer in advance. "I want to get out there myself. The Old Man says I can go to a rifle company in a couple of months."

"You aren't missing anything," I assured him. Max didn't want to come all this way to serve his time taking care of the Mess Hall. Somebody had to do it. The jerk who ran the Battalion picked Max. It was one of his better decisions, even if it broke Max's heart. Max went about his job with his normal high degree of enthusiasm. I occasionally exaggerated the truth about our patrol activities a bit, in hopes he might open his stockpile of beer. No way.

A heavy Charlie rocket attack on the main air base in Da Nang, some 75 miles north of Chu Lai, challenged the existing strategy of static defenses. We had to find something else to do besides being sitting ducks while we protected our land-based air units. The rocket attack killed a handful of Marine and Air Force personnel and destroyed a dozen planes on the ground. It was shocking. It was a surprise. Charlie was out there all right and moving with a great deal of freedom, despite all our patrolling. The attack used rocket launchers located three miles from the airstrip. Charlie had more long-range capability than we had previously thought. Our defenses were too close in to accomplish the mission against these particular weapons.

We had to reach out farther into the countryside and try to occupy and control all the territory in a five-mile radius from the center of the Chu Lai airstrip, which was now in full operation with a small number of jet squadrons and hundreds of helicopters of all sizes and shapes. It was clear we had to get more aggressive. Maybe now we'd start acting like marines and come blowing in from the sea, like some wild hyena, or drop in out of the sky, as we'd been trained. We sensed things were about to change, drastically.

Our new combat mission came just in time for the late-summer monsoons. Rain came from every direction and at every time of the day. It didn't stop. It became impossible to get dry. We patrolled, slept and ate in our rain-drenched clothes and were never without our less-than-comfortable ponchos, which kept some of the water out and were absolutely perfectly designed to keep all of the sweat in. Even with the rain, the days continued to be hot. Summer was not quite over. The heat from the seldom-seen sun turned the rain and the moisture in our clothes to steam. The steam turned life in the field to hell. No square inch of land or human body was dry. Mud dominated everything we touched or walked on. Those of us who were making a living with dirt as our base of operations found ourselves in less and less control of our surroundings. We slipped and slid and dripped with each step or sudden movement.

Our company got new marching orders. We were to move out to a series of hills three miles east of Battalion Headquarters and farther inland. Getting set up in these newly assigned positions became more tedious and difficult with each new storm that rolled in from the South China Sea, now several miles at our back. It took us almost half a day just to walk and crawl to our new home. We couldn't move in the mud. We resorted to the use of our Amtracs, a green turtlelike steel trap that is normally used to move marines from ship to shore, slightly below the water line and less vulnerable to shoreline fire that always threatened amphibious operations. These churning, clumsy, mechanical monsters were also of some use on land. They were of marginal use in the mud. Progress was very slow as we tried to climb the steep vertical incline leading to our new home but it beat trying to make it on hands and knees. Once we did arrive, it took the better part of two days to get our separate platoons into the desired positions, each miles away from the Company CP. The area of responsibility for the company would normally be occupied by a regiment. It took nearly a day of hard climbing to walk from one end of our position to the other.

To give ourselves any chance at all to properly defend the area and the routes which could lead to the airfield we had to place squads of 13 men in clumps of fortified positions nearly a quarter of a mile apart. Nobody was happy with this or believed that we were going to scare away any Charlies that felt like they wanted to disrupt things a little down at the airstrip, now more than five miles away. Regardless of the private feelings any of us had about the mission, we went about doing our jobs as best we could. We continued heavy patrolling during the day. Battalion was on a rampage. Their requirements for daily patrols grew past merely ridiculous levels. Bigger patrols, more patrols, larger patrols. Sleep and rest became a thing of the past. If we weren't on a patrol we were on a high degree of alert around our perimeter defenses. Days melted together, weeks flew by. We started to move like robots, going through the motions but not so sure why or how. We started to lose our edge. We made mistakes.

Battalion couldn't care less. The Old Man didn't want to hear about fatigue or lack of efficiency. He got his eight hours of sleep every night. I resented that. So did the troops. The Marine creed that instructed an officer not to ask his troops to do something you wouldn't do yourself was evidently on hold.

We couldn't cover much ground in one patrol, because of the weather and the mud. The hilltops, on which our platoons were placed, also contained a very thick undergrowth that seriously inhibited foot travel. Some of the grasses were nearly head-high. They grabbed and clawed at you when you attempted to move through. We had to become experts with the machete, carving paths from one position to another. And the rains kept coming. Our Company Command Post was located approximately in the middle of our geographic spread and about one mile to the rear of our most forward position. Battalion Headquarters was three miles further back. During most of the training we'd had in preparation for establishing a tactical defensive position, we could always see and hear and touch most of our company units. We should be able to trot back to Battalion Headquarters. This situation was very strange. We couldn't see anyone in any of our platoons from our Company Command Post. It was not a comfortable feeling. We were too spread out. An army could have marched through our positions, totally undetected. Charlie could launch 5,000 rockets from right in front of our noses.

Maybe our positions looked good on some map at Headquarters but out here on the ground it didn't seem to make any sense at all. Not only didn't it make sense to be so spread out, but worst of all we were totally tied down, big time. No longer could we jump in a chopper and go out deep into the countryside and provide a surprise party for Charlie. We were anchored in place, providing a static defense that was largely imaginary. It made no military sense. Or, at least, it didn't make any Marine sense. Even the Old Man didn't like this mission and openly discussed his concerns with Captain Swenson and me.

"Gentlemen, we've got a job to do and some specific orders on how to get the job done," the Colonel said, in one of his infrequent briefings of the battalion officers. "Don't get too comfortable though. Nobody is happy with this role at Regiment or Division. We need to get more aggressive. Plans are being put in place," he added, as we all listened with intense interest. "We're marines, we need to be moving by sea and by air, bringing fear and chaos into the life of the VC," he added, switching into his John Wayne impersonation, once again. "This just isn't our style. Things will change. Be ready," he warned. We settled into dull routines and concentrated on survival. Some days it was very difficult to remember we were at war. The troops got careless, frequently falling into the habit of taking off their helmets and body armor. Few who get caught making this mistake do it twice. Charlie lobs in a mortar or a few AK-47 rounds two or three nights a week, just to let us know he hasn't forgotten about us. Once in a while he finds a real target.

It was hard to concentrate on making war when most of the day was spent on more survival-oriented things, with no consistent encounters with the enemy. We built up our positions, making them easier to defend as well as more comfortable and more like home. Pictures get hung. Stoves were erected to try to make the C rations, which had by now grown beyond boredom, more palatable. Worrying about creature comforts was another potentially deadly mistake. We add concertina wire, camouflage, trip wires, mines and flares to give us a bit more security.

The troops bitched about everything, which was a very good sign. Troops bitch when things are going well. When things aren't going so well, they get quiet. They listen to their favorite music at each and every opportunity, which drives me crazy. I try to argue that big band music is more enjoyable than what they prefer and lose every argument. This is a black war. The music is mixed Motown and Soul. Somehow the system that supplies these wonderful marines picks a high percentage of blacks. Rich white kids aren't here. They never will be. Tough black kids with all the scars that their world has inflicted on them, along with country bumpkins from the backroads of America, form the heart of our organization. They accept their position, give gloriously to the Corps and revel in a world where one's skin color, accent or previous condition of income doesn't count for much. The color of one's uniform is what counts. They like the color of theirs. They brought their own language and music to the war. The language was crude but creative. "MFWIC" was their invention for "Mother Fucker, What's in Charge," the unofficial title for any high-ranking officer. They walked and crawled and fought to serve the Corps. They gave much more than their rightful share to this war without complaint. We gave up on them later.

I stayed busy by concentrating on making our Company Command Post a little more habitable and safe. With no reserve platoon to provide security, as required by the book, we had to be a little more innovative in the use of wire and trip flares. Friendly people would be coming and going from the CP quite frequently, so we couldn't have too many mines. We didn't want any good guys getting hurt with our own weapons. If the Battalion Operations Officer actually blundered up forward to see our operation and caught a claymore, the Birds and Stars would get some kind of pissed. No matter what I cooked up for our defense, we still remained exposed and vulnerable. We did the best we could, at night, with a guard group made up of clerks, cooks, radio operators and jeep drivers, but it wasn't really enough. We stayed at 50 percent alert every night to prevent any of Charlie's nasty surprises. This left everybody short on sleep but alive to face another day.

The conditions must have had an effect on Charlie too. He didn't often visit us, personally. The hill leading up to our forward positions was steep, sharply angled and covered with a thick grass and large thorn-infested bushes, not to mention our land mines and trip flares. It was not a friendly path. It wasn't clear to me why any self-respecting Charlie would ever want to make the trip.

Captain Swenson spent every other night out with one of the remote platoons, so I was often left with explaining to Battalion Headquarters why we had flares going off or who and what we were exchanging fire with. Do we see any Charlies? How many? Any confirmed kills? Radio traffic was guaranteed for hours, once one of these nuisances occurred. At 0300 hours, it's tough if not impossible to always make some sense of these things. A stray dog who has run into a tripwire isn't going to file the requisite forms on the incident in triplicate.

The platoons involved sent me reports. I passed them on to Battalion. Guesses got multiplied. Like the age-old children's game of passing along messages from one person to another, the end story wasn't what you started with. By the time the reports were written at Battalion, the events of the night probably sounded as if they really made sense. I'm sure they had very little to do with the actual events on the ground. The troops on the spot rarely knew what was really happening. The administrators at Battalion Headquarters thought they did. Most of the time it was not worth worrying about anyway, except that when a whole lot of absolute bullshit got up to the top brass and became absolute, certain truth, with a lot of numbers to prove it, big trouble was cooking. As the computer wizards were beginning to say, GIGO-Garbage In, Garbage Out.

The 7th Marine Regiment was the first stateside-based Marine unit to arrive in Vietnam because we were in the most combat-ready state. Our battalion was particularly ready, since we had returned from a 13-month tour in the Far East just five months earlier. A large number of us in the battalion had been together for well over two years now. We had become family, brought together by the common sweat we had spilled on the hills of Camp Pendleton, the hills and jungles of Okinawa and the jungles of the Philippines. We had pulled liberty together in ports from Yokohama to Hong Kong to San Diego. We had run together, fought together and written letters home together. Everywhere I looked I saw a familiar face and a friend. We protected each other and cared for one another. It provided a sense of security in our combat-oriented life. Get hurt and one of these guys will come to the rescue. You can count on it. Those of us who had been back in the U.S.A. only a few months before returning overseas for this tour had been informally informed we would be going home soon. It was only a matter of getting some replacements into the pipeline and we'd be on our way back to the real world. Every week found new sources of different versions of the same rumor. Several people claimed to have seen the actual orders sending us home during trips up to Regimental Headquarters. Official policy was that nobody had to serve more than one tour overseas without at least three years back in the States. Any day now the orders will be cut.

Tom Draude kept us posted as often as he could although he

had no desire to be anywhere but right here. "It looks like orders are about to come down from Regiment ordering us home," Tom said one night after dinner in the Mess Tent.

"Are you sure?" I asked.

"I talked with a captain at Regiment who swears he has seen them," he responded.

"California, here we come," Max yelled.

"I'm not going," Tom announced. "I'm staying until this is over." It's shooting time and Tom doesn't want to miss a minute. He does his job as Battalion Administrative Officer to perfection, but wants to get his uniform dirty and bloody, if necessary. He wants to be close to the troops. My uniform is muddy but so far I've been able to avoid the bloody part. When we get together, Tom wants to hear every detail about life on the front lines. I want to hear about the rumors. He would be elated if I got to go home. He would stay no matter what the orders said. If he went home and I was told to stay I'd be devastated. Tom's suffering from being stuck at Headquarters. He has always been a walking, talking example of dedication and hard work. That hasn't changed one bit but he is anxious to get away from the bureaucracy and paperwork at Battalion. It takes him three tours in Vietnam to get his fill. I do my job and count the days until I can go home. Tom is fully prepared in case a company commander gets hurt or needs replacing. He knows he will get a chance to command a rifle company. The question is, when? He's ready. I'm hoping no one important, especially me, gets hurt. When I ask Tom what he thinks of our defensive strategy, he spouts the party line but I can tell he doesn't mean it.

"Do you really think we're doing the right thing by sitting here on our asses?" I asked him, during one of his inspection trips to our Company CP.

"We've got a job to do. Let's keep it like that," he answered, dodging the question. "Maybe we could be a bit more aggressive," he adds.

He was not only struggling with his growing distaste for the Battalion Commander's style but also with the Battalion Executive Officer, Major Tom Baylor, who had, in my humble opinion, turned into something of a major-league wimp, and hid behind his paperwork most of the day. Move paper, publish orders, make schedules, just as if we were at Camp Pendleton. I guess he had his job to do too, but it was sure a lot different from ours. He made Tom's life miserable. Don't worry about the war going on around us, just make sure good order and discipline is maintained around camp. Conduct inspections, make sure everyone is wearing clean uniforms and is shaving every day. Police the area, keep the latrines cleaned on a regular basis. Keep the tents aired out. I never met Major Baylor without him calling me in his office to chew my butt out for something or another. His favorite time for butt chewing was when he called in all the company commanders and executive officers and went over violations of radio traffic protocol. All radio traffic was being recorded by some unknown and unidentified Division-level Communications group and inappropriate radio procedures were reported by these organizations. They were eavesdropping on our field radio operations. They don't like the use of profanity and the use of actual names over the tactical networks.

"Why is it necessary to use profanity, gentlemen?" the Major scolded. "Why do we use family names over the radio? Why all the small talk? Continued use of improper procedures or language on the Battalion tactical radio nets will lead to severe disciplinary action. Do I make myself clear, gentlemen?" He droned on, not expecting any sort of brilliant answer. "This is the Marine Corps, gentlemen, not the Boy Scouts." After an enlightening lecture like that, we just couldn't wait to get back to the troops and the bugs. I wondered if the Major ever tried to use a radio, with bullets flying all around, without using profanity. Maybe he'd never been shot at. Perhaps he never used profanity at all. Where did the Corps come up with these three-field-grade types?

I had met a few strange Marine officers with many different personalities and behavioral traits during my few years in the Corps. Tough guys. Wild men. And a few genuine weirdos. Never had I encountered such a collection of officers who were so down and dirty chickenshit to a younger officer. No other word could describe them. A very bizarre trait in any type of Marine officer I had been around. And we had three of them in one small group, the Commanding Officer, his Exec and Operations Officer. I'd always been in awe of my superiors in the Marines. Good, hard-charging, motivated and dedicated professionals. The Corps was filled with them. This battalion had what I thought were three chickenshit little pricks at the top. I wasn't alone in my thinking. I guessed the

Corps had rounded up the three worst officers they could find and tried to hide them all in 3/7. At least to me it looked that way. What did a lousy grunt know anyway?

Of course, as a member of a rifle company, I was really in no position to judge why the senior officers in Vietnam were choosing to fight so stupidly or why they chose to load this particular battalion with a bunch of no-talents to run it. We had a good battalion, in spite of them. We had good people and we did our job. And we bitched, a little.

Eventually sense prevailed and word came down from Division that we were to get more aggressive and go on the offensive. No more sitting around the airport waiting for Charlie to pull something. Let's start pacifying the area.

"Pacification" was the buzzword of the year. As best we could tell, it meant that we were to make the countryside free of Charlie's grasp and make the people living here hungry for democracy, or at least get interested in being on our side more than his. Get Charlie's butt out of the area, so that the farmers can get back to raising rice and kids. Make the entire area safe, so that the elections can be held, schools run and politicians bribed. It meant to be nice to villagers and kids, but kill Cong.

It took a few days for the orders from Division to get transformed into specific squad- and platoon-sized missions. We continued to visit a few of the minor villages to our rear each day, handing out medicine, candy and cigarettes while we waited in the rain and the mud for Battalion to decide how aggressive they really wanted to be.

The constant rain and heat was starting to get boring. It also brought up a few practical problems with the troops. Skin got softened in the humid atmosphere and became susceptible to severe blistering during any kind of heavy walking. Dry socks were impossible to find. Blisters became infected and sore. A marine, who must make his living on his feet, was at risk of being put out of action by the weather. Sick Bay became a busy place. Forced feet inspections became part of the routine. Keeping healthy had become an exercise requiring some vigilance. We'd been shot up with every type of vaccine known to man but bugs still found a way to live in our body. Dysentery devastated every stomach sooner or later, so dehydration in the rain was a constant companion. We were fighting a war and it was very unhealthy.

We also infected the local villagers with American germs, even though there was limited personal contact. Fraternizing was not allowed. There was no place to fraternize. We had no desire to fraternize. Beetlejuice pretty much took care of that. The locals all chewed the local bean, from an early age. It provided a high, not unlike caffeine. It also provided very black teeth. Young, pretty Vietnamese girls were rarely seen. Those that were seen had the black teeth. Even battle-hardened, old, lonely marines were turned off. This was redneck country, Vietnamese-style. One in 10 villages had a country store. Another might have a school. On very rare occasions we found one that had a cafe. Several versions of monkey meat were on every menu. We heard stories about the wild liberty in Saigon, with wild women and cold beer. None of that here. We didn't know it then but we were still eight months away from having a day off or an hour of liberty. Hollywood, and the journalistic fraternity, sent no spies to the war we were fighting. The ARVN, South Vietnam's fictional army, didn't either, though eventually we got a few interpreters who spoke no known language.

One of the really rare villages with some of everything, including a local hospital, was Lan Buc, a sort of county seat, located in the Tran Fo Valley. The valley started just forward of our central company position, on the hill we now called home, and ran north and southeast about three miles in each direction. On the far side of Lan Buc were the foothills and mountains that led to Cambodia, Laos and the vast network that came to be known as the Ho Chi Minh trail.

It was an unimposing valley made up of small hills and dense green outcroppings, interspersed with the never-ending rice paddies and small farming villages. One main trail, serving as a miserable excuse for a road, led into Lan Buc from the south, on our left, as we viewed the scene from our best vantage point, atop Hill 231. On the north side of the village two trails left the city, one northwesterly and one in a direct northward direction. Battalion decided that our first role in getting more aggressive was to get to know Lan Buc a little better.

Our company was to provide a total of six separate and independent eight man observation patrols, for the purpose of gathering road traffic data into and out of Lan Buc, over a period of a week. The general idea was to sneak these observation patrols into positions close to the city but far enough away to avoid detection. Gather data and observe patterns.

We were to find some high ground and make accurate records of foot and motor traffic in and out of the city. At night information-gathering would be accomplished by moving much closer to the road. The mission was to see if we could uncover any unusual goings-on. We would have to remain undetected to do our job. Units from up and down the battalion front would be participating at other villages near Lan Buc. There were going to be a lot of Jarheads snooping and pooping out there for the next seven days. Avoiding detection was going to be difficult and mandatory. It seemed unlikely to me that we could go totally undetected for too long. We'd have to find some local source of water. We'd be using the same source of water as the locals. They were mostly not blind and deaf.

No helicopter resupply on this mission. Radio silence would have to be maintained for seven days unless it was absolutely necessary to save lives. The troops liked this stuff. It broke the monotony. We took two days to get everything exactly right for the patrol. We had to be silent during every phase of the operation. Every piece of equipment was rigged for noiseless running. Dog tags were taped. Canteens were enclosed in dirty black socks. Metal surfaces were covered to make sure they didn't go bang in the night. This was going to be quite a different kind of mission and morale, which had only been a slight problem up to now, soared to lofty levels. Adrenaline was flowing again. This operation was meant for squad sized units, so corporals and a few sergeants took the brunt of the preparation activity and they were assigned as the leaders of all of the patrols. They loved taking charge. The Skipper had been told not to go on the patrols, but the orders were a little vague and easy to misinterpret, and he decided to go anyway. He would accompany the Blue Team into the southwesternmost position. He allowed me to tag along with Corporal Johnson's Red Team, which had as its destination a hill just north of Lan Bac and between the two roads leading northward from the city. One of the platoon commanders also got to go but the other two had to stay behind. We were not specific with Battalion about who belonged to each patrol so we did not jeopardize our chances of tagging along.

Preparations were checked and double-checked. From our 1st Platoon's position, high above Lan Buc, we could pinpoint the exact position we wanted to eventually reach. A piece of cake. I let Cpl. Johnson map out the entire plan for getting Red Team into our final position, some three and a half miles away. I agreed with his assessment that the simplest and best way to get us started was to step over the right side of the 1st Platoon's position and find our way down to a creek no more than a quarter of a mile away, down some rather steep and perhaps treacherous terrain. After reaching the creek we would merely have to make a hard left turn and head for Lan Buc. The creek led directly into the city. Before we actually reached the outskirts, we'd need to circle around to our right about a half mile until we reached one of our landmarks, the road north. Across the road would be a slight rise in the ground, covered with tall, thinly trunked trees, which would hide us during the day and give us the view we wanted for the next week.

It looked very easy from this vantage point. We should be able to make the three-plus miles in less than two hours, but planned for a maximum of five hours in case we bumped into something unexpected. The troops were excited by this simple mission, and the conversations during the last hot meal we expected to have for a while were upbeat and confident.

"Ain't nobody going to see me," one of our squad leaders said, in one of our preliminary briefings on the patrol mission.

"They'll know you're in the area by your body odor," answered another NCO.

"If they smell me, they'll barf when they smell you," the first squad leader came back. Precombat wit is a sign of good morale, and no one cares if it isn't funny.

Could we really go undetected for a week? It was a little like hide and seek, a kids' game with very serious penalties for getting caught. We watched a beautiful sunset and tried to relax before beginning our short trip. The eight groups would leave the area in 15-minute intervals starting at 2000 hours. Our Red Team would be the third to go. Sunset was at 1930 hours and darkness would be complete by the time we left our position. The patrol leaders made last minute checks of equipment. Even though we were not expecting to have any fighting, we were prepared for anything. We would be carrying big loads of ammo and lots of equipment. The troops applied camouflage paint to each other's faces and other exposed skin areas, to give us the maximum chance to fold into the background. Everyone was getting into the spirit.

"If you weren't so ugly, you wouldn't need that paint."

"Call me ugly one more time and I'll put my M-79 up your ass," came the response.

This was a rather strange application for this weapon that looked like a single-shot, sawed-off shotgun, but could launch a rocket grenade several hundred yards, supplying roughly the same damage as a hand grenade but at a greater distance. The remark required a very direct and well-articulated response.

"Your mother."

As the time for our departure gets closer pulse rates climb, and the humor gets more black and tempers shorten. The troops continue to tease each other. Patrol leaders break up the shoving matches, but tempers continue to flare every few minutes. The troops are getting themselves ready, getting themselves sharp. We'll need to be alert and sharp to pull this off. It will feel good to actually get going.

At 1800 hours, as day was turning to evening, a strong wind began to blow from the west and clouds which had been seaward during most of the pleasant, warm summer day came sliding overhead, spilling their watery contents on our helmets, first in refreshing drips, relief from the day's heat, shortly thereafter, an uncomfortable, ugly and very much unwanted and raging downpour. By the time the first patrol left our position, the rain was being driven by winds that approached 50 miles per hour. The temperature dropped 20 degrees in 50 minutes, and the rain kept coming. Combined with the now heavy darkness, it would certainly complicate the mission. More of a chance for mistakes and miscalculations. The night was moonless and the heavy cloud cover combined to make absolutely zero visibility.

Patrols were formed and moved out on their missions with great difficulty. A few minutes earlier, during the late-evening light, you could clearly see everyone on the patrol. Now it was necessary to yell and shout over the wind and rain to maintain contact with the group. You had to touch each other to gain positive identification, even though we were only inches apart. Once we left our departure point, silence would be mandatory. We were going to have to use the Braille method. We were going to have to move through the countryside and the night holding on to one another or we'd never make it to the final destination. If you got two feet away from the person next to you, you'd stand a good chance of never finding him again and consequently getting lost. We considered tying ourselves to each other but rejected the idea for fear somebody might fall down and drag everyone else with him. Of course a visit from Charlie when we were nicely roped together would quickly end the patrol.

Cpl. Johnson asked me to bring up the rear, a slight change in the plan, brought on as a special consideration of the weather conditions and the new problems we would be facing. He thought it would decrease our risk of losing someone on the way. I wasn't so sure. I'd rather have been in the middle of the patrol. It might feel a tad more comfortable and safe but I was supposed to be just an observer on this mission, so I kept my mouth shut and let Johnson run the show. He had done very well up to then. The Captain wished me luck as we passed his position. His group would be the last one to leave. Each patrol would head in a slightly different direction and would eventually be spaced a least a mile apart when we reached our final objectives.

Ten minutes after departure, I knew we were in trouble. The rain had made every inch of the terrain treacherous to move on. Once we started down the hill we found out it was impossible to stand up. Trying to hold on to the person in front of you couldn't always be done. I was flat on the ground much of the time. Both hands were needed to get up and once up, the next fall could be only seconds away. Unseen bushes and tree limbs brought unexpected sharp and painful slaps to the face and eyes. Each fall resulted in more pain. Things were going bump in the night. People crashed into one another and knocked one another down and came crashing on top of them. It is not easy to use a weapon when you are falling on your face or your ass. The Marine Band in full parade wouldn't have made more noise. I soon grew tired of trying to get the patrol to quiet down and passed the word forward to Cpl. Johnson to not worry about the noise or the fumbling around until we got down off this hill and reached the creek, a few hundred yards in front of us. A few minutes later he held up the column so that we could talk.

"This is the shits, Lieutenant," he said to me. "What do you think?"

"I think I'd like to start over, without the rain and the wind," I answered. "How about you?"

"We're behind schedule, aren't we?" he asked.

"Yeah, but we've got time," I answered.

We decided to slow the pace to a crawl, in an attempt to prevent the falls and to keep everyone together. It was hard to estimate how much progress we'd made. We had absolutely no landmark to guide on. Until we reached the creek we would be flying blind. Maybe we'd been through the worst. I was wet and cold and could have used a cup of coffee. This hadn't been a very smooth start to the week. It got worse. The rain refused to let up. The darkness got more intense. I was totally blind, but we stumbled forward, hoping to get a break. Then we got one. A bad one.

Cpl. Johnson fell off a 10-foot ledge and was seriously hurt. He may have broken his leg. We couldn't reach him right away, but we could hear his moaning. We finally discovered a path that wasn't too hard to traverse and soon the whole patrol was gathered in the darkness around Cpl. Johnson, who was in great pain, lying on the ground and unable to stand.

Any semblance of patrol discipline had evaporated. We lit cigarettes and took a good long break. I was tired and beat-up. So was the entire patrol. Cpl. Johnson was a horse with a broken leg. What the hell do we do? Shoot him?

I checked out the time on my watch, underneath my poncho, turned on a flashlight very carefully to avoid letting out any stray light into the unfriendly night, and made out that it was nearly 2200 hours. We should have been at least halfway to our target area. We probably hadn't covered 10 percent of the distance. I also noticed that in one of my many falls I'd lost my compass and one of my two canteens. No problem. I shouldn't need them anyway. I made the decision to leave Cpl. Johnson behind. He was hurt too bad to continue. We hadn't gone very far, so it would be pretty easy for him to straggle back to our initial position. I chose another marine from the patrol to stay behind with him, so he got back with minimum damage to the leg. I could have aborted the entire patrol, which was part of several possible emergency scenarios discussed in our preparation meetings, but that didn't seem necessary. I was beat to hell and my judgment probably wasn't too sharp, anyway. I took charge of the five-man patrol and continued to the bottom of the hill and the creek, the only landmark we can count on. The creek had to be there eventually. A no-brainer.

It was a little easier with only five people, but we were still making an incredible amount of noise. Every bush seemed to have finger-sized thorns which tore into flesh with each step. I couldn't see the blood, but I knew it was there.

When we reached the creek, I called a break and tried to regroup. The patrol was in some disarray. We had barely started our mission and it was already midnight. Four hours to traverse the first mile. Downhill. The rain continued to pour down on us and the wind howled. I had to shout to be heard above the sound of the rain beating on our helmets, for those of us who still had helmets. Two of the marines had lost theirs, in spills on the hill. No time to go back and look for them now. Just keep moving. In four more hours, the sun would begin its daily appearance over the ocean to the east. Time to get on our horse. We were hours behind schedule. We had better catch up. At least now we had the creek to guide us. Everyone seemed to be ready to continue. We'd just been through four hours of hell and were in one of God's great wind and rain storms. There were five marines, whom I couldn't see and didn't know by name, who were ready to get with the program. It was a bizarre scene. We moved on.

I was filled with a renewed sense of confidence thanks to the enthusiasm I felt coming from the characters standing next to me in the blinding darkness. The five green clad marines behind me gave me a strange sense of well-being. I felt in control and ready for whatever was ahead of us. I tried to pick up the pace a little now that we were off the hill and had the creek to guide us. It should be pretty straightforward from here to Lan Buc. We found a trail near the edge of the creek and moved out at full stride, without the fear of falling down. Smoother, more level footing. The rain continued to come down very hard. It was impossible to know exactly where we were. I had to hold up the column, from time to time, to count heads. We got increasingly more conscious of our noise as we neared our objective and reverted to better patrol discipline. We were getting close to Charlie country.

At 0100 hours, I started to get worried about not having reached Lan Buc. By 0200 I was starting to panic. We should have been there by now. Maybe all the stops we made were slowing our progress more than I had calculated. We continued forward hour after hour, step after step. The trail widened, as did the creek, which was now more of a stream, swollen with the newly fallen rain. It had its own distinctive roar that could be heard above the sound of the wind. On one of the rest breaks, two of the marines asked in hushed voices if we were lost. "Of course not," I responded, somehow sounding much more confident than I really was. By 0300 hours, my panic worsened. It would be light in a little more than two hours. If we hadn't reached our objective by first light, we might be caught in the open and compromise the patrol and maybe even the entire battalion mission. What the hell had gone wrong? Where the hell was Lan Buc? Why wouldn't it stop raining? What the hell should I do? At 0400, we were still on the trail, still short of Lan Buc. I couldn't take any further risks. I had to get us into a hiding place before the sun came up and caught us in the open. I passed the word to the patrol.

"We're stopping here until I can see where we are," I told them. "Get off the trail and find some concealment." We moved off the trail and found some cover among the heavy bushes which lined both sides of the entire trail. I sat down in the water and the mud, pulled my poncho over my head, and tried to get comfortable. It was not easy. But it felt so good to sit down. We'd been under way seven hours. I was soaked with sweat and my teeth were chattering from the predawn cold. I didn't feel much like a big tough marine at that moment. I was tired, wet, cold and miserable. Every bone and muscle ached. I needed some sleep and a chance to clear my head. I couldn't let these guys down. We had struggled forward despite the injuries, lost direction and unbelievable weather conditions. If I told them right now to saddle up and move out they'd be ready before I was.

Despite the possible danger and misery, I could hear a slight snore coming from beneath one of the nearby ponchos. These guys didn't get too excited about anything. It was now time to start earning my lieutenant's pay and act like I knew what the silver bars

on my collar were for. I had to dig deep into some silent reserve to
search through the last three years of training, to find something
that would prepare me for what to do next. I knew I had to stay in
control. Evaluate and react. I tried to formulate a plan to get out of
this mess. I'd have to wait until I could see something. We'd have
to be prepared for anything. It was not Sunday but I said my
prayers, anyway. I was going to need any help I could get. The
Chaplain said God was open for business at all hours of the day or
night. This ought to be a good test of his theory.

As dawn broke and the rain finally faded into a thin mist, we all
began to be able to make out some of the details of our immediate
surroundings. We were very near housing structures and civilization
of some kind. Bodies moved in and out of the mist. We had to be
prepared to fight our way out of here. People were all around us.
That was the bad news. The good news became apparent to me as
soon as I heard the first words of English being spoken by one of
the passing bodies. All of the people walking around us were
wearing green, not black. Where the hell was I? And what were all
these marines doing here?

Feeling very stupid and confused but convinced I couldn't sit
here in the bushes much longer, I stood up and moved out of my
hiding place. So did the rest of the patrol. They all looked at me,
begging for but afraid to ask for an explanation, which I was not
about to provide.

Once I was out of the bushes, I got a better look at the
surroundings. There on my left, not more than 75 yards away, was
our Battalion Headquarters. I was three miles east of the kick off
point. I was supposed to be three miles west. I was more than six
miles from our final target.

I was a dead man. There was no way to explain this. How
embarrassing, not to mention dangerous. Our patrol must have
passed through our own lines and must have walked within yards
of many other marine positions. We were lucky we didn't get our
heads blown off.

I figured I'd better take my medicine and directed the five
members of the patrol to follow me to the Operations Tent, where
there was certain to be activity and maybe a friendly face. The other
patrol members waited outside the tent, while I went inside to find
someone to report to. A friendly face was indeed there to greet me.

Tom Draude was on duty inside and approached me quickly as I entered.

"Where have you been?" he asked. "The Colonel has been looking everywhere for you."

"I've been on patrol all night. Why is he looking for me?" I asked, hoping we could avoid the subject of the lost patrol.

"Haven't you heard?" Tom said, sounding surprised. "Captain Swenson and his patrol ran into a minefield. He and four others are very badly hurt and had to be med-evaced last night. In all that rain, it was hard to get a chopper there. It took most of the night. Want some coffee?" he offered.

"Please," I replied, wondering when I was going to get an earful from the Old Man.

The Captain and four other India Company marines had evidently seen the last of this war. Tom went over the details with me. Captain Swenson's patrol was the last to leave our position, with a mission to set up a listening post just a few meters south of Lan Buc's outskirts. Properly positioned, they would be looking directly into the town center from a small patch of trees, along the creek that ran through the center of the town. They didn't get there. After jumping off of our company position, they ran into the same sort of problems my patrol had, getting further and further behind schedule as they cut and dragged their way through the impossible growth that lay between our lines and Lan Buc. About halfway to their target, they decided to move along a main trail that led from a small farming cluster, one mile east of their target, directly into Lan Buc. We had not seen this trail on the map. Walking out in the open like that wasn't a real good idea, even at night, especially at night. They wanted to make up some of the lost time. Bad decision. This was Charlie's territory.

The point man found the first mine and it separated him from his left leg. Two other marines were less seriously wounded from the same explosion. In an attempt to get to his wounded troops, Captain Swenson hit another trip mine that opened up his lower torso and sent shrapnel into the rest of the column. It took a couple of hours to get a helicopter in there and it was a miracle that nobody died from the large loss of blood that went with that type of wound. The end of the exercise had been a real nightmare for those marines.

All the other patrols had been contacted and had aborted their missions without further incident. Attempts to reach my patrol by radio didn't work because we were in the wrong place. I knew that. Did the Colonel? Anyway, the coffee tasted like heaven and it was warm and dry in the Operations Tent. And the best part was that up to now, no one had asked about the lost patrol. A half hour went by without much of anything for me to do but mull over my private thoughts about the events of the previous night. Not much fun, but on the other hand I hadn't run into a minefield either.

At precisely 0700, the Old Man and the Operations Officer, Major Bob Austin, arrived in the operations tent fresh from the Mess Tent and a nice hot breakfast, which I could smell coming from off in the distance. I was hungry but decided to stay and discover how much trouble I was in with the Old Man. After he got done taking me apart, maybe I'd still be able to enjoy some hot chow.

"Lieutenant, where in the hell have you been all night?" he asks, not really waiting for an answer. "I've been trying to get hold of you on the radio since midnight," he yells, at the top of his voice.

"On patrol, Sir," I reply, hoping not to have this conversation go too much further.

"What the hell were you two cowboys doing up there?" he blurts out, starting to really get warmed up now. "Nobody gave you the permission to go on these patrols. What the hell is going on? Are you guys playing games or is this still the Marines?"

I knew better than to answer that one and for once in my life kept my big mouth shut.

"I don't want any heroes out there, Lieutenant, I want commanders. Do I make myself perfectly clear, Mister?" he asks, in a way that suggests only one answer will satisfy him.

"Yes, Sir," I reply, taking a wild guess at the answer he was looking for.

I was now starting to get this wonderfully strange feeling that this guy didn't have a clue I'd been lost all night. Not only that but between the lines I sensed that somehow I'd won a few brownie points with him for having gone out with the patrol.

The marine facing me from across the table was a dour, strict, unpleasant man, who lacked even a trace of humor. He also had a mean streak, which he seemed to save for some of his best people. It was clear that his method for motivating people was to scream, yell and demean, in public. A pat on the back was not in his repertoire. He was a lonely man and very private. A mystery man. He shared none of his private life. He was close to no one. When his boss, Col. Henning, the Regimental Commander, was in the area, the guy turned to putty. Insecurity and fear seemed to grip his personality. On this day and under the bizarre events of last night, he seemed less frantic than I would have suspected. He'd given me more shit than this for laughing too much in the Chow Hall. He was almost under control and in a reasonable mood. For him. Could it really be going so well? Could I get out of this thing with only a mild ass-chewing and some hard-to-get credits on my side of the ledger?

Having vented his slightly faked rage over not being able to find me the minute he wanted to, he got down to new business.

"Lieutenant, you're now my India Company Commander. Think you can handle it?" he asked, looking again for that one correct answer.

"Yes, Sir," I replied, with as much genuine enthusiasm as I could muster.

"Then get your ass up to your company position and start taking care of business. And no more of this cowboy stuff," he advised.

I didn't bother to reply. I didn't know how to reply. I put on one of my best about-faces and departed the scene in a very militaristically precise fashion. I was having trouble comprehending this whole scene. My boss had just gotten his butt blown off. I'd been totally lost on a dangerous patrol and now I'd been rewarded with a promotion. I was now a company commander. The best job the Marines had to offer. It didn't get better than this for a Jarhead. I was supposed to have five more years of experience and training to qualify for the job. There were several other officers around the Battalion who were more senior and experienced. Why me?

One look at Tom and I had the answer. He had convinced the Old Man to let me have a try. I was sure of it. Tom and I caught a little breakfast before I started on my new assignment.

"How does it feel, Marine?" Tom asked, knowing in advance the answer.

"Tom, I think I can handle it but I don't understand why the Old Man picked me. He has never liked me. Did you have something to do with it?" I asked, knowing the answer.

"He asked me what I thought and I told him you were the best guy for the job," Tom said, with the help of a small smirk. "Just doing my job, Marine."

"Sure. Thanks pal," I offered, starting to sense how far he had gone for me.

I knew that Tom wanted the job himself. Probably wanted it more than anyone could imagine. He was better prepared and senior to me by a few months. He certainly could have asked for and gotten the job but he was too special for that. He went out on a limb for me. He sacrificed his own strong and well-deserved ambitions for me.

To Tom, being a Marine officer was a never-ending quest for perfection. He had such a positive attitude and sense of purpose that it set him clearly apart from the rest of us, who also worked hard, did our job and gave it our all for Country and Corps. We knew how to do our jobs and were very good at it. Tom was always prepared to do any job including those requiring more rank, more experience or more training. His inner light was shining bright and very intensely. It gave him the strength to do his assignment, enough of a challenge for even the most motivated of us, and then find the time and energy to read, study and practice the skills necessary to accelerate his preparation for a bigger task. The extra work load never diminished his taste for life. Months in the field, immersed in the battalion business and constantly surrounded by our disappointing battalion senior officers, couldn't dent his enthusiasm and love for the Corps. The smile was always there. The urge to take this first open company commander's job must have been enormous.

I didn't deserve all this, especially after last night, now a fading memory for the six of us on the patrol and a nonevent for the rest of the world. The three-mile jeep ride back to India Company Headquarters gave me more time to reflect on what had just transpired, my incredible luck and to start worrying about what might lie ahead.

Command felt comfortable. I inherited two excellent platoon commanders and an all-time gunny. We were short a couple of officers and NCOs, but true to best Marine tradition, the next senior person took over every open billet and went about getting the job done. We had plenty of horsepower and I was very glad of it. And I was absolutely in love with being a company commander.

We returned to running night patrols, fortifying our positions and looking for Charlie whenever we had a chance. The Old Man confined his visits to my area to a weekly tour of the line platoons, an event I didn't look forward to with much pleasure. Except on occasional trips to Battalion Headquarters, I never saw the Executive Officer or the Operations Officer. They didn't seem to like it much out there with the mud and the bugs and the grunts. Those three didn't provide me with much leadership, or help me much. The three of them seemed, to this lieutenant, to be more interested in paperwork than in seeing firsthand how the war was being fought. They spent their days making sure everything looked good to Regimental Headquarters. This may be good for careers, but it doesn't win firefights. And, as it turned out, this type of attitude probably helped us lose the war by stroking high-level fantasies. This war was being fought by the smaller combat units and sometimes the powers that be weren't much help to me.

I saw the Regimental Chaplain more often. He managed to find one or more of my units each week, like clockwork. He'd usually arrive by helicopter, uniform rumpled and unkempt, helmet slightly askew, looking not unlike the warriors around him. He passed out Bibles, songbooks, and built an altar with whatever resources he could find. I learned that it was not a cliché to say that there are no atheists in a foxhole, or in slit trenches, which is what we dug and lived in. There weren't, and the Padre's services were always well attended. Many were conducted while an air strike or artillery duel was taking place nearby. He never paused or let on that he was concerned for his safety. I wonder what Charlie thought as he heard "Amazing Grace" come floating off the hill we called home.

The Padre would share a postservice meal out of cans with anyone who cared to join in, and chatted privately with a few individuals before his helicopter service arrived to take him to his next stop. A smile and hearty wave and off he would go. I'm sure his big boss enjoyed the effort. We did.

7

Proud to Claim
the Title

Vietnam was still a small-unit war. Battalion, Regiment, Division, Corps, MACV, and so on up to the Joint Chiefs, SecDef and C-in-C, no doubt lots of people looked at maps, read reports, conceived strategy, issued orders and created scenarios. To men in the field, this did not count for much. A company is the largest unit that can be personally controlled by one officer. He knows his platoon leaders, is aware of quirks which range from bizarre, personal superstitions to extraordinary individual courage, and shares water, food, the constant presence of death and the exhilaration of great achievement with his men. He provides leadership, and is expected to lead. It's the best job in the world, coveted by every young marine officer.

I lost mine quite unexpectedly to an ovarian cyst. My wife underwent a sudden operation, and I was ordered home on compassionate leave. Naturally, someone else took my job. The Marines had now firmly established that Vietnam tours would last 13 months. No more rumors about going home soon. They rotated units around, so that at the end of 13 months, entire units didn't go home all at one time. It was a version of musical chairs, Marine-style. Each battalion lost a couple of companies and gained a couple from one of the other battalions. When I returned from compassionate leave I learned that I had been transferred from 3/7 to 2/4. It was a long jeep ride to find my new home. The driver was evidently quite familiar with the roads and villages and Marine units which we passed. He clicked off the names and unit designations without me asking, as if we were on some sort of guided tour.

We didn't talk much, although he did want to know what was going on in the States and how serious was this antiwar stuff? During my trip to the U.S.A., I really hadn't seen evidence of any, except on TV, so I reassured him it was a small, isolated group of idiots, being exploited by the press. I was sure it was. He wasn't.

We pulled into an area near the beach, behind some sand dunes, which contained a few large command tents and an assortment of military vehicles. It all looked dirty and unorganized. Near the entrance to the area was a handmade sign stuck casually in the ground that proclaimed we had just entered the HOME OF THE 2ND BATTALION, 4TH MARINE REGIMENT and underneath in large black letters the words THE MAGNIFICENT BAS-TARDS, a nickname the battalion had picked up several wars ago. Might be a good omen. The jeep driver helped me unload my few belongings on the sand near the Battalion Command Post and sped away, leaving me standing alone and not at all comfortable with the world. People were moving from tent to tent, vehicles came and went and life in this place looked familiar, except that I didn't know anyone. The uniforms and the weapons were identical to what I had just left, yet it was somehow very different. I gathered up my courage, walked to the door of the tent identified as the home of the Battalion Executive Officer, and knocked.

"Enter," came a friendly-sounding voice from behind the screen door that covered the entrance to the tent.

"Sir, I'm First Lieutenant Van Zanten, reporting for duty."

"Have a seat, Lieutenant. We've been expecting you." The person on the far side of the desk hadn't moved or lifted his head from the work in front of him. He didn't seem to be expecting me too much. The silence of the room continued as the unidentified body across the desk grunted and groaned over some multipart form that evidently contained an arithmetic problem or two. He erased a few parts, entered new figures and looked again. I'd rather do almost anything than watch someone else struggle with trying to add and subtract.

"This paperwork shit bugs the hell out of me. How about you, Lieutenant?" the voice behind the desk asked, without facing me directly.

"Yes, Sir."

He finally turned toward me and I was now able to match up

the voice with a real face. And what a face it was. A grizzled, heavily lined face. An old face. Much older than I'd expected.

"What the hell took you so long to get here?" he challenged rather abruptly, catching me slightly off guard.

"Just arrived from stateside late yesterday afternoon, Sir," I apologized, sounding hurt. "Got here as soon as I could."

"Don't bullshit me, Lieutenant, you been screwing off for the past 10 days and you think I ain't ever going to find out," he spit out, measuring me all the while, with two very cold eyes that were well set back in his head. "I heard you were back in the States screwing off with civilians. By the way, I'm Major Ernie Defazio," he said, offering his large, thick, right hand. "I've been around this man's Marine Corps so long I forget what civilians look like. Don't need to know either, just need to get this paperwork done so I can get this battalion off its ass and back in the war," he said mostly addressing himself. "Welcome, anyway, this here's the 2nd Battalion, 4th Marines, and I'm the XO. We're supposed to get a new CO next week but for the moment, I'm it. We need an Executive Officer for Echo Company. You're it," he announced. I was sure there wasn't going to be any discussion about it. "Captain Jerry Ledin is the CO, you can find them over behind the water buffalo, there," he said, pointing to a spot about 20 yards down the beach and a little closer to the sand. "Welcome aboard, Lieutenant, and now get the hell out of here and let me get these reports done."

I exited quickly after a sharp "Aye, aye, Sir," not particularly anxious to continue the one-way conversation.

I wondered to myself about what I had gotten into. He was grouchy but seemed like the kind of guy that was going to be out in the field with the troops, not hiding behind some desk. Maybe this would work out OK after all. Months later I would find out just how crusty the Major was and how much he deserved to be crusty and grouchy. He had first spilled his own blood for the Corps on Guadalcanal, a long and distinguished career ago. He had a chestful of medals from WWII, another chestful from Korea and he was still at it. The Marine generals who came visiting from time to time called him Ernie. He sometimes called them by their first names. To me he was always "Major Defazio" or simply "Sir."

I spotted the landmark the Major had given me, headed off toward the large green water tank we called a buffalo and walked quickly in that direction, hoping to find Captain Ledin and the rest of the company before it turned dark. Captain Ledin was catching a small nap in his tent as I arrived in the company area. He wasn't particularly happy to be awakened, or to have a new addition to his staff, and nearly took my hand off on our first handshake even though he was still about half asleep. He talked with a slight southern drawl and with a sense of confidence brought about by eight or nine years of training for this particular job. He also had the obvious confidence of those around him. When he gave orders, they were immediately carried out with no fuss or delay. His voice never had to be raised to get attention, he didn't give much time to small talk or kidding around, he was all business.

The company had just returned from six days of patrolling in an area south of the airstrip and they were catching some rest. They had operated without an executive officer for a couple of months and no one seemed to be particularly relieved to have one again. It was freezing outside and everybody was wrapped in lined field jackets and gloves. The wind from the ocean further cooled the evening air. The uniforms and the language were all the same, but there was little other familiarity. The faces were all new. Nobody seemed to care if I was here or not. Extra baggage. I would obviously have to work my way onto this team. The company had been together since the battalion had landed in Vietnam direct from its peacetime home in Hawaii. They had taken a number of casualties through the months. Most of the company leadership was still in place and they were very confident-sounding veterans. I was the only unknown.

The company officers and staff NCOs enjoyed a C ration dinner by candlelight my first night with the Magnificent Bastards. They grumbled about the awful taste of the rations, just like the marines back in 3/7. Captain Ledin broke up the bitch session by spreading out a map on a makeshift desk. Seven of us gathered around it.

"Tomorrow we move out to hill 69," he started, placing a short thick finger on a point on the map that represented a location several miles north and east of the main airstrip. "I don't know how long we'll be there but it may be awhile," he added. "Division wants this area kept clear of any possibility of mortar attack."

"Any reports of recent VC activity?" asked Second Lieutenant

Gary Brown, our 1st Platoon Leader, a wiry, mature-looking, recent graduate of Georgia Tech.

"Nothing."

"Any other units in the area?" questioned Second Lieutenant Fred Williamson, our 2nd Platoon Commander, a taller, stocky, more baby-faced type, who two years ago played his last game of football for Wagner College in New York City.

"None. We'll be alone out there for the time being. We'll be about five miles from the nearest unit, here at the Phu Ma bridge," he said, gesturing to another spot on the map in front of us. "Anything between Hill 69 and the bridge is considered Indian country. We'll take some mortars with us and we'll have Lt. Henry for artillery support. I want us to get set up fast once we get there. Dig in and dig in fast. Get wire up quick. I want to be ready for anything by tomorrow night. Helicopters will pick us up at 0700 tomorrow morning. First Platoon will go in first with me, then 2nd Platoon and the rest. Any questions?"

None were asked. There were hundreds of other details to work out by 0700 but these guys seemed to be operating by ESP. Everybody knew the routine. I waited for Captain Ledin to say something to me about what he wanted me to do. Nothing was offered. He assumed I knew what to do. I did. It wasn't much. As Executive Officer, I had learned that the best thing to do was to stay out of the way, keep the clerks out of the way, and wait for someone to get hurt. I was back in the war.

Hill 69 was a hill in name only, a pimple on the landscape that barely rose above the surrounding flat terrain, a small village nestled comfortably in a tree line 500 yards to the west of our position along Highway One. Hill 69 seemed to be the only place within a mile in any direction that wasn't planted in rice. Not one tree. A barren five-acre plot with no amenities of home, but with plenty of views that would make it easy to defend. Recent rains had turned the thick, dark brown dirt into a very unfriendly, slippery mud that made each step treacherous. I was on my butt twice on the short trip from where the helicopters set us down to the location on the top of the knoll that Captain Ledin designated as the Company Command Post. Activity was well under way in every direction. Entrenching tools dug into hard-packed earth immediately below the few inches of mud that coated the top of the earth. Foxholes and trenches and firing positions for the machine guns and mortars were starting to take form. Concertina wire was being strung in seemingly odd patterns, intended to discourage intruders and to lead them into streams of 7.62mm rounds from machine-gun emplacements with interlocking fields of fire. The mortar crews were having trouble finding flat enough places for the large base plates that were necessary to deliver an accurate fire, so they dug them. The Gunny and I concentrated on getting our supplies and ammunition below ground and protected from possible incoming rounds. It felt good to be back at work and I could now call a few of the 200 marines by name.

By dark, our defensive positions were about as good as they were going to get. Creature comforts would have to wait. For now safety had a far higher priority than comfort. Captain Ledin inspected every position just as the sun was moving behind the hills far to the west of us, liking what he saw and only occasionally making small adjustments in people or machinery. He tried to make sure that everyone was ready for any eventuality and talked in a hushed, confident voice to each of the troops as he moved through their area. "If they're going to hit us, it'll be tonight," he told one of the squad leaders, in the 2nd Platoon. "They'll figure we haven't got set up yet. Stay alert."

"Right, Sir," came the confident answer. I tagged along, not offering much help. He didn't need much. This guy knew what he was doing and exactly what he wanted. Our only major concern was the younger local population.

"Gunny, get those damn kids out of here," the Captain yelled, pointing to a group of seven or eight near the ammo dump.

"I'm trying, Sir," the Gunny answered. "Every time I move five of em, seven more show up." No matter how much we threatened or screamed we were overrun with kids begging for food and cigarettes. They were irresistible but this was becoming a very unsafe place for them. Like a green Pied Piper, the Gunny took a couple cases of C's to a position well outside the wired perimeter. The little rats followed quickly, when they figured out that free food was available from the Gunny.

From that day forward the Gunny was in control and so were the kids. They weren't allowed in or near the wire. It cost him a couple of cases a day to keep the peace. He also had to agree to let them scavenge through our garbage. Two hundred marines generate a lot of garbage every day. The kids utilized every scrap and pestered us to death for more. Their parents were seldom visible, except when one of the kids found something useful in our garbage pit. As usual, the marines and the kids became close friends quickly. Even the gruff old Gunny had his favorite urchins, and always made sure they got their share.

Something important was going on in the area. All we knew was that we were kept busy. Daylight patrols of platoon size, every day. We were going out in force, aggressively pursuing something. We weren't sure exactly what. At night we were kept in a high state of readiness although it was seldom necessary. Every four or five days a lone rifleman would approach the wire, pull off five or six rounds, and be gone before we could respond. Each night we put a squad or more near the village to check on nighttime VC activity. There wasn't any. We knew Charlie was somewhere close as our daylight patrols found more and more booby traps when our patrolling increased through the area. Sometimes we located booby traps the hard way.

Charlie was an expert with booby traps. Trip wires that tossed a Bouncing Betty a few feet in the air before exploding violently at gonad or chest level were one of his favorites. Buried Punji Stakes, poisonous, sharpened wooden stakes hidden a foot or so beneath the ground, another. One killed, the other crippled. We could fight a war of attrition or keep well out of areas where he didn't want us moving. Or we could go find Charlie first. We either learned to spot booby traps or took unacceptable casualties. We tried to be careful. We didn't always succeed. The locals took casualties from the same devices. Highway One was only a few hundred yards away and it was a constant source of problems with Charlie. He kept it mined and no amount of mine sweeping activity seemed to keep it clear. The buses, bicycles and handcarts the local population used to travel this main country transportation artery were a frequently found target. Human carcasses and burnt-out buses lined the side of the road, a grim reminder of Charlie's presence.

Marines tried to avoid the main road. There weren't that many choices if you had to get somewhere fast. We often paid the price for having to move from one area to another by vehicle. Charlie wanted to paralyze movement and thus gain control of the population and of the area. It worked pretty effectively. Only those who had no other choice would use the road. But there were enough of those. Very few days went by without us seeing evidence of a busload of civilians having been blown to the sky with one or another of Charlie's special weapons. The civilians considered running through the mine-filled road as part of their lives. We treated the presence of the mines as the threat to our lives they really were. Charlie killed and maimed too many marines with these things, but it was nothing compared to what he did to his own countrymen.

We became immune to the constant fear of death and accepted our position of kill or be killed. Very few days went by without casualties of some sort. Those of us who weren't casualties sometimes found ourselves envious of those who sustained some minor wound that would get them back to the world. We never doubted our own ability to kill, if put in that position. It became automatic. Too much so. When given the chance, we'd pour it on, justified as getting even for some buddy that got it last week. We measured things more carefully now, taking few unnecessary risks, yet willing to risk everything at the right time. We had become complete professionals. When we saddled up and moved out into Indian country, somebody had better be damn careful about taking us on. Weapons were kept in perfect working order. No marine would leave the area without being totally loaded down with every conceivable type of ammunition, for his weapon and for other weapons in the company. Captain Ledin was extremely well schooled in the application and use of supporting weapons and wasn't afraid to use them, as often as necessary. We went by the book. No wasted time or energy. Everyone in his place. Everyone aware of his part in the drama and to the others around him, protecting, covering, working together. Teamwork. The large investment the Corps had put forth in training each of us was paying dividends and Captain Ledin was the banker making sure the dividends kept getting paid.

Not yet completely a part of the family, I watched with some envy as the entire company functioned and prepared and executed their assigned tasks as if they had been doing it all their life. My old battalion, with the exception of the three senior officers, had been good too, but not like this. I wanted to be a part of it, no matter the miserable conditions under which we lived. This was the real thing. This was what Leon Uris had talked about, what I had trained for. I had to find a way to become part of the team quickly.

I found a way to be absolutely indispensable. Captain Ledin loved beer. He could live with C rations 21 meals a week. He could live without hot showers for weeks at a time. He could live without mail, but he was worthless without a cold beer once in a while. He had the need. We all did. I had to find the supply.

Every few days or weeks, at the end of any exercise away from Hill 69, I was given a jeep, a driver, a machine-gun crew, lots of money, a map and told to go find some cold beer for the Skipper and the troops. We had to drive along Highway One to get near to something resembling civilization. Most of the 10 to 12 miles we had to traverse was territory to which Charlie held the deed, particularly at night.

Max Sanders helped make me a hero in the eyes of the Echo Company marines of 2/4. He couldn't resist my tale of woe. By now he had amassed such a cache of beer it required a full-time guard detail. Our battalion had no beer. His was drowning in it. My only real problem in settling this inequity was getting the beer I wanted to buy past the miserable old bastard who ran 3/7. He spotted me every time I came driving into his Command Post.

"What the hell are you doing here, Lieutenant?" he greeted me, soon after the jeep came to a halt.

"Just stopping by to say hello to all my friends, Sir," I answered. "How are you doing, Colonel?" I replied, hoping to see him respond in something resembling human terms but not expecting too much.

"We're pretty busy here, no time for much visiting in this battalion."

"Right, Sir, I won't be long. Got to get back to my company before nightfall," I responded.

"Keep your hands off my beer, Lieutenant," he added, not bothering to return my salute.

I found Max conducting some training for new members of his 81mm Mortar Platoon. The drill worked its magic every time. Set up the simple rugged base plate, tube and tripods structures. Then the more complicated aiming stakes that were the hardest part of the system to understand and responsible for getting the mortar rounds onto the target and away from friendly bodies. It was a system that had been worked out decades before and required very little creativity. Practice, practice, practice. It worked. In Max's capable hands it looked easy. These guys could get set up and be in operation in a minute or two, even while under fire themselves. Max had become expert by studying the instruction manuals over and over again. He knew the procedures by heart and he passed along his love of perfection to the marines who carried out the job. I watched from a distance, not wanting to interfere with my friend's work. I could sense his enjoyment in all this. It also made me realize how far we'd both come in the last two and a half years together. We had become really comfortable with the lethal tools of the deadly trade.

After turning the practice session over to his Platoon Sergeant, Max made his way to where I was standing. "Looks like life is treating you OK," he opened, as he extended his right hand for a hearty, Texas-style handshake.

"You don't look so bad yourself, ugly as ever," I teased.

"I may be ugly, but I'm still better looking than you," he added weakly. "Need some beer?"

"Yeah, in the worst way. Man, we haven't had any for weeks," I said, hoping to enlist sufficient sympathy. "But the Old Man already warned me to stay away from your stock."

"We'll have to wait until dark, then. We've got too much anyway," he replied, increasing my hopes that I could be a hero to the troops of Echo Company, and a worthwhile lieutenant to Captain Ledin.

I didn't much want to wait until after dark, because getting back to Hill 69, 11 miles away, in the dark of night would be a little treacherous. But I didn't have much of a choice, it seemed. Share and share alike was not part of the stingy Battalion Commander's makeup, even for one of his former employees. Max and I shared a dinner in the Mess Tent and afterwards I drove a mile down the road and waited for darkness to set in. About 2100, Max drove up and handed off 10 lovely cases of American beer. I had hit the jackpot.

"If the Old Man ever hears about this I'm a dead man," Max offered, not sounding quite as concerned as he might be. "Cover my ass, will you. Lie about where you got this stuff."

"No problem, friend, nobody'll ever know. Thanks again, Max, and take care of yourself."

"You too," he yelled as we raced off down the dark, pothole-filled road, toward Hill 69.

At a top speed of 30 miles per hour the lack of shock absorbers accentuated each and every lump or hole in the road. It was too dangerous to have lights on and we were also, technically, violating curfew regulations. My idea of a good time did not include being spotted by an itchy-fingered helicopter door-gunner with a sudden urge for nighttime practice.

Racing through the darkness, keeping the jeep on the road, was a trick requiring great skill. I held on to my seat with both hands to avoid being thrown out of the jeep. My backseat machine-gunner, sitting on 10 cases of beer, could hardly keep the M-60 pointed out at potential targets. Charlie owned this territory after the sun went down, and his calling cards were buried randomly, just out of sight. This was not fun, even though Captain Ledin considered it one of the more important operations of the war. But this time, we made it back without an incident. All of the marines on Hill 69 were glad to see us, most especially the Skipper.

"Gunny, make sure that everyone who wants beer gets two cans," he ordered. "Whatever is left over bring back to my tent and we'll finish it," came the instruction from the Captain, carefully supervising, as usual, every important aspect of company activity. He took care of the troops first, according to the best traditions of the Marine Officer's Creed, but he would have died had the Gunny come back empty-handed. He didn't.

The Captain put down a quick six-pack and told me to watch the radios, while he hit the sack. He needed the sleep worse than I did, so I let him sleep most of the night, while the Gunny and I took turns listening to the quiet and the constant static of the company radios, which were unused except for an occasional time check to ensure the radio operators were awake. They weren't always.

From that day forward, Captain Ledin called me by my first name. I had passed his supreme test. I could be counted on, so I was tasked with several beer runs during the next few months. I tried to find multiple sources in order not to wear out my welcome at Max's place. Too many visits and the Colonel would know exactly what was going on. He might be a prick, but he did have a sense of self-interest.

One such hunt for beer led me to the Officer's Club at the Air Wing Headquarters near the beach at Chu Lai, nearly 15 miles from Hill 69. The pilots had more combat action, on the average, than the grunts like myself did, but when they weren't fighting and flying combat missions they lived like kings, compared to us. Nicely constructed tents to sleep in, with cots to lie on. And an Officer's Club, right on the beach, that was open 24 hours a day, seven days a week. Unlimited cold beer and three hot meals a day. Paradise for a grunt.

I felt highly out of place as my jeep pulled up in front of their Club. I had been in the field for more than five weeks without a shower or a change of clothes. I probably looked and smelled a little out of place as well. I got a funny feeling that I was being noticed when I walked up to the bar, and before I could get a beer ordered everybody moved out at least 10 paces from where I stood. I asked the sergeant behind the bar whether or not I could buy some beer to go.

"How much you got in mind, Lieutenant?" he asked, knowing it looked like I could use quite a few.

"Ten or 15 cases," I said, hoping he would approve so I could get out of here.

"Come on, Lieutenant, I can sell you a six-pack but no way can I let you have that much," he laughed.

"Sergeant, my men haven't had a beer in six weeks. You won't miss 15 cases," I replied, hoping that if I asked for 15, he might settle for five.

"Sir, I can't do that. Sorry, but I got my orders," he said, hiding now behind military protocol that probably didn't exist. We were interrupted before I could make any progress in this conversation by a clean-uniformed major from the Air Wing, who stepped up beside me at the bar.

"Lieutenant, why don't you find your own bar to drink at?" he opened in a snotty tone. "This Club is for Air Wing officers. You look and smell like a grunt."

"Yes, Sir, I am a grunt. A thirsty one, too. Sorry about breaking your rules, Major, but I thought the sign on the door said OFFI-CER'S CLUB/OPEN MESS. I thought that meant the Club was open to all officers," I offered, knowing the correct answer and that I was on safe ground.

"It does, but we don't have enough booze for everybody in Vietnam," he said. "Go get your own. We'd very much appreciate it if you took your business elsewhere."

"Major, Sir, you and I both know that I have every right to drink here, same as you do," I answered, completely sure of my position now. "If you'll sell me 10 cases of beer at a decent price, I'll leave. Otherwise, I ain't leaving."

"All right, smartass, you can talk to the Colonel," he promised, walking away from the bar. I drank my cold beer in relative solitude. The pilots kept their distance and I concentrated on enjoying the view of the sunset and the clear blue sea, out the glassless window of the Club. A gentle, warm breeze, uncommon for this time of year, came in off the water and moved through the open Club, giving the place a feeling like one of the popular Marine pubs in Laguna Beach, except there were no women schoolteachers. I felt a long way from Hill 69 and the mud-covered marines who lived there. This was pretty special. What every grunt in Echo Company wouldn't give for a few minutes of this every few days. It might even make war tolerable. These guys lived like this all the time. I guess I should have been an aviator, just like the big, tall, gray-haired colonel charging my way from the other end of the Club.

"Lieutenant, I hear you're causing a riot and refuse to leave even after being ordered to do so," he stated. "And what the hell are you doing here in such an unkempt condition and while we're at it what in the hell are you doing in here with your weapon?"

"Colonel, I've made it very clear that I'll leave, if you guys will share some of your precious stockpile of beer. My troops have been without any for weeks and you guys have more than you can ever drink."

"Lieutenant, we don't sell beer to go here," he retorted.

"Colonel, if you won't sell me beer to go, then I'm going to stay here and drink a few more and enjoy myself until I feel like leaving," I said, not sure how far I could go with this. "Regulations require we wear sidearms at all times, as far as I know, Colonel, and I'm not taking mine off. As a matter of fact I think you're out of uniform without one, Sir. This is a pretty dangerous place. Can I buy you a beer, Colonel?" His face turned bright red and the veins on his neck seemed close to bursting. I was bluffing all the way but what were they going to do to me for being a smartass? Send me to Vietnam to serve in a Marine infantry company?

"We don't need smart-mouthed, nasty-smelling grunts around here, Lieutenant, and I want you out of here now," he ordered. "How much beer do you need to get on your way?"

"Fifteen cases, Sir," I replied, knowing that I was treading on very thin ice.

"That's outrageous, Lieutenant, but if you'll promise me you won't ever show your face in here again, I'll arrange it."

"Yes, Sir, no problem. Be glad to oblige, Sir. Could I also have some ice, Sir? Warm beer isn't very good," I asked, really stretching my luck. "Up in Indian country we've got no refrigerators, you know."

"Sergeant, take care of the Lieutenant and make sure he gets his stinky ass out of here right now," he yelled at the bartender. "Do I make myself absolutely clear, Lieutenant?" he blurted out, not waiting for an answer. The Sergeant helped us load 15 cases of beer into the jeep, a smile a foot wide splitting his face in two.

"Anything else I can do for you, Sir?" he offered, still enjoying the entire show.

"Yeah, could we have a cold six-pack to go?" I asked, hoping to get more sympathy from the Sergeant than I got from the Colonel. "My driver has worked up quite a thirst today and it's a long way back to our unit."

Our trip back to Hill 69 was a little less tense knowing that I'd screwed the Air Wing out of some of their treasure. The guys who flew the airplanes saved our butts time and time again during that year, often risking their lives unnecessarily to get our wounded out or to bring us in some much-needed ammo. When it mattered most you could always count on them, but they were a breed apart and didn't want to have much to do with the grunts after the firing stopped. I guess they figured that anyone who couldn't fly an airplane didn't amount to much. One-way bastards, I thought to myself as we cruised down the road in our military convertible, hoping Charlie didn't interrupt our party.

A few trips like this and Captain Ledin became downright friendly. He now referred to me as "Bill" or "Van Z" and always included me in the planning and execution phases of any operation,

big or small. I was working my way onto the team. Every man has
his vulnerabilities and Captain Ledin had his.

By November most of our battalion had moved out to Hill 69,
protecting Chu Lai's northeastern outer perimeter. We now had a
tent for the Battalion CO, probably stolen or "borrowed," never to
be returned, by Major DeFazio. We also had a wooden-framed,
screened-in toilet, an eight-holer, that really gave us the feeling of
permanency, and the most glorious outdoor shower installation
ever seen. As long as the water held out, 15 to 20 marines at a time
could take a cold shower. I don't know how the Major worked that
one, but it was worth every bit of it.

But our larger unit missions kept us out in the field for longer
and longer periods of time. Winter was about to arrive in full force
and it was cold and damp most of the time, especially after the sun
went down. We didn't have much cold-weather clothing and had to
write home for gloves and ski caps. I'm not sure how you could
find a place on earth that had such terrible year-round weather. It
was miserable four seasons a year. Each season did bring a new set
of obnoxious bugs, so there were many environmental changes one
could observe. If one gave a damn.

I sometimes missed my friends back at 3/7 but after two or
three times out into the field with Echo Company 2/4, I knew I
wouldn't change places, even if they gave me the choice. Sometimes
I regretted that during a particularly low period just before I left
3/7 I had sent in my resignation as a regular officer, a lifer. My
resignation was effective September 1, 1966, the earliest the Marines were going to let any of us out. Maybe I should stay in? Deep
in my heart, I knew that I had done the right thing in resigning. I
was a warrior now and yet I wasn't. I knew how to be a warrior and
was pretty good at it, too. People looked to me for strength and
leadership under combat conditions. I gave it. I had it to give. But
I couldn't see myself still doing this when I was an old man like the
Major. Combat is mostly a young man's sport.

We continued to lose people through attrition. Small firefights,
snipers and booby traps were our daily fare. We chased Charlie over
every square foot of the territory within 25 miles of Chu Lai. For
some reason 2/4 seemed to get more than its share of this duty. We
almost never laid our heads down in the same place two nights in a

row. We were on the move. It felt comfortable in a very strange way. Even though we were continuing to take casualties they were never in great numbers on any given day and we had the certain feeling that Charlie had no intention of taking us on head to head. We, however, wanted to take him on, big-time, rather than taking a sniper round today and a booby trap tomorrow. But we almost never found Charlie working in big groups. On a good day, we might see three or four of him, running together out of some village we were approaching and disappearing into the jungle beyond or into a tunnel, far faster than we could get a rifle trained on him. We grew frustrated. We were tired and weary of this game. I noticed with some surprise one day, during a run through the streets of a small village, that I was quickly out of breath. I was also getting out of shape.

Living on three or four hours of sleep a night, night after night, for months now, was taking its toll on the body. I was strong enough but losing endurance. All of us could sit down under a tree in a driving rainstorm and be asleep before our head came to rest against the tree. People slept through minor firefights, if they weren't directly involved. We were wearing out, and replacements weren't arriving fast enough. We were going to the field with 10 to 15 people short of normal and then 20 and then 25 and more. We were being asked to do more with less. Our company, in particular, seemed hardest hit and we had to continually reorganize into smaller and smaller groups. But we figured Charlie must be having the same problems, so we unhesitatingly adjusted to fit the conditions. The Marines had been doing this for 190 years. Semper Fi.

By December 1965, I had fully integrated into life in a new outfit and felt good about the situation. My tour was now about half over. There were no more rumors about an early return to the U.S.A., but halfway sounded pretty good. I had drawn close to the two young second lieutenants, Gary Brown and Fred Williamson, and to Captain Ledin. Even Gunny Howard seemed to like and accept me. I was no longer afraid of getting hurt and nobody knowing about it, or caring. We worked very hard together and now we could laugh together and trust together. And kill together. We had incredible skills in that area. We needed them.

A South Vietnamese Army outpost near the city of Bi Phu, 21 miles south of Chu Lai, had been overrun by Charlie. Since Bi Phu had been manned by nearly 400 ARVN soldiers, the fact that a group of Charlies made them all disappear was rather interesting to the Marine high command. Evidently, a rather large group of the enemy had been gathered here on this day. Four hundred South Vietnamese troops had vanished. They were dead, or they had deserted. Neither Charlie nor the ARVN bothered taking the other prisoner.

Echo Company 2/4 was sent to find out what the hell was going on. We got our assignment from Battalion about noon on the day after the outpost had been overrun. The Army had lost track of the ARVN troops at this outpost the previous day. No radio contact had been established in 24 hours. They wanted us in there to find some clue to what was going on and where the hell were 400 supposedly first-line troops. Not much else to go on. We were to land by helicopter, two miles west of the outpost, and make our way in there, as fast as we could. Find the ARVN folk and return things to normal as quickly as possible. Sounded easy enough. Maybe they were taking in a double-feature Bob Hope movie festival.

We boarded trucks that would take us from Hill 69 down to the airstrip, where enough helicopters could be mustered to get us all into the landing zone in only two trips. The HR-34 helicopter is designed to carry 13 fully loaded marines, and there were 200 or so of us. No way. We had become used to loading no more than six or seven. The choppers were too tired or something. Their engines couldn't lift that much weight at one time. But in another of the famous Marine accommodations and adjustments to local conditions, the Air Wing built an inclined ramp that led from the airstrip down to the ocean. It extended 200 yards or so, with one end of the ramp raised perhaps 20 to 30 feet in the air at the farthest point from the water line. Helicopters would taxi onto the ramp near the bottom and work their way to the top by increasing the power in the machine. How this thing held together was a mystery. It creaked and groaned under the weight of the fully-loaded helicopter. Near the top of the ramp, the pilot turned 180 degrees and headed straight down in a mad race to the sea. The ride down allowed the chopper to get sufficient ground speed to provide enough lift for takeoff. It was a pretty exciting ride. And every chopper carried 13 marines.

Captain Ledin went in with the first wave and two of the rifle platoons. I followed up in the second wave with the other platoon and most of the support personnel. We got there, as planned, in two quick, unopposed assault landings. As soon as the Captain saw me on the ground, he ordered the first part of the company, which had been waiting for us, on to the road which led in the direction of Bi Phu. We had landed in a rice paddy area in the middle of nothing in particular, only the odd group of two or three huts in all directions. There were few landmarks on the maps we had to give us much of a clue as to where we were, but if our landing was in the right place, we just had to get on the road and head inland until we arrived at the desired location. Nothing in the landing indicated it would be anything but a cakewalk. It looked much like the kind of work and kind of day we'd been having for the last several months, chasing Charlie and finding his presence, but not him. Nothing new here. If Charlie was in the area, he was hiding and staying out of our way.

I quickly gathered up the last people into the landing zone and ran the column for about a half mile until we caught up with the first group. With my group I had an artillery liaison officer, who would be useless, since the artillery bases were 20 miles away, a Marine aviation officer, who could call in air strikes if needed, and who was already in touch with a group of F-4 Phantoms flying overhead. We also had a naval gunfire officer, who was able to talk to some ship 15 miles offshore. The ship had guns that could deliver an 8″ shell to within 400 yards of any target we gave them. If Charlie was around and he wanted to play tough, we had a few surprises for him.

Captain Ledin wanted to get there quickly and the rear end of the column had to continue to run to keep up with the pace he set. It would be dark in about three hours and he had no intention of letting darkness catch us out here in the open.

The road was in pretty good shape and we were making good time except for two occasions, when the forward units in the column saw something that looked suspicious moving through one or another of the several small villages that we were passing. We halted while fireteams from the 1st Platoon looked into the activity. It turned out to be nothing. Villagers were running away, making their way to safety, assuming that our presence in the area meant that bullets and bombs were going to start flying through the air any minute now. They must have known something about what had been happening at Bi Phu.

About an hour and a half before darkness set in, we arrived at Bi Phu, hot and thirsty from the running we had been doing, but alert and in a combative mood, not knowing what this situation held in store for us. The village seemed to contain a rather large Catholic church, perhaps 10 houses and a large barracks building which must have housed the missing ARVN. Several even smaller clusters of hooches were from 100 to 200 yards from the center of Bi Phu in virtually every direction. The church and its steeple tower dominated the local landscape. The town itself seemed to be deserted.

"Bill, I'm going to lay in the three platoons in a triangle formation around the church. While I'm getting them set up and in position, set up the mortars in the church courtyard over there, where they can get a 360-degree shooting position," the Captain yelled at me, as I brought the last elements of the column through the gate to the churchyard. "See how much you can get done before I get back."

"Aye, aye, Sir," I answered quickly, letting him know that I completely understood what he wanted. "We'll get right on it," I replied again, knowing that the units he wanted me to get set up could do this blindfolded. The Mortar Platoon Sergeant overheard the conversation and didn't need it repeated. He started immediately to yell orders to his small unit leaders and within seconds they were digging positions for the four mortar tubes that accompanied us. I was busy keeping Battalion informed of what we had found. For so little action they sure had lots of questions. I had the clerks and cooks set up a sort of Company Command Post and start digging some firing positions that could protect us and hold off any attack through the main gate area.

The center of the CP area was behind a small tin-roofed shed a few feet away from the church, slightly behind the 2nd Platoon, which was being put in place directly south of the church, about 50 yards away from our position. A small white fence separated the CP from the 2nd Platoon. The fence bordered the church property on all four sides. This didn't afford any protection, but did give a solid landmark that might be useful after dark if we had to traverse the area. The shed was set on a slab of asphalt and offered a bit of cover from enemy fire or the weather.

The Air, Artillery and Naval Gunfire officers plopped down on the ground and got busy with their maps and radios, making sure everybody knew where we were and where we might need some friendly fire in case of an attack. Prearranged targets were agreed on, marked and numbered, in quick order. The entire company was at a high-activity level. Nobody had to yell or shout orders. Work came easy, knowing that the preparation might save our lives in the night to come. This place had a smell of Charlie. Let's get ready for him, before it turns dark.

The Vietnamese Marines had provided us with one of their second lieutenants to act as an interpreter for the company. He had two young Vietnamese enlisted assistants. All three of them were running through the village, out in front of our 2nd Platoon, interrogating villagers and trying to gather some intelligence data on what had happened to the garrison that had occupied the clump of villages one day before. There was no sign of them. They had just disappeared. I looked through the barracks where the missing 400 men had lived. It was adjacent to and not far from the rear of the church. It was a small building where no more than 100 could sleep at a time. It had a small kitchen that was about the size of a kitchen in a normal American house. Most of the 400 must have slept and eaten somewhere else. Maybe most of them were locals and just lived at home. There was almost no evidence that anyone had been in the barracks recently. No clothes lying around. Nothing. It looked like when they moved out they had time to organize the move. They certainly weren't caught by surprise. They took everything with them.

Lt. Dong Phucy, or whatever his name was, hit pay dirt. Without warning, groups of five and then 10 and then 20 ARVN soldiers came out of hiding. They came out of houses. Out of bushes. Out of tunnels. From everywhere. Hands raised, rifles above their heads, they started walking back towards the church. Bunches of them. All jabbering away as fast as they could talk, hoping that we could understand the language and they could somehow convince us that they weren't Charlies. More came. And then some more. First they came out of the village directly south of our position, with all the thatched huts. Then from the village to our west. Then our 3rd Platoon announced the arrival of some from the north side.

The missing army all headed directly for the church, and as they passed through the gate into the courtyard, they would call out at the top of their voice for their still-hiding brothers-in-arms to join them in the safety of Bi Phu. They all appeared very shaken and wary of the marines herding them to one corner of the courtyard, nearest the road. They wouldn't stop talking, even though marines from the CP tried to quiet them down. We wanted to get them more under control, so we could evaluate what the hell was going on. The interpreter was of very little help. He seemed to be doing his best to give them a lecture and a scolding about deserting their post. He shoved a few and took a quick kick at one of them before the marines nearest him put a stop to it. They were obviously very afraid of Charlie. They weren't so sure of us, either.

"Hey, V.Z., I don't trust these bastards. Tell the interpreter to tell them to drop their weapons and lay down in the prone position," the Skipper yelled at me, indicating that he too was somewhat overwhelmed by this nonsense. By now, perhaps as many as 150 and maybe more of the uniformed South Vietnamese soldiers were surrendering to us from every direction and to anybody who would take them. They had their hands raised, giving up evidently, through with fighting for their country for a while. They had given up Bi Phu without much of a fight. Now they were surrendering to their allies. Every time I looked around, there were more of them, coming in from every direction. Some were carrying weapons. Some had shed their uniforms and tried to fold into the general population when Charlie showed up early yesterday morning. The interpreter tried to interview as many of them as possible but they were all yelling and jabbering at once. And it was getting dark. He thought some maybe were Charlies in disguise. All of them were deserters. I didn't think it sounded like a real good idea to count on these ARVN being part of our defense for the night.

"Go find the Captain, tell him we've got our hands full with ARVN troops," I yelled at one of my clerks, who was helping the interpreter move this mass into one large group near the hut where we were setting up the Company CP. I looked at the Interpreter for help. He raised his arms in the universal manner. He didn't have a clue, so kept up the interviewing process. There didn't seem to be any ARVN officers or leadership of any kind in the group that had come in. I was getting a little uncomfortable with more than 200 of these guys wandering around at random inside our defensive perimeter.

"Sir, the Captain says he's busy and that you should do whatever you think necessary with the ARVN," the clerk informed me upon his return.

"Great," I whispered under my breath. This is one not covered at Quantico. I had 200 strange-looking question marks with rifles inside our lines. Outside the lines were Charlies, number unknown. I decided to interest my new charges in religion.

"Gunny, grab a couple of the troops and help me get this mess inside the church. Let's get them out of the way, until we can figure out what all of this means. I want em searched and disarmed before they go through the door. I don't trust any of them," I added, as the Gunny and several of the clerks started in. One by one they were searched, disarmed and led into the church sanctuary, which was meant to hold 50 or 60 parishioners. It was a crowded service that night. We put two armed marines and the interpreter in there to keep things under control until we could figure out this puzzle. We locked the door and began piling their rifles and gear against the church wall, then we got back to preparing our defenses. Captain Ledin wasn't pleased with the way it was progressing. Too slow. He summoned the platoon commanders.

"Damn it, gentlemen, I want those holes deeper and I want to see more Bangalore Torpedoes put out. From what I see, your troops are taking this too lightly. We have no idea what's out there. I don't like the smell of things. I want you to go back and bang some heads. It's dark but keep working until I say stop. Do I make myself absolutely clear?"

"Yes, Sir," came the response from the three of them, in unison.

"Sir, can I have two machine-gun teams? I've got an area between those two large sheds over near my left flank. Anyone who wants to take me on tonight will probably come right through there," Fred Williamson, our 2nd Platoon Commander, offered.

"I could use some extra help too. You've got me spread out pretty thin all along my position," pitched in Gary Brown, who had the 1st Platoon. "I'd like to set up one at either end to cover my whole front," he added.

"OK, you got em. Van Z, you see those things get used properly," he ordered me. "I'm going to check out the mortars. Tell the Naval Gunfire Observer I want to meet him here in 15 minutes," he added. The Captain seemed a little tense tonight. None of his usual banter and good humor. All business. All serious. I set about on the tasks he had given me, a little more familiar with the terrain we were holding. Even though it was completely dark, I could move from position to position, platoon to platoon, without bumping into too many objects or falling in one of the many holes which now dotted the landscape.

It didn't take long to get four of the six machine guns located in positions that could cause the most damage to intruding bad guys. We kept two others in reserve, ready for quick deployment, back near the shed that now served as the Company Command Post. It had suddenly become a very busy place. We had lots of room to prepare firing positions around the shed. The courtyard had a surface that had once been asphalt but now was a mixture of asphalt and hard dirt. It was not possible to dig holes through it. We had to use some old beat-up tables and chairs to improvise defensive positions. Our Mortar Squad was set up in a small area just behind the church, but far enough away from the building to give them a full 360-degree firing capability. The Skipper had given them 10 prearranged targets on the maps that we all had and they were kept busy plotting these targets on their aiming stakes, so they could take out those 10 targets within seconds. They lobbed a couple of rounds out into the night, just to make sure everything was in working order. It was. The Gunny had already arranged all of our extra ammunition into two small stacks, several yards away from each other, well surrounded and protected by sandbags. I occupied myself with organizing the radio crews we had with us.

The Captain had announced that he would occupy the church belltower during the night, which would put him 20 to 30 feet above ground and give him a panoramic view of the entire area. I sent the radio operator up the steeple steps to establish and keep contact with the platoons, but kept the battalion radio operator inside the small tin shed. The Arty radio wasn't going to be much use since we were out of range. I decided to keep the Air Officer, Lt. Duram, and his radio operator near me in the shed and had Navy Lt. Stonehouse and his Naval Gunfire Team a few yards away against the church wall. We had very little practice with these guys. They could call in 8-inch shells from a ship 15 miles away and well out to sea, but it seemed unlikely we'd use them tonight.

We had two corpsmen. I kept one with me and I sent the other to the area occupied by the Mortar Squad, so that he could get to our 3rd Platoon quickly if necessary, then formed a fire team out of the six clerks and the Captain's jeep driver and had them positioned around the gate which led into the courtyard, at the front of the church. Everybody had a place in the defense and a job to do. All of the radios were working, which was a bit unusual, so we were in contact with the world if the world wanted to know what was going on. Only the 200 friendly prisoners made for anything but a dull night. Nothing much to report. So far. The Captain finished his third inspection of the platoon positions, returned through the darkness, and called the Gunny and me to join him.

"Who's got some chow?" he asked, sounding a bit out of wind.

"Everything OK out there, Skipper?" I asked, knowing he wouldn't come back here until it was.

"Yeah, we're as ready as we can be but I have a strange feeling this is not going to be a quiet night. What has the interpreter come up with?"

"All I can make out is that the ARVN outpost was attacked early yesterday morning while most of them were asleep," I told him, knowing that he wished I had more than that. "They suspect that maybe as many as 100 Charlies came out of the north side of town soon after mortars started pouring in the church. All of the officers were gone on leave so they decided to make a run for it. After they dropped their uniforms, they went out into the local villages and laid low till we arrived. They think Charlie has left the area."

"I don't like it," the Skipper offered, pushing down some cold spaghetti and meatballs. "I want everyone alert on this one. It doesn't smell right to me. You in touch with Battalion?" he asked me.

"Yes, Sir, everything seem to be in perfect order so far. All of the support groups are working too, except Arty is not going to be of much use unless Regiment moves some of them a bit closer."

"What do we have on station for air support?" he asked me, polishing off the spaghetti with some stale white bread.

"We've got the Phantoms from Chu Lai but with this cloud cover they won't be too helpful either," I offered. "Puff the Magic Dragon will be on station from 2200 to 0200 if we need him," I answered, knowing that the Captain didn't have much use for the slow-flying cargo plane. Its dual-mounted Gatling guns fired several thousand rounds per minute each, but couldn't be counted on for very accurate fire. Puff might scare someone, and it could always deliver a steady supply of flares. Flares might be handy tonight, since cloud cover masked what little moonlight was available.

"I don't think we'll need all that stuff, but we'd better be ready. Ask them to stay on station," he said, looking straight at me. "I'm going up the tower. Stay close so we can talk," he said, continuing to look in my direction. "Let me know if anything changes down here."

It was starting to get cold and I had to walk around a bit to take some of the chill off my body. The platoon positions were quiet and the only sounds in the area came from inside the church, where the ARVNs were evidently getting a bit tired of house arrest. I walked to the church door. The room was lit by one small set of candles near the altar. The interpreter had one of the prisoners by the throat, conducting an interrogation session that didn't follow Swedish Red Cross rules.

"Lt. Hu, knock off the noise and put out those candles," I yelled at him. "I don't want any more noise out of this area and I want you out of here. Tell them that anyone leaving this room will be shot on sight. Is that clear?" I sounded as stern as I could. He nodded his head, indicating he probably didn't understand a word of it, shouted a few words in Vietnamese, and left the room right behind me. It grew immediately quiet and the candlelight disappeared.

By 2300 hours, it started to look like it was going to be a quiet night after all and Captain Ledin called the platoon commanders into the CP, more to make sure everyone was awake than anything else. The cool night air was a big sleep aid and twice I had dozed off as I sat with my back to the shed, listening to the crickets singing in Vietnamese.

I would bet anything I wasn't the only one of the 200-plus

people here tonight with droopy eyelids. It didn't look like we needed all this alertness, anyway. It was also probably getting a little too dull for the Skipper, up in the tower with just him and Kilmer, his favorite radio operator. The three platoon commanders arrived before the Captain got down from his loft.

"God, it's cold out there," Fred whispered as he came through the gate and approached the shed. "Dark too, I can't see a damn thing."

"Quit bitching, Lieutenant, quiet nights are the best kind," I answered, sympathetic to his concerns but not about to let him know it. Gary and Bob Wallace, our 3rd Platoon Leader, showed up a few seconds later, needing only a nod of their heads to let us know they had arrived.

"This is too damn quiet. I don't like it. Anyone hear anything out there?" the Captain blurted out, as he came striding up to our little huddle.

"I think I can hear some movement out in front of my area," Gary responded. "I can't get a fix on it though. Maybe just a buffalo or some other animal. Want me to put out a listening post?"

"No, I don't think we've got enough people for that. We're too spread out already. Let's just keep our eyes and ears open and see how it goes," the Captain added, sounding less concerned. "Anything new on Battalion getting Arty moved closer in our direction?" he asked me.

"No, Sir, we've got no Arty support yet and it doesn't look like we can count on any but we still got Air and Navy guns," I pitched in. The Captain was satisfied we were in no unusual danger. We could handle anything that came up and he ordered a stand-down alert status. Just as the Captain was finishing, a loud thumping sound came from the direction of Gary's 2nd Platoon. We all heard the same horrible sound simultaneously. A mortar going down a metal tube and being sent on its destructive way by a small explosive charge.

"Incoming," came a yell from a chorus of at least 15 voices. Bodies hit the ground and scurried for what little cover existed. I hit the deck beside the hut, where I had only minutes before been resting peacefully. I closed my eyes, hoping that would protect me from the explosion, which couldn't be far away. The impact of the incoming mortar round and the associated noise and light ended the evening quiet. It may have been a lucky shot, but luck or not, it got the job done. The round hit one of the asphalt patches about 10 feet from the shed and just short of the church wall. Because of the hard surface, it sprayed shrapnel in every direction from the impact area. Captain Ledin was hit. So were six or seven others. I felt my arms and legs and was surprised to find out that I had no new openings. A large hole in the shed just above where my head had been made me take a deep breath and a look, long and hard. Close, but no cigar, Charlie. I didn't have time to sit and think about it. The night had come alive. Time to earn our pay.

"Send the corpsman up to see me when you get the others taken care of," the Captain shouted to me, pressing a handkerchief to his left arm as he ran towards the tower.

The 2nd Platoon was returning fire by now in the direction from which the mortar had been fired. The platoon commanders rushed back to their platoons. The Gunny and I were left with several screaming, moaning marines.

We hardly had time to notice the next two incoming rounds. The first hit off the wall of the church, which absorbed most of the blow, leaving a gaping hole about a foot in diameter, and created a giant cloud of dust in the air. The second hit the shed squarely on top and collapsed it in one gigantic shove. One more marine caught some metal from the second round.

The corpsman had the wounded charted by the severity of their wounds in quick order, spending most of his time with the one most seriously wounded. None of them were in immediate danger of dying, but a couple were in a great deal of pain.

"Let's get an aid station set up over against the wall," I shouted at one of the clerks. "Help the Gunny get the wounded over there and out of the way." I helped one of the least wounded walk to the wall before the Captain started getting involved in the fight and needing my help.

"Hey, Bill, see if you can get Puff to drop a few flares so we can see what the hell is going on," he called down between instructions he was giving to his platoon commanders and the Mortar Squad.

Gary thought he and his people had the location of the source of the incoming mortar rounds. He passed the information on to Captain Ledin and within seconds our mortars were sending out an answer.

The Air Officer was already on the job by the time I got back to where he and the other support groups were gathered, in a small foxhole near where the tin shed used to stand. The corpsman had just finished putting a bandage on his hand to cover a mostly superficial wound he received from the first incoming shell.

"I've got Puff on the radio. They're ready to drop flares," he half whispered to me, as I jumped in his hole beside him. "Where do you want em?"

"Let's try to drop some south of the 2nd Platoon, about 200 to 300 yards out, so we can backlight them," I asked.

The firing from the 2nd Platoon area had pretty much quieted down, so it was easy to hear the drone of the C-130 floating high above us, well above the clouds that blanketed our immediate world. I could hear the chatter of the Captain speaking with Gary over the phone, and Gary's answers. I wasn't on the radio. Without gunfire to ruin the quiet of the night they could talk to each other in normal voices, but neither seemed to know it.

The flare came through the cloud layer like an airborne spotlight announcing the opening of some new supermarket. Lights and shadows bounced off each new layer of clouds as the parachute-held illumination bomb came floating toward earth. The light irritated our eyes, now accustomed to the last several hours of darkness. It robbed our night vision. Several hundred pairs of squinting eyes peered out at the landscape, trying to catch a glimpse of something out of place in the otherwise peaceful country setting. During the 30 seconds where we had light no trace of Charlie could be seen. We had another flare dropped east of our 1st Platoon with the same results. It was quiet again.

"What's the status of the wounded?" came a calm voice from the tower area.

"We've got seven wounded so far, Skipper. Only one might need a med-evac," I replied, hoping the trembling I felt wouldn't affect my voice in some strange way.

"Check with the corpsman again and see what he thinks. We should be able to get a chopper in here next to the mortars," he added. I walked over to the spot near the wall of the church where the wounded were now laid out in a neat row and looking more comfortable.

"Hey, Doc, got a minute?" I asked, grabbing the corpsman by the shoulder as he was working on one of the patients.

"Give me a minute, Lieutenant, I'm just about through here," he replied. Morphine injections eased the pain that had ripped through the bodies now covered by blankets and sleeping bags. The darkness covered the blood, open wounds and contorted faces. I wasn't very good with that stuff and having me vomit right now probably wasn't good form.

"Have you checked out the Captain?" I asked the Doc, as he completed his rounds and ambled over to where I was resting.

"No, Sir, he says he's not hurt bad. I'll go see him in a minute," he promised.

"Any of those guys need an immediate med-evac?" I quizzed.

"Well, Hanson was bleeding pretty bad for a while, but I think I have it stopped. I'd like to get him out of here if possible just in case there's something I can't see in this light."

"OK, I'll get on it," I said. "Make sure you check the Captain," I added, as I headed to find the Air Liaison Officer. "All right, Bob, let's see if we can get some help in here, we've got some wounded we need to get out of here," I spit out when I found Bob Hendricks and his radio operator talking to Chu Lai and the Air Wing.

"They're ready to go whenever we are," he informed me.

"If they have time, have them bring a resupply of mortar rounds," I added at the last minute, remembering that the mortars had answered Charlie with a good percentage of what we had brought with us.

"Roger," he answered, getting back on the radio, and returning to the aviation talk he felt more familiar with.

"Hey, Skipper, you all right up there?" I whispered loud enough for the steeple dwellers to hear, but quiet enough so that the rest of the world couldn't.

"Yeah, I'm OK," he answered, sounding like he really wasn't. "You get a med-evac on the way?"

"Yes, Sir, on its way."

"Good, let me know when it gets close. Hey, Van, let's see if Puff can shed us some more light on the subject here. Have him drop a couple in front of 2nd Platoon again and then a couple out in front of 1st Platoon. I'd like to have a look out there before the choppers get here," the Captain ordered.

"Aye, aye, Sir," I answered, moving back toward the Company CP. I asked the Air Liaison Officer to let me know when the med-evac helicopter got close and relayed the instructions I had on illuminating the area. The Gunny informed me the wounded were ready to go if med-evac had room for them. The corpsman was kept busy comforting the wounded, who no longer moaned and groaned. A small amount of radio static and chatter was the only noise that broke the silence of the still, pitch-black night. Puff the Magic Dragon returned to the area and right on cue and gave us four consecutive parachute flares exactly where the Skipper had requested. As each floated to the ground, a temporary band of light brought our small world into focus, simultaneously easing fears and yet reminding us of how remote the area was and how little support we had should Charlie come marching through the villages and jungles that stretched forever, in every direction. Wherever he was hiding, the flares didn't give us any further information about him or what he had in mind. This was the first time any of us had been on the receiving end of a mortar attack. It might mean Charlie was moving with a big group, which would also jibe with his ability to scare the hell out of 400 ARVN troops, most of which were now attending services at the local church.

"Med-evac's about eight miles out now," the Air Officer informed me. "I'm going to bring them in from the west and drop in over there by the mortars," he said, as he motioned toward the rear of the church. "We've got two Hueys. We'll only be able to get the two most critically wounded on board the first ship. The others will have to wait for the next one. I've asked the Gunny to get 'em all lined up, because I don't want these birds on the ground for any longer than necessary as long as Charlie has mortars targeted on us," he added, becoming quite possessive about his airplanes.

"Roger, I'll go over and help. Hey, Skipper, birds incoming," I whispered at the tower. Within a few seconds we could all hear the familiar chop-chop-chop of a helicopter in the distance. The Air Officer couldn't see the chopper because of the cloud cover and the pilot couldn't see us for the same reason. The radio, now in full and constant use, was the only landing aid. As the pilot broke through the clouds, I could see that he wasn't using his running lights. No use giving Charlie a clearer target. Only the fiery exhaust pinpointed his position in the sky. The Air Liaison Officer was providing the navigation, by radio. As the helicopter descended and started to zero in on our position, we had two Headquarters troops light up the area as much as possible with two miserable, low-illumination flashlights. The pilot spotted them at once.

He had no warning. None of us did. The rat-a-tat-tat of a .50-caliber machine gun from a position perhaps 100 yards west of the church and directly in the helicopter flight path burst upon the night and ended any speculation about whether Charlie was still in the area. Where the hell did they get a weapon like that? Must have taken it from the ARVN. Two rounds ripped through the cockpit near the pilot's head, causing him to lose momentary control of the helicopter's flight. He spun left, then right and went into a slight dive, at a dangerous altitude for such things, before he gained control and applied maximum power and executed a steep climb out to his right. The radio traffic got instantly heavier.

"What the shit was that?" he bellowed, loud enough for all of us standing near the Air Liaison Officer to hear. "I thought you guys said this zone was quiet," he added, knowing that grunts always lied about such things.

The peaceful scene was no more. A flurry of activity aimed at responding to the incoming .50-caliber rounds came automatically. Our 3rd Platoon was returning fire and the Captain was busy getting our mortars on target.

The incoming mortar rounds caught us by surprise. Too much noise to hear the rounds going down the tubes this time. The first one landed on the church roof, blowing lumber and shingles into the air, providing a dirt and wood shower for those of us standing near the church. The next two hit right in the middle of our Mortar Squad. The Captain dispensed with his radio traffic and leaned out the bell tower to get a quicker answer.

"Anyone see where they're coming from?" he broadcast into the night, ready to accept an answer from anyone except Charlie.

No answer came from our side. Charlie gave the Captain a clue by getting a direct hit on the bell tower with a 75mm recoilless rocket launcher. It blew out one of the corner support posts of the steeple, leaving the roof being held up in only three places. The Captain had to be directly in the path of that baby.

Even though we had new wounded in the Mortar Squad and a helicopter trying to decide whether to call it a night, and we had two of our platoons firing at something very real out there, I headed for the tower. Most likely I was in charge now but I had to see for myself. There was no response to calls to the tower. This eats shit. Just before I arrived at the stairs leading up to the tower, I bumped into the interpreter coming out of the side door of the church.

"They no want stay in church," he informed me, obviously sharing their concern about the new holes in the roof and the wall. "Some hurt, not bad," he added.

"You tell those bastards if they set one foot out of the door, I'll open fire on them," I yelled, hoping they wouldn't take me up on my offer, which was mostly bluff. "I can't handle any more confusion right now, so you get back in there and get em quieted down. Do you understand me, marine?" I spit out while we were nose to nose. I didn't have a clue what I would do if the doors burst open and they started pouring out of the church.

The stairs leading to the top of the tower were filled with debris. So far, we'd been hit with mortars, .50-caliber machine guns and a rocket attack. What the hell were we up against? I asked myself as I made my way on my hands and knees up the darkened stairs, not knowing what sort of mess I'd find at the top.

"Captain, Captain you up there?" I pleaded, knowing that if there wasn't an answer pretty soon my nuts would be on the chopping block. "Captain Ledin, can you hear me?" I called again, as I crawled over fallen boards and bricks that used to be part of the bell tower structure.

I found the Captain on his knees trying his best to get to his feet. I don't think he could hear me. As I reached down to help him to his feet, he jerked as a reaction to my presence. I had surprised him.

"What the hell was that?" he heaved, trying carefully to catch his breath.

"A rocket, Skipper, it came from over there," I said, pointing off to the east toward the 1st Platoon, which was now engaged in a lively firefight of their own.

His radio operator was sitting against the wall, opposite from where the Captain had now managed to get into a sitting position. The young marine was very dead.

One of the platoon commanders was trying to reach the Captain by radio. I took the receiver from the dead man's hand.

"Echo Six, Echo Six, this is Echo One, over," Fred repeated into the headset on his end.

"Echo One, this is Echo Five," I yelled into the headset, letting Fred know it was me on the other end. "I'm here with Six and I think he should be back on the air any minute," I said, hoping my judgment about the Captain's condition was correct. "What's going on, Echo One?" I asked, pretty sure I knew the answer, since I could see his platoon position pretty clearly by looking over the edge of the side of the tower, something I didn't want to make a career of doing.

Puff was providing a large moving lamp every few minutes. Tracer rounds from both sides and muzzle flashes provided the other light. The miniguns spat out enough tracers to look like some kind of sci-fi ray gun.

"I must have been knocked out by the blast," the Captain said, rubbing a spot on the side of his head. "I can't hear too well yet but I think I'm OK now," he said to me, not sounding too confident.

"Echo Five, this is Echo One, I've got a shit pot of Charlies at my front," Fred said in a very calm voice, considering the circumstances. "Echo Five, can you see them?" he asked.

A new parachute flare popped just in time to give me a perfect view of 1st Platoon's front. I wasn't so sure how glad I was to be able to see them. There were hundreds. Moving in small groups of five or ten, attacking our 1st Platoon, at what must have been point-blank range in some spots. We had found Charlie. No doubt about it. When the parachute light came on, they ducked behind trees and paddy dikes and any other thing that could offer protection. Judging by the bodies which were lying on the ground not moving, 1st Platoon was doing some damage too. I could see 10 or 12 of Charlie's troops dragging bodies back to a tree line 50 to 75 yards directly in front of the Platoon CP. A couple of enterprising young marines from Fred's platoon were lobbing M-79 grenades into Charlie's hiding place in the tree line with incredible accuracy, lighting it up with the special sound and music of a rifle platoon. One round, a white phosphorous type, lit up the night and all the trees for several yards around. The M-79 was a handy way to be able to lob a grenade 100 yards.

"I'm OK now, Lieutenant," the Captain said, looking straight at me with a face that still showed pain. "Get the hell out of here and get me a new radio operator. I'm not hurt bad. Just stunned a little," he said, hoping I would believe him.

"Are you sure, Skipper?" I asked, knowing he wasn't all that OK.

"Don't argue with me, Lieutenant, and go see what the squids can do for us," he insisted, making sure I didn't get too involved with offering any pity for his condition. His face was bleeding and pockmarked from the flying debris caused by the rocket hit.

As I crawled back down the stairs, I could hear him start to take charge of the company again, and I heard him acknowledge to Fred that he was aware that Fred had some new casualties.

By now, it had become exceedingly clear Charlie was going for the throat. No more sniping and booby traps. Tonight he planned to wipe us out, see if he could eliminate Echo/2/4, end this particular ball game permanently. He obviously figured the odds were in his favor tonight. He was ready to pay any price.

Captain Ledin, once again in command, ordered the Mortar Squad to open up on the predetermined firing positions eight, nine and 10. There was a free fire. Charlie was out in the open. Let him have it, with all we could muster.

I could hear our mortar people yelling out commands for more and more rounds. I could hear Captain Ledin celebrating the success. We were inflicting heavy casualties on Charlie. He kept coming. We kept hitting back.

Harry James joined Charlie's fighting band. A trumpet, perhaps a bugle, blaring an earsplitting sound, urged Charlie forward by sending strange musical tones floating through the night air, lending more of the bizarre to this deadly scene. More mortars. More trumpet. More death. Captain Ledin called for more firepower.

Fred's 1st Platoon was fighting hand-to-hand along his front. They were using bayonets.

"Gunny, get the corpsman up to see the Captain again," I ordered, finding Gunny Howard waiting for me at the bottom of the stairs. "He also needs a radio operator."

"We're running low on mortar ammo, Lieutenant," the Gunny informed me, as he sped off to find the Doc.

I found my way back to what had been the Company CP. It was alive with confusion and pain. We now had 13 wounded and one dead, in the tower. The med-evac helicopter had told us to go to hell. He wasn't landing. Puff was running out of candles. Artillery was still out of range. Mortars were almost out of ammo. Charlie was still blowing that damned trumpet. We were taking fire everywhere.

The Naval Gunfire Officer outranked me but we weren't arguing about seniority right now. This was our show.

"Can you give us some help?" I asked, as I jumped into a foxhole next to him.

"Ready when you are," he promised, calmly. "Where do you want it?" he asked, with a continued sense of assurance.

"Let me look at your map," I asked, hoping I could find the target quickly.

There wasn't much sense in being overly careful now, so we lit two flashlights to look more carefully at the details on the map. As we searched for the desired point, another rocket hit the bell tower and several more incoming mortars exploded around us in the courtyard. To the west I could hear the .50-caliber ripping into our 3rd Platoon position. Reading a map was one thing, reading one while under intense fire was another.

"Sir, Lt. Williamson is on the hook. He wants some more machine guns up there if possible," my radio operator in the next foxhole informed me.

"OK, OK, tell him we're working on it," I shouted back, searching frantically for familiar territory on the map with my finger. "Right here," I gestured. "Coordinates 165-326," I added.

"Too frigging close," the Navy officer sitting next to me announced.

"Lieutenant, that's exactly where we need it. I could care less that you think it's too close," I said, conveying my sense of urgency.

"We're not authorized to bring this fire closer than 400 yards from friendly position. I can't do it," he instructed me.

"Unless you figure out something clever to do with those eight-inch shells sitting out there on your ship, Lieutenant, Charlie is going to come through that gate in a couple of minutes and cut your balls off," I promised, absolutely sure I was correct in my assessment.

"Can I walk them in?" he asked, responding to my logic.

"Sure, I think the 1st Platoon will appreciate that," I said, trying to inject some humor into a completely unfunny situation. "Move closer to the bell tower so you can talk directly to the Skipper," I ordered.

I called for the Gunny. He was standing a few feet away, ready as always.

"Gunny, grab a couple of the headquarters types. We're going to need some help on the one," I ordered.

"Be right back, Lieutenant," he answered, shuffling off into the darkness.

We grabbed two machine-gun crews and three clerks to act as stretcher bearers and headed quickly for the front gate. My little group and I turned left at the gate and slowly worked our way down the main road which divided the church area and Fred's 1st Platoon. We couldn't see much from this position but it was obvious that fighting was still going on in the entire area. I could still hear the Vietnamese Harry James getting in his hot licks. Somebody wanted Charlie to keep moving forward. He did. He also paid for it. Small arms fire kicked up dust all around us. I halted our column on several occasions when it appeared to me that we were the main target. A shallow ditch ran along the road and gave us some protection from the intense rifle fire that was coming into the area all around us.

"Fred, Fred, this is Five, where are you," I blurted into the night. "Echo One Actual, it's the Five. Where the hell are you," I shouted in code, hoping Charlie didn't speak much English.

"Over here, Van," I heard a voice whisper through the sounds of gunfire.

A quick dash across the road and we were in Fred Williamson's Platoon CP, or what was left of it.

"I've got to have some help here," he told me, in a very matter-of-fact way.

"I brought two more machine guns and their ammo," I stated, hoping this might be enough to handle his need. It wasn't what he needed at all. He had six or seven severely wounded marines and was running short of ammo all across his front. He had already told his troops to fix bayonets. By the numbers. This kid was doing OK. I told him about the naval gunfire that would soon be arriving. I told him we would bring it in close, too close. I told him to pass the word to keep heads down. Big stuff coming in.

"I'll see what I can do about ammo," I promised. "Where are the wounded?"

"Laying over there," he said, pointing to a hole a few feet away.

"OK, I'll get 'em," I said, hearing that the Gunny and the stretcher bearers were already moving the bodies. Incoming bullets struck the ground very near our hiding place.

"I'll be back," I said, hoping I would.

"Hurry," he said, with no sign of panic but lots of urgency in his voice.

We got the wounded back to the main CP area after three quick trips. The First Aid Station was starting to get crowded and the corpsman was running low on supplies. I had to remind him that daylight was still several hours away and that we probably would not be resupplied until then.

The Captain was still operating from the tower despite one more direct hit and one more close call.

"Give me two more rounds on target 12," he yelled at the mortar people, no longer worrying about transmitting messages over the radio. "Where is that naval gunfire?" he screamed.

"On the way, Sir, should be no more than a few more seconds," the Liaison Officer answered.

"I need it now, Lieutenant," he screamed back before getting on to his next subject. "Air, what the hell happened to Puff? I need more light," he said, now completely in high gear.

"Puff is getting low on candles, Captain, we're trying to get a backup," came a response from a tired Air Officer, who along with the Naval Gun Fire Officer had moved to the base of the tower so they could talk more openly and quickly with the Skipper above them.

Based on the shouting and yelling coming from Fred's position I fully expected to see a swarm of black-uniformed Charlies come rushing through the gate at any moment. I had my .45 pistol at the ready, hoping that if they did make it to the gate the 15 or so of us waiting for them could push them back. If they were going to wipe Echo Company off the map, they were going to have to pay a high price. As accurate as I was with a .45, they probably weren't sweating it.

The first round of eight-inch fire from a ship 15 miles away exploded with an earthshaking thud, several hundred yards east of where the Captain wanted it.

"Not bad, Navy, let's walk it in 50 yards at a time from there," he blurted out, obviously somewhat jubilant about his new firepower. By the fourth round we had it right on top of them and about 100 yards from our most advanced position.

"Fire for effect," came the order from the tower.

The Naval Officer relayed the order to the faraway ship and within a couple of minutes shells were raking the area. Evidently it was doing the job.

"You can see bodies flying everywhere," the Captain shouted and then gave out an Oklahoma war cry. "Keep it coming, Navy, this is beautiful," he said, sounding overjoyed.

I had missed most of the fun. I went searching through the 3rd Platoon area for extra and excess ammunition. There wasn't a whole lot. They had to keep that .50-caliber off our back and every time he opened up they returned it five times over.

I did manage to collect about 25 magazines of rifle ammo and wrapped them in a poncho to get ready for another quick trip out to Fred's position. On my way back, I decided to stop by Gary's 2nd Platoon and see if they had any extra bullets to donate.

"Are you kidding?" Gary asked me, with a pained look on his face. "We're running low here too. Any chance of getting resupplied tonight?" he asked.

"No way. Not tonight, I'm afraid," I answered.

"Hey, Van, if you get wounded tonight, can I have your radio?" he asked, through the darkness.

"Kiss my ass, Brown, I ain't going nowhere." I told him to pass the word to be more selective in their rifle fire. This was the time for maximum fire discipline. We couldn't afford anything else. The Gunny found time to scavenge around the ARVN barracks and found two cans of machine-gun ammo hidden in one of the back rooms. He gathered a couple of marines and took all the ammo we could muster out to Fred and his people. He went back later with 25 ARVN rifles and their ammo, which we had confiscated from the deserters now in church. Off and on, the remainder of the night, Charlie's Harry James kept at it, first from one location and then another, but after a while Charlie wasn't having much of it. Several more attacks were short-lived and had very little follow-up or staying power. They probed and felt their way along our three fronts but never found the weak spot they were looking for.

"I'd like to find that bugle boy and jam that noisy thing up his ass," the Gunny said, as he rushed by me on one of his many details that night.

"I'll help," I offered.

We were confident of the naval gunfire now and brought it to within 50 yards and then 25 during one of Charlie's last-gasp attacks. He quit for the night about 0400. The Captain reported every time we got some illumination he could see groups of soldiers out in the killing zone pulling casualties back to a safer position. They were starting to exit the battlefield. It looked like a big job.

By 0500 hours, we were pretty sure we had survived. Reinforcements in the form of two rifle companies would start landing at first light. Resupply and med-evac helicopters were standing by to get airborne at first light. Charlie's window of opportunity to really kick butt was just about closed. The cavalry was coming to the rescue and not a minute too early either. We had long since been out of mortar rounds and grenades, Puff had gone home for the night, after emptying out his last few hundred rounds from the door-mounted Gatling gun. We had almost no rifle ammo left. And we had a pile of wounded. Twenty that I knew of and two dead. Hurry sun.

First light brought in some beautiful-looking helicopters. They carried the two rifle companies from the 1st Battalion, 4th Marines, who immediately set off in hot pursuit of what was left of Charlie's troops. We let our prisoners see the light of day. They staggered out of the church door half expecting good morning with Charlie. The church was now much holier than before. And air-conditioned, as a result of numerous direct hits by mortar and rocket rounds. The .50-caliber had taken most of the plaster off the back wall.

Captain Ledin came down from the tower, bloodstained but still in charge. And happy. He held a staff meeting inside the church, while we shared a cold meatloaf breakfast.

"Gentlemen, I hope I never have another night like that. Bravo

1/4 is reporting that they've discovered 145 fresh graves just east of here. We done good and I'm proud of all of you."

"You didn't do so bad yourself Skipper," Fred said, speaking for all of us. "You OK?"

"Yeah, I'm fine, couple of scrapes and bruises is all. Let's get packed up and get the hell out of here."

He had bleeding pockmarks all over his face, from flying cement and bricks. He would look much better 30 days later, when on his way home the Commandant would pin the Silver Star, Bronze Star and Purple Heart on his chest, in a spit-and-polish ceremony at Marine Headquarters. Fred would receive his first Silver Star on a dirty, dusty parade field at the Chu Lai headquarters of the 4th Marine Regiment.

I waived good-bye to Bu Pai from the door of the HR-34 helicopter that took us back to Hill 69. I had a full membership in the Echo Company Club now. I was a paid-up member in good standing. We had held off a substantial enemy force, during one long ferocious night. I knew that walking away from here had been less than certain a few hours earlier, a lot less than certain. Charlie had us on the ropes but couldn't finish us, and destroyed himself in the process.

It wasn't the first time I had been afraid of dying, but it was the first time that I was absolutely certain I was going to die. A strange place for my life to end. It didn't happen. Luck? Or something else? Looking down on the countryside from the door of our helicopter, and catching the clear cool fresh air provided by our increasing altitude, I felt the answer. God was saving me for another day.

8

To Keep Our Honor Clean

Captain Ledin left soon after the first of the year, getting in the doghouse with the Battalion Commander on New Year's Eve. The Captain went to a party at Regimental Headquarters and never quite made it back that night. Charlie decided to pay a visit about 0100, hoping to catch us drunk or asleep. The plan was good, but unfortunately for him we didn't have the means with which to get wasted and nobody wanted to sleep that particular night. The troops were not only fully sober, they were incredibly awake. We caught Charlie out in the open before he could muster much of an attack. Illumination rounds from our mortar section lit him up like a Broadway stage. The backlighting was particularly nice, because it put Charlie in silhouette and made lovely targets out of the damn black pajamas. Gotcha! And Happy New Year to you, too, Charlie.

Gary Brown's 2nd Platoon was having most of the fun, but he decided he might as well make it dramatically successful, so he asked me over the radio if he could have some help from the artillery guys. Sounded like a good idea to me and I got busy trying to make the arrangements. As I was doing so, the Battalion Commander came on the radio net and asked to speak to the Captain.

"Lieutenant, this is the Big Six, let me talk to the local Six," he said, throwing me into cardiac arrest.

"Sorry, Sir, he's not here right now. I think he's out with the 1st Platoon, taking in some of the action," I lied, hoping we could all change the subject and get back to taking care of Charlie.

"You tell him I want to talk to him."

"Aye, aye, Sir," I responded, thinking to myself that I could probably obey that order and still avoid a court-martial.

"By the way, how are you guys doing up there?" he asked earnestly. "Need any help?"

"I think we got this one pretty much in control, Sir. Soon as I get some Arty, this thing should be over pretty quick," I said, sounding like I needed just a little encouragement.

"OK, keep up the good work and have Ledin get back to me right away," came the words I was hoping not to hear. I got the First Sergeant working on trying to track down the Captain, while I began to pay attention to the 1st Platoon's attempt to spoil the New Year's party for several dozen Charlies. After the second round of artillery came on target, what remained of Charlie's forces limped back into the jungle. Hill 69 and surrounding territory was once again safe for democracy.

"Lieutenant, did you tell the Captain I wanted to talk to him?" came a slightly louder and stronger question from the Battalion Commander.

"No, Sir, I haven't seen him yet and he hasn't been in radio contact with me. I'll have him call the minute he gets back," I said, meaning every word but praying that the mean old man on the other end of the radio didn't get my true meaning.

"You're not shitting me are you, Lieutenant? He is around there, isn't he?"

I was doomed. So was the Captain. The radio operator looked at me and then turned his face to the blackened night. I was alone on this one. My lack of an immediate response gave the Colonel all the answer he needed.

"OK, Lieutenant, I respect you for trying to cover up for the Captain, but cut out the crap now and tell me where you think he is," he ordered in a calm and controlled voice, which for him was very unusual.

"I think he planned to spend the night back at Regiment, Sir," I offered rather meekly.

"Thank you, Lieutenant, and you did a good job up there tonight. I'll talk to you about it later," he said, sounding very sincere.

The Captain was in big trouble. Maybe I was too, but I didn't think so after the way the Colonel finally responded. Oh well, what the hell were they going to do? Captain Ledin was one of the first highly decorated veterans of this campaign. They couldn't get on him too bad. I hoped.

The Captain spent his last seven days with us in hack, meaning he was under house arrest. He was not allowed to leave his foxhole. Big deal. He was a little embarrassed at having been caught, but not at taking a night off. He hadn't had one in over 10 months. He deserved the night off and we all tried to help him forget the trouble he was in by bringing him a steady supply of beer to his office in the ground.

"The Colonel told me you lied your ass off trying to cover for me," the Captain said on his last day with us. "Thanks."

"No problem, Skipper, you'd have done the same for me," I answered.

"I would have broken your neck," he laughed.

Captain Brad Thompson showed up a few days later and it didn't take long for us to find out what his priorities were.

"Boy, you guys sure took good care of Captain Ledin," he said with a big smile when he first sat down with the four officers on his staff. "He's got all the medals he needs to make General now," he added. "If you guys do the same for me, I'll take care of all of you."

Over the next several weeks we all came to realize that he was serious about this stuff. He wanted medals and he wanted them bad. He had been in the Corps for eight years and had one skinny ribbon on his chest. He wanted more. Every time we got into a firefight over the next couple of months, he would go out of his way to get in the middle of it and expose himself in whatever way he could so that he could get wounded and appear brave in case anyone was interested in writing him up for a medal. We didn't feel like it. We thought he was stupid.

He finally got a Purple Heart one day when we were ambushed by about 15 Charlies, while sweeping a series of villages just north and west of Hill 69. They got in some pretty good licks before most of us could find some cover and get out of the direct line of their fire. He walked right at them and caught a round in the left hand. He wasn't hurt real bad and he came walking back into the Company CP with a big smile on his face. I was behind the biggest tree I could find and was working the radio to get some of our forward units to engage this ambushing party. He sat down next to me and announced that I now had control of the company and that he was going back to the Battalion Aid Station.

"Take control Bill, and if you're lucky you can get one of these million-dollar babies yourself," he said, as he sat inspecting his wound. "I'll be back in a day or two, so don't get things too screwed up," he said jokingly. "Think this is good enough for a Bronze Star?" he asked, in a very serious tone.

"I don't know, Captain, I'm a little too busy right now to worry about it," I said, hoping he would just get the hell out of there. "Need any help getting back to Battalion?" I asked as he started to walk away.

My three platoon commanders became increasingly concerned that Captain Thompson's quest for medals would sooner or later have an unnecessarily bad effect on their well-being, and discussed the situation with me in hushed voices, well away from any witnesses. As long as he was there and still alive, I didn't think we had too many options. This was not a democracy. He called the shots and we followed orders. We had all signed up for that deal, including him. We all missed Captain Ledin, particularly when the shooting started. He had taken chances too. And he had been aggressive. But he was not stupid. He didn't take stupid chances. He took calculated, high-payback chances. And sometimes people got hurt and killed, but we always felt that the price we paid in wounds and death was measured and proportional to the situation at hand, at least to the extent it was within our control. Captain Thompson was different. He took chances when none were called for, not only with his own life but with everyone else's. In addition, he was not skilled at running a rifle company. It figured he was a lousy poker player too. He seemed to like to lose. He played a wild style, unafraid to bet with any set of cards. My conservative style was not very popular at his table, but he let me play anyway. Once he arrived at the company, I never needed a paycheck. I took his. A pair of fives is going to beat drawing to an inside straight 12 out of 13 times.

Somewhere there had been a void in his training. Or else, he hadn't been paying attention during years of training. Some big expert in military theory once said that three minutes of actual combat is worth more than three years of training in making a fighting man. Maybe so. But an untrained or poorly trained soldier isn't likely to live three minutes in combat unless he also has very good luck, God on his side, some mighty helpful buddies and lousy opposition. Charlie was not lousy opposition. Charlie was good, damn good. But Captain Thompson didn't know how to move and maneuver and strike and defend and attack and call in help. He grabbed his saber and rushed the enemy. A perfectly good tactic under certain conditions, but not under every condition, every day, every fight. Since he made no secret of why he did things like this, it was hard to convince the young second lieutenants that we were in a winning situation. The three of them already had lots of medals, won for very wonderful work they had done when it needed to be done. They knew a good company commander when they saw one and the contrast with Captain Ledin was not good and probably unfair.

Two of my platoon commanders, Gary Brown and Fred Williamson, were the best I'd ever seen. They were extremely competent. They were exceedingly brave. And they were very funny in an unfunny situation. The combination was unbeatable. They took good care of the troops and would never consider putting one of their men in a dangerous position unless it was absolutely necessary, which, of course, it often was. They didn't crave medals. They tried to avoid getting the Purple Heart for themselves or anyone in their platoon. They just concentrated on killing bad guys and trying to avoid being killed by the bad guys. Pretty simple really.

One evening, after an unusually bad day of trying to win some medals for the Captain, the platoon commanders called me to a private meeting near the shower facility that had just been constructed on Hill 69.

"Did you see what he did when we reached the edges of the village today?" Gary asked me, as he slammed his helmet to the ground.

"He had our two platoons facing each other, 50 yards apart," Fred added in a tense but quiet voice. "We're very lucky somebody didn't get hurt real bad today for no good reason," he continued.

"We were looking right down the barrel at each other," Gary went on, after he retrieved his headgear. "The asshole doesn't know what he's doing out there and we're just flatassed lucky he hasn't gotten us all killed," Gary blurted out.

I was in an uncomfortable position. I knew they were dead right about the Captain. I also had a responsibility to stop the criticism. This was more than just the normal bitching you expect from hardworking and frustrated marines. This was full-fledged breaking of the rules we were all sworn to live by, somewhere between insubordination and mutiny. Don't question orders from superior officers. Just do it. Obey orders. Mutiny is an out-and-out capital offense in the Marine Corps. I should have chewed their ass for talk like this. I should have stopped it right there. It wasn't proper. But boy, was it right.

"What can we do?" I asked, truly perplexed by the situation and how to react to it.

"Go tell him that he's acting like a shithead and see if he won't start acting like a company commander instead of John Wayne," Fred suggested.

"We've had a couple of conversations like that," I said, letting them know for the first time that I had tried to put a halt to this type of behavior on several occasions. "He thinks that we've been out here too long and that we're getting gun-shy," I added.

"Well, he can kiss my ass then," Fred offered.

"We're not talking about heroism here, we're talking about competence," Gary said, hitting the nail squarely on the head.

"He doesn't see it that way," I repeated.

"He won't listen to me, either," Gary mumbled under his breath. "Why not write him up for a Congressional Medal of Honor and maybe then they'd send him home," he added.

"Why not go speak to the Colonel?" Fred asked, after a long silence.

"Are you crazy?" I answered. "He'd kill us."

"So will the Captain, if we don't stop him," Gary reminded me.

Get the job done and take care of the troops. Where did this problem fit in the simple-sounding equation? I wondered about how the weather was this time of year at Leavenworth Prison. I had to do something.

"Enter," came the command from inside the tent of Major Ernest DeFazio, the Battalion Executive Officer, after my knocking at the wooden door interrupted the silence that filled the night air around the Battalion CP.

"Good evening, Major, can I talk to you for a minute?" I

opened, knowing that the unusual request would bring up the antennas on the Major's audio system.

"Yeah, sure," he answered, looking at me over the top of his glasses, trying to guess what kind of trouble I was in and how much. "Want a drink?" he asked, holding out a bottle of gin.

"No thank you, Sir," I answered, wishing I could grab that bottle and take a quick slug.

"Take a seat," he said, in a soft, low voice so unusual for this gruff old veteran of three wars. "How's it going?" he asked, opening the door for me to come out with it.

"I've got a big problem, Sir, and I really need your help and advice," I started, my voice not quite under full control.

"You're a marine, Lieutenant, you ain't supposed to have problems," he said, with the hint of a smile coming from his unshaven face.

"Normally, I don't, Sir, but this is really something different and nothing I've learned so far in the Corps has taught me how I ought to handle it," I went on.

"Sounds serious," he said, sparring with me a little.

"Sir, I've got something like a mutiny on my hands," I said, making sure he got the seriousness of my drift right away. "I've got the best damn platoon commanders I've ever seen."

"Absolutely the best," he agreed.

"They're brave and competent and dedicated and the men adore them," I went on, slowly. "They've been through lots of shit and they've never complained about anything, it's just not their style. I can't imagine how we could get much better," I added.

"I totally agree," the Major said, nodding his head with everything I had said so far. "What the hell's your problem then?" he quizzed.

"The Skipper, Sir," I said, hoping it came out without me choking on the words. His eyes narrowed and the smile left his face but he didn't say anything. He continued to look straight at me with eyes that didn't seem to contain a lot of sympathy. I took it straight on. "Sir, Captain Thompson is a really brave guy," I said, trying to explain my problem while presenting a fair evaluation. "He's very Gung Ho and aggressive but he is a disaster as Company Commander," I added, feeling better that it was now mostly out, and the Major hadn't killed me. "He can't read a map and he doesn't know how to use supporting arms and his tactics were never taught at any Marine school," I continued, keeping it going as best I could. "He's going to get people hurt unnecessarily and all the platoon commanders have about had it." I paused, and hit the bottom line. "He wants medals and he'll do anything to get them but I don't think it's smart to put other marines in jeopardy just to let him have his fun. I don't know how to handle this with the platoon commanders. Sir, I need your help. These lieutenants really are the best, Sir."

He took a long swig of gin and tonic and continued to look at me over the top of his glasses. I'm sure he didn't want this problem in his lap and I'm sure I didn't endear myself to him by dropping it on him like this. He knew I had few options and that it wasn't easy for me to have walked in here like this. He could can me. He could arrest me. He could chew me out or punch me out. His expression didn't give me a clue about which of these options he was about to execute.

"Thank you, Lieutenant," he finally whispered, tensely. "I'll take care of it and we never had this conversation, do you understand me?" he said, looking at me with his sternest glare. "Get out of here."

"Aye, aye, Sir."

The next morning Captain John Fredrickson joined Echo Company as its new Company Commander and Captain Thompson was assigned to the Battalion S-3 organization. The grizzly-faced old man had protected my ass. We never spoke of it but he always treated me a little distantly afterwards. I always had a lot of respect for the guy and now I had a bunch more. Gruff and grouchy most of the time, he had a marine teddy bear heart. He loved the troops, respected that my concern was for their safety, not just my own self-serving concern.

He was a class act, as were all the battalion officers of 2/4. A marked difference from my experience of a few months earlier with 3/7. Major DeFazio and Major Sam Adams, the S-3, were two of the finest officers I'd ever served with. Major Adams had also worked his way up the ranks. This was his second war. He had been one of my instructors in Basic School. An aggressive, offensive-oriented teacher, he had been a favorite of the students in Quantico. Out in the field he was even more popular. He and I had shared an airplane ride on our way to Okinawa for three days of R and R. I spent the days playing golf and drinking beer. He relaxed by taking long, solitary walks. He ate and drank at the Officers' Club by himself. I tried to buy him a beer once but he politely declined and made it clear he didn't want any company on his three-day vacation. He was a loner all the way. He was a strong figure among strong figures. The two majors made a dynamic duo. Then there were three.

One cold day in February 1966, our battalion got a new commander. I met him while he was shaving outside his Command Tent the second or third day he had been our new boss. Lt. Col. P. X. Kelley was quite a specimen, tall, built like Superman and very pleasant.

"Glad to meet you, Bill," he said, while continuing to scrape the cream off his face. "I want to know about you and the men of Echo Company," he continued, a slight, sincere smile on his face. "Start talking." This guy was confident, totally unpretentious and smart. He had been around the Corps for 16 or 18 years, most recently as a battalion commander with the 1st Marine Division, Force Recon Unit, the most prestigious unit the Corps had. It was a combination of frogmen, parachutists, and the Green Berets, plus some of Superman's younger brothers. He also had a couple of advanced degrees, used words with lots of syllables, could cuss out any sailor, and was at home in grunt dialect. Colonel Kelley was ready for this job and he made that clear, from the very start. Each week he made it even more clear. He was also a protege of Lt. General Lewis Walt, the top-ranked marine in Vietnam. General Walt naturally took a personal liking to our battalion. He gave it every dirty job that came up. We jumped, ran and crawled our way through every emergency in the country for the next several months. It was as if in some crazy way his admiration for Colonel Kelley was a license to abuse us. We got much more than our share of dirty details. He called. We went. Colonel Kelley led the way, with a smile on his face and a twinkle in his eye.

"You look as though you could use a drink," the Colonel said to me one evening, when I made my way back to the Battalion CP during one of our many trips out into the boonies.

"Sure, Colonel, I usually have a drink this time of night," I laughed, enjoying his ridiculous invitation. We hadn't had an alcoholic drink in months. We were in the middle of the jungle. Nothing could have been further from my thoughts at that moment. He didn't comment further. From behind his pack, which was lying against a small tree near the edge of a clearing where the CP was settling in for the night, he lifted out a large plastic bottle. He offered to pour some of the contents into a paper cup for me. The cup contained four ice cubes.

"Dry martini OK?" he asked, as he shoved the cup towards me. I inspected the clear white liquid with my nose first, half expecting some sort of trick. It wasn't a trick. A genuine vodka martini. On the rocks, with a lemon twist. This was quite bizarre.

"A little on the dry side," I said. "But what the hell," I said, as I relaxed for one brief moment with my unusual cocktail and the small talk I was having with a future Marine Corps Commandant.

P. X. Kelley played war like Ernie Banks played baseball. "It's a beautiful day, let's play two." He didn't need a breaking-in period. It was his battalion from the minute he showed up. I had served with and under some fine, talented people during the three and a half years that I had been a commissioned officer. Nothing like this guy.

When the three of them, the Colonel and Majors DeFazio and Adams, got together, something good always seemed to happen. They knew how to make a battalion hum. We ran and flew and shot and killed, according to the rules and according to the Marine doctrine covering such subjects. Working hard and working smart. No obstacle too high or job too tough. And we loved it. Having bosses like this made all the misery and hardships tolerable. They shared the sweat and dirt. Side by side with the troops. In charge, yet totally a part of us. I was proud of our unit. Proud to be a part of it. We got up every morning ready for some new action. And it came.

OPERATION TEXAS started innocently enough on the first day of spring, 21 March 1966. One battalion was dropped into a blocking position, four miles south of the village of My Li (not the village made famous years later by Army Lt. Calley) and alongside the Phong River. Our battalion and one other would be dropped in just north of the village and sweep toward the blocking battalion. This was standard tactics, typical of several operations we had run since the decision to get more aggressive. Captain Fredrickson was preparing to jump off with the 1st and 2nd Platoons when I walked into the Company CP after an uneventful helicopter landing with the 3rd Platoon, in an open rice paddy on the outskirts of Dong Chi, a small village that was a part of the My Li complex.

Helicopters were landing and taking off on both sides of our position. Artillery rounds were arriving randomly in the general vicinity of My Li. Radios were crowded with routine operational traffic. Nothing seemed to be abnormal. No big enemy units had been encountered. None were expected. I moved with the 3rd Platoon about 75 yards behind our main forward positions as we swept forward in a broad company front and had a good view of the Captain as he moved his two rifle platoons toward the outskirts of Dong Chi.

Without warning, small arms fire engulfed the 1st and 2nd Platoons, raking our entire company front. Bodies were flying through the air, trying to find cover. This wasn't a random burst that came quickly then faded just as quickly. It started hard and got harder. Everybody on the forward line was involved in the firefight.

I knelt down to get out of the line of fire, now coming our way. The kneeling not only kept me safer, it also helped me see a little about what was happening in front of me. People were moving forward, slumped in firing positions. Others were firing from prone positions. Others were just prone. The 2nd Platoon entered the tree line which defined the Dong Chi boundary on my right side. Hand grenades were exploding. Their report sounded like a big bass drum, keeping time to some high-speed rock music. Thump. Thump. Thump. And more rifle and machine-gun fire. I saw a couple of M-79 grenades launched high above the tree line making a long, slow arc toward a couple of shacks at the back of the village. It was going on too long.

I could see people down on the ground who were not moving or taking part in the fight. Some of these rounds were finding targets. I zigged and zagged forward, found a dike separating a rice paddy and the town about 30 yards away and dove behind it. Two marines lay bleeding on my left from leg wounds. No corpsman had found them yet and they lay quietly with their wounds. Another marine was hunched over on my right. He was dead. The rest of the company was beyond the dike I was hiding behind.

After catching my breath for a second, I peered over the edge. Staff Sgt. Black, the Weapons Platoon Commander, and five other marines were flat on their back, a few yards in front of my position in the middle of the open area between me and the tree line where all of the firing was coming from. They were all wounded. All down hard. Some of them were screaming in pain. Others not.

The Captain and most of the 1st Platoon were just inside the tree line off to my right, engaged in a furious exchange of rifle fire and hand grenades. They seemed to be trying to move further to the right. People were moving in short sprints, jumping and running in brief spurts, firing as they moved. Orders were being screamed and encouragement voiced. They had their hands full.

So did Charlie. I could see black-pajama-clad bodies moving from tree to tree, house to house, firing on the run, stopping from time to time to reload and toss a grenade. Our 1st Platoon was at such close range with a group of Charlies that they could be fighting hand-to-hand, except no one had a free hand.

Above the din, chaotic noise, automatic fire booms, I could hear the moans and cries of the wounded marines lying a few feet away from me. Our artillery units were delivering heavy fire somewhere in the rear of the village. I couldn't see the Captain. He must be not too far. No company radio traffic. Everyone fighting. No time for talking. I had to move. Do something. Lying there behind the paddy dike isn't getting the job done. Look around. Five, six of HQ group. Followed me this far. Third Platoon, scattered out, another 20 yards behind.

"OK, Robinson, I need some help getting these wounded back behind the dike," I said over the noise, pulsing and throbbing all around us, making verbal communications almost impossible. He nodded, understanding what we were going to do. Another marine back to find the 3rd Platoon Commander, have him and his men move up closer. Going to need help. Messenger to Battalion, only a few yards farther back, see if he can scare up some medical help. Casualties going to be high. We have to have help.

I closed my eyes and tried to catch another deep breath. Adrenaline flowing in every vein. Breathing forced and unnatural. I said a small, short prayer asking for protection from my God, and took a step into the open field.

Pfc. Robinson and I reached SSgt. Black about the same time.

His eyes were still open and slightly rolled back in his head. A gaping hole in his neck was preventing normal breathing. Blood and air spilled from the wound. He was choking from vomit that spewed from his mouth and nose. We didn't have time to do a careful examination but as we each grabbed an arm and started to haul him the few yards back toward the dike, I noticed a large bloody spot on the upper portion of his right leg.

"Let's move," I said, grabbing one of the Sergeant's arms.

"I'm ready, Lieutenant," Robinson answered, darting forward with more than his share of the load. Sgt. Black was a large man and the load was heavy. The two of us struggled forward under the strain. As we stepped up over the dike, Pfc. Robinson took a round between the shoulder blades. The dull thump from the sound of the bullet driving into his body echoed above the clamor. As he fell face first to the ground, he blurted one last human thought. "Father, forgive me," he said, from a body that was already dead.

SSgt. Black was now half draped over the raised dike and before I could get some help in pulling his body up and over the dirt mound to a more protected location, two more rifle rounds came thumping into his prone figure, rounds that were probably meant for me. Mortars were now being fired into our hiding place behind the dike. Fortunately, the ground was mostly filled with water and the rounds exhausted themselves in vertical explosions. Just a little of their shrapnel found the intended targets.

"The Captain's wounded and the Gunny's dead," one of the corpsmen shouted as he skittered back to the Battalion Aid Station with a wounded marine.

"Where are they?" I asked, looking up at him from my hiding place.

"Over there, other side of the trail." He pointed 30, 40 yards off to the right.

"Skipper hurt bad?" I asked.

"Arm wound," he answered, trying for the Aid Station. The corpsman looked like he was on a springtime walk through the countryside. He just kept walking with his arm around the wounded marine, as if he didn't have a care in the world. The air had no air in it, almost none. Sweat gets in your eyes.

During my second trip out into the open rice paddy to pick up more wounded marines, I took three other marines to speed up the process. Two didn't make it back alive. One caught most of a mortar round near his left foot. The other caught a grenade tossed by a Charlie just inside the tree line near Dong Chi, a tree line that still contained too many bad guys. Two of us who survived dragged another body back behind the dike. I could end up with the whole company lying out there in the open.

The entire 3rd Platoon moved up behind the dike. The Colonel came to take a look, too. Help coming. Help.

"You got enough help now?" he asked me.

"Yes, Sir. We should have 'em all in a few minutes, if it doesn't get any worse," I answered.

"Yell if you need more help," he said, moving away. "We need to get this area cleared up."

We were still receiving incoming mortar rounds, with rifle fire and grenades. We had to get some heavy stuff on those Charlies. We couldn't do it with the eight or ten bodies still lying out there in the open, some maybe not dead.

The rest of the company was moving off to the right of the village, so we could clear a firing zone. We were taking a frightful number of casualties. The area around me looked like—like a war zone. It took me four more horrifying trips over the dike and the help of an uncounted number of marines to clear the area of dead and wounded. There was instant death and maiming out there for my helpers. There was no shortage of volunteers for the trip. I asked. They came. Some of them died. I believe all of them were hurt. They never stopped coming. I would wave a hand. They moved.

"Who's ready?" I asked, ready for another trip out into the paddy.

"Right behind you, Lieutenant," came three or four answers, at once.

Was this heaven or hell? Why wasn't I dead? Why was it so easy to get men to rush to their death? Why were black-skinned marines rushing to pick up a white marine and getting splattered before they could get there? Why were white-skinned marines crawling towards wounded black ones, only to die in the attempt? Man trying to help man and giving their all in the attempt. The best and the worst the world had to offer, all right there in a few square yards of a damp, dirty piece of Vietnamese soil and mud.

I was exhausted by the time we had all the wounded extracted and I lay for a few minutes behind the dike, resting in my own vomit, blood and bandages decorating the evacuation area. We were still under fire. I didn't have the strength to lift myself up again. I reached for my canteen. The canteen had a bullet hole through it. It was empty. I borrowed water from the Air Liaison Officer who was lying next to me.

The Colonel had sent the Air Liaison Officer up here to my position so we could bring in some airborne firepower as soon as the area was cleared of friendly personnel. He was in radio contact with his buddies in the sky.

"Can somebody give us red smoke on the target?" the pilot calmly asked from his seat atop a Phantom jet 3,000 feet above us. The Air Officer handed me a smoke grenade.

"Let's see how far you can toss this baby," he said. This toss wasn't going to set any world records.

While a couple of riflemen opened up at the tree line to keep heads down across the way, I let heave. It barely made it to the tree line. Within seconds red, billowing smoke made its way into the sky.

"I've got it," said the voice in the sky. "How close are friendly troops to the target area?" he asked.

"About 30 yards to the north," the Air Officer next to me responded.

"Then let's keep those heads down, marines. Here comes the cavalry," the pilot responded.

The jet jockeys, one by one, pointed their planes at the red-smoke-filled area, and released a steady stream of high-explosive rockets. They came from our back. Halfway down it was certain the rockets would come crashing into our own position. Trapped in place, we had no choice but to wait and look with stark terror at rocketing death.

"Oh, shit, they're going to hit us," I screamed, as the first rounds were released from overhead.

"Nah, they've got us spotted. Don't sweat it," the Air Liaison Officer lying next to me said, confidently. The rockets whooshed over our heads and thudded the target with a shrieking set of explosions. Trees, parts of trees, dirt, little bits of whatever ripped high into the air. Then again. And again. We hardly noticed that the incoming fire from Dong Chi slowed down dramatically the moment the rockets arrived. Charlie must have been watching the air show too. The Phantoms kept coming until all rockets had been spent, each one delivered with pinpoint precision. Charlie was backing off. The pilots didn't want to.

"We're out of rockets guys but we've got lots of .50-caliber left. Want us to do a little strafing before we go home?" the lead pilot asked, as his four-plane formation continued to circle the area. The Air Officer lying next to me raised his eyebrows, indicating the decision was mine. We were awfully close to the target to be directing strafing runs. The margin of error was very small. A few feet off target and we would have some friendly casualties. On the other hand we could use the help. I nodded at the Air Liaison Officer and listened intently to his detailed instructions to the zoomies overhead. They knew the risks too but had supreme confidence in their ability to bust up the intended target and simultaneously keep the good guys safe from harm.

He brought them low and slow over the target area, moving from our left to our right, down on top of the tree line where only minutes before Charlie had been creaming us with rifle fire and grenades. Low and slow meant about 240 miles per hour at 10 feet. No noise until they were over and gone, and then the explosion of a wailing scream that shook the ground and rattled the trees.

I peeked out of one eye at one or two of the 12 strafing runs. Mostly I tried to see how close to the ground I could get every ounce of my body. They arrived over the target with little or no notice, only a blur in the sky. Despite the speed and their short time over the target, I could make out the pilots' faces. Serious, concentrating heavily. And enjoying it. One of the Phantoms had to leave the area prematurely due to an engine problem. Bamboo in the intake.

Colonel Kelley wanted us to move back a bit now, so we could clear up some space for the Arty to have a chance at Charlie and Dong Chi. I was not disappointed to move. In three hours I had seen more death and destruction than I cared to remember, without even knowing how bad the rest of the company had been hurt or just where they were. I crawled most of the 40 or so yards back to another series of dike formations, where the Battalion CP had been set up. As I began to get my bearings, I caught sight of familiar figures approaching our position from the south. It was bits and pieces of the 2nd Platoon.

"Where's Lt. Brown?" I asked one of the passing troops, who was holding a bandage against a bloody shoulder.

"I think he's right behind us, Sir," he answered.

"He's been hit, Sir, but I think he's OK," came some additional information from another marine who seemed to be free of wounds but not quite lucid. He looked right past me, as if he were somewhere else.

I made my way down the long file of men until I found Gary Brown. Although he had taken a round through the right forearm, he was barking orders to his squad leaders and actively assisting with the evacuation of the wounded.

"Are you OK?" I asked.

"Yeah, I'm OK, but we still got lots of people out there and we're still taking casualties," he said, sternly.

Colonel Kelley was standing a few feet away observing the same scene I was and trying to make assessments about what he should do next and with what.

"Colonel, do you think we can get some artillery smoke over there to cover our movements?" I asked, as the Colonel walked by.

"Let's do that," he said. "Too many people in the open," he added. It only took a few seconds for him to arrange for the smoke rounds and get them on target. We were no longer visible from Dong Chi.

Fred Williamson had taken a round in the stomach. Two marines were carrying him, one under each arm. He was still on his feet and pale. Pained, scared and still doing his job. He had new body holes in the front and in the back. He refused to let us put him on a helicopter until he was convinced all of his troops that were getting back, were back.

"I'm hurt bad, Van," he said, as he and the two helpers came into the Battalion CP. "We caught some heavy shit in there."

"Get him over there by the helicopter landing area," I told his two crutches.

"Make sure they all get out, Van, I haven't seen my 2nd Squad in the last few minutes," he requested, as he was moved away.

Within 10 minutes the rest of the column had found its way into the CP. The Captain had a bad gash on his arm from a well-placed grenade, but he wouldn't leave either. He tried collecting bits and pieces of the company, while I supervised the evacuation of the last few wounded. Gary cradled Fred in his arms on the floor of one of the last helicopters to leave. Fred was hurt real bad. The corpsman who was looking after him told me that he wouldn't make it.

"I think he's already dead, Lieutenant," he yelled over the rotor blade noise, as we backed away to let the helicopter do its thing.

I waved good-bye to Gary, as he stared at me out of the helicopter door, and I cried. I didn't stop until the helicopter had disappeared over the trees. What was I going to do without those two guys? I walked back to where the Captain was trying to assemble Echo 2/4 and make a damage assessment. It was not pretty. We had 62 people still on their feet. We had started the day with 157. A fully loaded rifle company had 196 marines. There wasn't much left of the company. We had lost nearly 100 men in three hours. It would take days to find out about some of the wounded and dead. Anyone who wasn't still here we assumed must be a casualty and already evacuated. The only exception was the Gunny. He had been decapitated by a rocket round to the head. His body was lying somewhere in Dong Chi, now under heavy artillery attack.

Captain Fredrickson and I were kept busy organizing our survivors into some sort of fighting unit. He didn't feel like moving around much. I was too tired. We organized into two 25 man platoons, one commanded by the last sergeant we had, and one commanded by a corporal. We were a hurting group except for one important fact. All 62 survivors were still marines. We'd be out here fighting and helping each other until a bullet stopped us. No question. Not a doubt in my mind.

I fell asleep with little trouble shortly after the sun went down. I fell asleep while I was gazing up at the stars. In addition to the bullet hole in my canteen, a bullet had penetrated my backpack, another had creased the heel of my left boot and my poncho was full of shrapnel holes. My body was untouched. How long would this go on? Why so many near misses? Chance? Divine intervention? If so, why? I asked myself and the stars.

About 0200 a group of three marines dragging two Charlies by the neck woke me. It couldn't have been easy. These Charlies had tried to infiltrate our lines and had been captured in a silent hand-to-hand skirmish that had attracted no attention. These two were well dressed and appeared to be North Vietnamese regulars. Hard-core guys. They looked scared and hateful. They had been carrying pipe bombs and satchel charges when the three marines coldcocked them.

"Caught this little asshole trying to blow us up," the corporal hauling the two Charlies said to me.

"You guys didn't make much noise," I said, steering the group toward my little admin area.

"Didn't need no noise, Lieutenant. These guys can't fight worth a shit," the corporal added. It was typically modest Marine Corps bravado. Charlie had just eliminated nearly two-thirds of Echo 2/4. Being marines, the survivors were still an active fighting force. Ten percent casualties is—literally—decimation. Two remaining marines is a unit. These Charlies seemed to feel the same way about it. Battalion had an interpreter, so I assigned a couple of clerks to take the prisoners back there for interrogation and sent the three marines back to their original defensive positions.

We ordered our alert level to a full 100 percent but it was unnecessary. Nobody could sleep now. We needed the sleep but we needed to stay alive even more. Let the bastards try that one again. If the airplanes and the artillery hadn't done the complete job, we'd have to see about it ourselves, in the morning. We received a couple of incoming mortar rounds, but each time the Colonel ordered a retaliation with about 100 artillery rounds and the firing from Charlie's side soon stopped.

We had breakfast with General Walt. He and a bevy of reporters came in at first light to see what all the fuss was about. A no-nonsense guy. Gimme the facts. And he listened. And he cared. And he roared. Not at us, but at his own staff, which wasn't here. They were going to catch hell when he got back. I think he took our wounds personally. We had all been surprised by the size of the force we had encountered. Bad surprises are not good in war. He would not tolerate them. After taking so many casualties, we decided that the best course of action was to lick our wounds and then attack. We hit Dong Chi head-on again, approaching this time with a bit more caution.

Charlie was still there but in much smaller numbers. The few of them still around exchanged small arms fire with us for less than 10 minutes. A few escaped down the ever-present tunnels. The others disappeared into the jungle, in small groups. We had what was left of the village totally under control before I had my second cup of coffee.

We found the Gunny. His body was booby trapped and both his arms and legs had been removed with some sort of a machete. His head lay nearby. He died carrying a wounded marine to safety on his shoulder. How was I going to get along without him? I didn't cry. It was too gruesome and revolting. I saved the tears until I touched his name on the Wall, 22 years later.

We counted 165 freshly dug grave sites in Dong Chi. We tore up four or five to check the contents. Freshly dead hard-core North Vietnamese Regulars. A lot of them. We had encountered a large force of their best troops. Very unusual. Very expensive. Deadly. We mopped up the area for the next three days. No more furious action. No more casualties. Captain Fredrickson finally left to have his wounds looked after and I was left to bring the company home to Hill 69.

A few days later, Lt. Col. Kelley and I were picked to drive down to Chu Lai and receive a medal from an arrogant, flashy South Vietnamese general with a wide, toothy grin. We stood in line with a dozen or so other marines while the General put some cheap ribbon and tin around our neck. Good dog, Rover, that's a good boy. It was like shaking hands with a dead chicken. The Colonel was embarrassed. So was I. Mister Creepy Vietnamese General, who led the parade, was a well-known crook and legendary coward. He adored TV, and would ceremoniously pimp the Pope's mother or award the Vietnamese Cross of Gallantry to Ho's barber if CBS would send a reporter and camera crew, and could even smile at a big stupid marine.

"Think you can handle all this notoriety?" the Colonel asked me, as we drove away from the ceremony.

"Sure. All marines love to eat shit, Colonel," I said.

"No kidding. The General gave me the willies," the Colonel answered. "Let's get the hell away from this mess," he added.

We would find out later that my Silver Star had been reduced to a Bronze Star and the Colonel's Navy Cross had been reduced to a Silver Star because somebody had picked us to be a recipient of a Vietnamese Cross of Gallantry. If it weren't for the honor of the thing, we'd have preferred to pass.

Epilogue

When I left Vietnam, I was a 26-year-old Marine captain, battle-hardened and war-weary, but eager to take on new challenges and new risks. Like Danny Forrester in *Battle Cry*, I had longed for adventure and found more than I had really bargained on.

I had learned a lot about myself. I learned that I could be a good marine. When necessary, I could kill my enemy. I knew the job and could do it well but also knew it wasn't my life's calling. I didn't like it enough. I didn't have it as a permanent part of my soul. Not withstanding a chestful of medals, I knew I wasn't a hero. I never did one thing that I didn't need to do or shouldn't have done, one thing I wasn't trained to do. Thank God for the training.

The Vietnam War was a lousy war, as wars go. We won every battle and still lost the stupid thing. In my mind, our side was clearly the good guys. I believe history has already shown that the North Vietnamese leadership and soldiers were dedicated and tough. They were also indescribably barbaric, cruel and devastating, to their own people, and to their neighbors. We were branded "baby killers." I was called that by antiwar activists on the campus of Arizona State University the first day I arrived, some 60 days after I had left Vietnam. I never saw one of our guys kill a baby. I saw the North Vietnamese do it day in and day out for a year. They've been doing it over and over again since 1975. I never doubted who the bad guys were, and still don't. Could we have kicked them out of South Vietnam? Sure. Should we have been there trying to? Probably not.

Probably most people in South Vietnam just wanted to be left alone so they could get on with life. Sometimes, however, you have to fight to be left alone. While the "leadership" there was quite willing to steal, and did a lot of it, and while they were happy enough to let people die for them, not many people were willing to fight. Not enough of them, anyhow. So none of them, in the end, were left alone. It was a rotten deal. I'm sorry. But I don't think it was the responsibility of the U.S. one way or the other. I'm sure it's not my fault the North Vietnamese and their Cambodian allies killed two or three million people.

Clearly our strategic plans to help them were extremely flawed. Our tactics may have been worse. Those flaws led to the unnecessary death of too many people. For one thing, we never had a strategy for winning. The Pentagon Papers make clear that President Johnson's concern was *not losing*. In consequence, we lost. President Nixon proclaimed the war must continue until we achieved "Peace with honor." Whatever may have been achieved, it wasn't peace, and it wasn't honor.

I love a bumper sticker "Vietnam. What the hell happened? We were ahead when I left." This rings true in my story. I was there during the early part of the war and I'm sure as it drug on, our execution there lost focus and meaning. But during my tour we had to go find Charlie. He stayed away from us. His fight was with the civilian population. He tried to change their politics through intimidation, fear and murder. He convinced us to fight a war of attrition. This was stupidity on our part, and mostly luck on his part. Too much politics. Deadly politics. Those master politicians, LBJ and Nixon, tried to grab control of old Ho's precinct when he wanted the whole district. And a whole lot of people got very dead.

Each person's Vietnam story is unique. All the stories have their share of ugliness. Tragic, ugly stories. I hope this book proved that point. War is indeed hell, stupid, heartbreaking, painful and evil, the worst man has to offer. With moments of the best. I'm glad I can still tell mine. One could come to the conclusion after viewing Hollywood's version of the war that my war must have been extremely rare. I doubt it. I saw no drugs. We seldom had access to alcoholic beverages. We didn't have time off. I never saw a whorehouse or a Saigon bar. No marine shot another marine. Nobody shot their drill instructor. There was no fragging. The young officers that led the troops were not stupid. While I was there we took care of each other. We risked our lives for each other. We loved each other. We trusted each other.

And we were well trained. The young platoon commanders, squad leaders and individual marines were absolutely magnificent in their execution of their duties. This war mostly involved small units fighting at the squad and platoon level. If I see another movie depicting a second lieutenant as an incompetent wimp, I'm going to throw up, or say something very impolite, very loudly. The ones I knew were aggressive, disciplined, competent, dedicated, brave and tough guys. If somebody saw something different, I pity them.

I almost never meet veterans of the war anymore. At the time, it seemed everyone was sharing these experiences. Of course, they weren't. It's probably not rational to think of war as some sort of "highlight" of one's life, but I've heard veterans express this feeling and I believe I understand it. Many wonderful things have happened to me in the 25 years since I left Nam. But I miss the war. To say it more honestly, I miss not the war but the people. Funny people, crazy people, good people. Dedicated, disciplined and honest people. I wish I had more contact with these guys and I often find myself wondering what they're doing and how they are. Life was simple there. You didn't need money. There wasn't any. Our world was free of racism and hatred, except against the faceless enemy. There were no luxuries. We worked together, shoulder to shoulder, in a life-and-death struggle to survive. Few backed away. Almost no one let me down. Far too many died or were maimed.

Most of the people I work with and know now didn't go to Vietnam, some for good reasons, some not. Many of them now regret not going. They can't go back. I don't resent them not going. I do worry a lot about a nation where its young men and its young women fail to answer the call, or don't have the idealism, discipline, courage and self-respect to give of themselves. Killing, per se, is none of these things, and the most universally respected guys in Nam were the medical corpsmen. They were the bravest, too, the most courageous of the very brave. Nearly all of us cried in Nam. None of us whined. Men and women cry. Puppies and spoiled brats whine.

It's well documented that our country didn't treat Vietnam veterans very well. What has been less well documented, and seems to me a larger disgrace, is the treatment of black vets. They carried far too great a burden during the war. For the first time in our history we not only had integrated services, we had overintegrated fighting units, at every field combat level. If there was a dangerous, dirty, demanding job to do, be sure there would be a lot of black faces, black backs, black arms and legs. The country has not acknowledged their unselfish contribution nor does it want to. I miss these guys and wonder how much I've let them down over the years. Racism is not unique to the U.S.A. but we have certainly taken it to a fine art. This is a terrible legacy to bequeath our children.

War is full of horror, more than anyone should have to remember. I saw my share. I never want to see it again. I never want my children to see it. Even worse than going to war would have been to go to war with a poorly trained or unprepared team. I may have at times, during my marine life, cursed the requirement to practice and practice and do it again, as we prepared for war when there wasn't one. More times than I can ever recall during the heat of combat my response to the crazy situation was a spontaneous, reflex reaction to the training I had received. It saved my life. Of this, I am absolutely certain. It also saved the lives of the men I was leading.

We must live to avoid war, avoid it with great vigor. But not preparing for what we least want is a good way to get killed. So far, at least, conflict has been a human activity. Unlike cauliflowers or avocados, humans actively and consciously strive. So we make mistakes. Mistakes are a big part of life. I made plenty of them, and always will. I trust the reader can understand that in my view and judging from my own experiences recovering from mistakes is almost always possible. Living life purely for the purpose of avoiding mistakes is self-defeating. Life has to be lived with the fervent belief that the attempt is what counts. Failure can be overcome. Sometimes you reach your goal, sometimes not. If we only try those things that involve certain success, we will try few things. Fear of failure is healthy. Fear itself is healthy, and can be dealt with. Fear of failure should not alone dictate our actions and directions in life. The god-forged shield of Achilles did not protect his mortal life forever, but it did picture for eternity a world worth living in, or dying in and for.